Jubilee

Jubilee

RECIPES FROM TWO CENTURIES OF AFRICAN AMERICAN COOKING

Toni Tipton-Martin

CLARKSON POTTER/PUBLISHERS

NEW YORK

CONSECRATE THE FIFTIETH YEAR AND
PROCLAIM LIBERTY THROUGHOUT
THE LAND TO ALL ITS INHABITANTS.
IT SHALL BE A JUBILEE FOR YOU; EACH
OF YOU IS TO RETURN TO YOUR FAMILY
PROPERTY AND TO YOUR OWN CLAN.
—LEVITICUS 25:10,
NEW INTERNATIONAL VERSION

Contents

Introduction

As I knelt on the cool hardwood floor in my home office, surrounded by books that span nearly two hundred years of black cooking, I realized my ancestors had left us a very special gift: a gift of freedom, culinary freedom. And like the Biblical Jubilee that marks restoration of a people through deliverance, rest, and land conservation, and like Jubilee Day celebrations marking the emancipation of enslaved Americans, our culinary Jubilee is also about liberation and resilience. Our cooking, our cooks, shall be free from caricature and stereotype. We have earned the freedom to cook with creativity and joy.

I had spent a near fortune in musty secondhand and antique bookstores, tracing the elusive history of talented, professional black cooks whose legacies have been overshadowed throughout history by the famous caricatures. You know their names—Aunt Jemima, Mammy, Uncle So-and-So—while the names of the women and men who have created so much of American cuisine have been obscured or lost. Before I knew it, I had recovered nearly 400 black cookbooks—many of them rare—dating to 1827, with themes that reflect not just Southern cooking or the soul food African Americans are known for and pigeonholed in, but immensely broad culinary interests and recipes. These books convey a wide range of technical skills and knowledge, each one written with determination and a sense of pride.

More than half of these fascinating books received new life when I wrote about them in *The Jemima Code: Two Centuries of African American Cookbooks*. For that annotated bibliography, I surveyed and analyzed these books, recognizing the hidden figures of their authors. These were largely self-published experts who resisted prejudice, often reclaiming classic American recipes as their own. Their writings showed me what is possible when social boundaries no longer prohibit black cooks from choosing their ingredients and tools; from traveling, cooking, eating, and celebrating their independence.

And in that moment in my office, I reflected on the wonderful foods I ate growing up in Southern California, and on the decidedly bourgeois, vegetarian, and Latin sensibilities of Mom's cooking that permeates some of my favorite things to cook. The memories of food and family made me hungry; they also exhausted me. Let me explain.

My parents were among the professional African American migrants to leave their community in South Central Los Angeles during the early 1960s, integrating a breezy Los Angeles hillside neighborhood that had been the site of the 1932 Olympic Village. Developers promoted the area to middle-class and affluent whites as a "haven for the homeowner who wants something more than just a house, with access to the city and a haven from it." Eventually, that sales pitch appealed to black families, too. The hamlet with panoramic views became known as the "Black Beverly Hills," home to the black elite—doctors, lawyers, entrepreneurs, and white-collar professionals.

By the time my family found this special place, athletes like Curt Flood and entertainment industry celebrities including Nancy Wilson had settled there as well. We were "movin' on up" just like the lyrics said in the theme song to the 1970s sitcom *The Jeffersons*.

Together, View Park, Baldwin, and Windsor Hills created a privileged LA oasis—similar to communities that existed nationwide, in cities like St. Louis, Mobile, Nashville, New Orleans, Cleveland, and Philadelphia. These places are rarely recognized or discussed in media, an omission of the black middle and upper classes that serves to stereotype African Americans as poor, uneducated, and possibly dangerous. This neighborhood was where we would see Berry Gordy's family limousine roll by, or one of Ike and Tina Turner's sons showing up on the block riding the family Great Dane, Onyx, like a pony. It was a sanctuary my friends and I took for granted during the Watts rebellion. And it was here, amid the perennial sweet scent of bright lavender jacaranda blooms on palm tree-lined streets, that my culinary sense of place was established.

My mother treated our home like an urban farm, where she nurtured our appreciation for healthy living. A duck we called Corky served as the family mascot. Fruits and vegetables filled Mom's harvest basket—from tender lettuces, crisp cucumbers, and ruby red tomatoes to squashes and gnarly roots, plus every kind of California stone fruit, melons, a half-dozen types of citrus, apples, avocados, persimmons, blackberries, raspberries, and strawberries.

As school-age kids, we ate her fresh fruits and vegetables before heading out to trick-or-treat—a counterweight to all that sugary Halloween candy and the McDonald's cheeseburgers handed out at Ray Charles's home. In middle school, during long, hot summers, we balanced out junk food lunches by walking a mile to the local supermarket, pooling our allowance money, and purchasing the ingredients to make tacos with corn tortilla shells we fried ourselves.

In high school and college, we used that same extra spending money to support the food businesses in our midst: fried chicken at Golden Bird or a Double-King Chili Cheese Fatburger topped with a fried egg, which eased the transition from last call to morning hangover. (The original Fatburger was a walk-up shack on Western Avenue where the owner, Lovie Yancey, served homestyle hamburgers to our parents. The tradition continued when she expanded to a second location on the southern tip of Beverly Hills's prestigious Restaurant Row. It also was the spot chosen for an episode of *The Beverly Hillbillies.* Today Yancey is still looking over the shoulders of Fatburger customers; her portrait hangs in franchises around the globe.)

It is against the backdrop of a diverse culinary upbringing that I set a global table when I had a family of my own. When we sit down to eat, cast-iron abides with bone china, crystal, and damask, and iconic Southern and international dishes are served alongside one another and seem right at home. I commingle Mexican *migas* with flaky Southern biscuits at breakfast. Asian-style coleslaw is the side dish everyone insists I bring to the cookout. A dash of chili powder is the secret to my savory red beans, a trick I learned from my Aunt Jewel. I serve tortilla soup, crab cakes with chipotle mayonnaise, beef tenderloin with chimichurri sauce, roast turkey rubbed with chiles, Asian-spiced back ribs, and guacamole—often.

Before I wrote *The Jemima Code*, my family history was like a mirage. I had wonderful food memories and endowed my family with traditions centered around food, but those remembrances and practices had always made me feel isolated as a food writer. My culinary heritage—and the larger story of African American food that encompasses the middle class and the well-to-do—was lost in a world that confined the black experience to poverty, survival, and soul food.

I knew what my family and our friends and community ate, and yet, traditional written history and modern social media consistently ignored our style of cooking. Some restaurant critics mischaracterized inventive Afro-Asian fine dining as "inauthentic." Others panned mid- to upscale African American restaurants that didn't serve soul food or Southern fare. Whenever I searched the Internet for mentions of food I could relate to, the few stories I encountered conflated key words such as "black California cooking," "black middle class food," or "African American cuisine" with the legacy of slave food. All I saw were questions like, "How do black people cook fried chicken?" or "How do you cook neck bones and cabbage?"

I wanted to scream.

For more than two hundred years, black cookbook authors have tried to tell a *multifaceted* story of African American food that includes, but also looks beyond, what people call "soul food" today. I spent at least thirty of those years collecting their writings in search of nimble cooks like Freda DeKnight and the members of the Negro Culinary Arts Club of Los Angeles, who resisted tropes by publishing the recipes of middle-class black folks. I gave them back their dignity in *The Jemima Code,* and in turn, they set me free to tell the part of our food story that I grew up in and love.

Previously, when thinking about African American, Southern, and soul food, my angle of vision had always been through race; but discovering their lost legacy opened the view to an unexpected characteristic: class. This book broadens the African American food story. It celebrates the enslaved and the free, the working class, the middle class, and the elite. It honors cooking with intentionality and skill, for a purpose and with pleasure. And it level sets notions of hospitality and confident cooking when resources are plentiful, as well as when they were less so. It is a culinary Jubilee!

At its core, African American cuisine reflects the blending of two distinct culinary styles. One was crafted by ingenious and industrious field hands in the slave cabin, from meager ingredients, informed by African techniques. The other signifies the lavish cooking—in the plantation kitchen or in kitchens staffed or owned by people educated formally and informally in culinary arts.

We know the story of the "magical negro" cooks who fashioned their food customs "in sorrow's kitchen," as Jessica B. Harris has written. These were people who'd lost their indigenous cultures. Their food habits were stripped away. They were forbidden to display any traditions of their own, from the continuation of African names and languages to remembered customs and celebrations. But forced to fend for themselves, they applied remembered African practices and impressive survival skills to make-do provisions in their cabins, creating a highly seasoned, "soul-satisfying" catalogue of dishes known as the roots of soul food. Farmers and rural agricultural migrants took these dishes with them out of the South following Emancipation. They emphasized cooking with feelings and down-home tastes. They served this comfort food in spaces that gave black workers a place to restore themselves, to recover and relax, for a moment freed from social indignities. They claimed their intellectual property: Black-eyed peas, greens, cornbreads, pork dishes, and the like became the soul foods that celebrate African American heritage.

We hear less, though, about the cooking that can be traced to free people of color, the well-trained enslaved and skilled working class, entrepreneurs, and the black privileged class. Some prepared luxurious fare for their owners as cooks in plantation kitchens; others built reputations for fancy food "in freedom" as food business operators who established and maintained their independence while building wealth for the next generation.

Through the embrace of classic techniques, formal training, global flavors, and local ingredients, African American cooks of all three of these groups demonstrated habits that break the soul code, while inspiring pleasurable cooking with style.

WELCOME TO THE JUBILEE

In *Jubilee*, I have tried to honor the kind of joyous cooking that would have turned yesterday's enslaved and free cooks into today's celebrity chefs with glittering reputations grounded in restaurant fare and cookbook publishing. I have reclaimed their timeless wisdom and the new light it sheds on the meaning of African American cuisine. And I have tried to end dependency on the labels "Southern" and "soul," and on the assumptions that limit my ancestors' contributions to mindlessly working the fields where the food was grown, stirring the pot where the food was cooked, and passively serving food in the homes of the master class.

On the following pages, you will find graceful recipes developed by the black professional culinary class on the job—expressive butlers, waiters, bartenders, well-trained plantation cooks, operators of oyster cellars, grogshops, hotels and boardinghouses, rice and nut cake vendors, bakery shop owners, caterers, railroad chefs, ranch and stagecoach hands, cooking school teachers, home demonstration agents (itinerant teachers who helped rural cooks maximize their resources), nutritionists and dietitians, and classically trained chefs. You'll also find delicious dishes that reveal aspects of living well, from the luxurious hospitality embraced by the black bourgeoisie to the sturdy but refined cooking that supported community activism by women's social clubs, sorority sisters, and civil rights leaders.

I gathered these recipes from the cookbooks in my collection, presenting and translating them for today's kitchens.

To guide my selection of dishes, I started with the inspiring work of the Afro-Puerto Rican historian Arturo Schomburg, also known as Arthur, who was a star of the Harlem Renaissance dedicated to unearthing black contributions to history and culture. His personal collection was eventually purchased by the New York Public Library and named the Arthur Schomburg Center for Research in Black Culture. In the 1920s, Schomburg voiced his interest in black cooking as an expression of black achievement, and he wrote an untitled proposal for an African American cookbook, listing more than four hundred dishes he believed represented our culinary style.

I first encountered Schomburg's outline in *Black Hunger: Food and the Politics of U.S. Identity*, Doris Witt's compelling study of African American foodways, but it wasn't until I had the full catalogue of black cookbooks in front of me that I saw the framework of a distinct African American canon.

Schomburg believed that black cooking "developed along two lines"—cabin cooking, known for ingenuity with less-desirable ingredients, and cooking for the wealthy, where an elaborate table set with fancy food marked a family's wealth and social standing. The book was never completed, and the outline contains just one recipe: "Gumbo of Okra or Filee."

Schomburg described his plan to "divide the book into three parts: morning, noon, and night, with appropriate meal time victuals and between-time snacks . . . from the hearty egg breads and sugar-baked apples of Virginia to brains in brown butter and batter cakes with borders of crisp black embroidery in the Blue Grass, on down to rice calas and the ineffable steeped coffee, cinnamon-flavored chocolate and hot toddies served in the early hours behind the sun-streaked jalousies of the Vieux Carré in New Orleans." He also intended to show "how the negro genius has adapted the English, French, Spanish and Colonial receipts . . . to his own temperamental needs; and how he has modified them to express his own peculiar artistic powers."

The draft provided a blueprint of black culinary history.

Schomburg cited famous cooks and their dishes—Black Sam, Nancy at Monticello, Bones the Atlanta fish fryer—as well as Baltimore and Philadelphia caterers Dan Singleton, Charles Shipley, and Bernard Smith, and food vendors from Carolina, New Orleans, and Harlem. He touched upon the religious customs and cultural influences behind certain dishes, and furnished a comprehensive recipe list that ranged from unpretentious to elegant, featuring early American classics such as salt-rising bread and turtle soup; dishes requiring knowledge of culinary technique like oyster vol-au-vents and baked shad roe timbales with hollandaise; those flavored with ethnic character such as West Indian deviled crab, Charleston roast squab with rice pilau, Haitian tasso, Brazilian onions, and Italian *salumi*; and the African penchant for fried things; along with updated and standard Southern fare—sweet potato pone with orange peel flavor, yams in sherry, turnip greens with salt pork, cowpeas with molasses, Dixie biscuits.

With the Schomburg recipe list as my guide, I combed the cookbooks featured in *The Jemima Code,* documenting dishes that reoccurred often—showing that they are durable in the African American canon—as well as those that would show influences all the way back to Africa before the slave trade. I looked for aspects of African cooking in Old South menus and in black cookbooks, the Africanisms— ingredients, techniques, and folkways—that survived the Middle Passage.

Anthropologist William Bascom once identified five traditional cooking techniques of the West African Yoruba—smoking, frying, baking in ashes, roasting near the fire, and boiling in water. *The Peppers, Cracklings, and Knots of Wool Cookbook*, written by Diane Spivey, expanded upon the Bascom list, adding cooking with seeds, stewing in milk, high seasoning, beekeeping, fermenting (honey for wine), creating sweetener from sugar cane pressed and pulled by elephant, marinating and slow-roasting skewered meat, flavoring the stew pot with palm oil, frying bits of dough as snack food, and stirring yam flour into biscuits.

Jessica B. Harris added a few more traditional culinary practices associated with the African diaspora: composing dishes like Hoppin' John, red beans and rice, and jollof rice that mix grain with bits of meat and vegetables into a one-pot dish; garnishing with spicy sauces; making dumplings and fritters; seasoning with pastes like sofrito (herbs, green peppers, garlic); abundantly using okra; flavoring with dried, smoked, and pickled ingredients; and preparing confections using nuts, fruit pastes, and cane sugar or molasses.

When I tied all of these diasporic practices together, I observed a culinary IQ that is both African and American, the very definition of fusion cooking. You might think this intelligence is not all that different when compared to other world cuisines. And you would be right. But the idea that African Americans shared these qualities with the rest of society has been ignored for far too long. *Jubilee* documents these practices as they undergird a culinary African American repertoire that is much more expansive than has been known outside our community.

The recipes in *Jubilee* also bring African botanical heritage to light. A scholar, William Ed Grimé, in his 1979 book, *Ethno-Botany of the Black Americans*, identified *more than fifty* African crops/plants transferred with the first generations of Middle Passage survivors to the New World, such as benne, okra, and yams. Nutmeg, allspice, cinnamon, prickly pear, alligator pear/avocado, beans (broad, kidney, and lima), dates, wild grape, sour/wild plum, mulberry, acerola, cloven-berry/wild coffee . . . were all used by African enslaved peoples throughout the Caribbean and the United States.

And finally, I wanted these recipes to show the profound influence of westward expansion and the Great Migration on African American cooking. The dishes in *Jubilee* reflect expertise with regional ingredients around this country; use of expensive convenience foods; and exposure to new cultures, new culinary techniques, and kitchen tools. Whether cooks adapted kosher dishes in Jewish homes across the South, mingled with Cuban and Puerto Rican immigrants in Harlem, or experimented with Mexican ingredients in the West, a varied and beautiful cuisine blossomed.

ABOUT THE RECIPES

I've organized the recipes in *Jubilee* into groupings that showcase delicious variations on a theme or, in some cases, how a dish has evolved over time. For example, I started by searching for a recipe or a recipe type from Schomburg's list, such as "batter breads." In the first black cookbooks, I encountered a handful of leavened doughs we now call "quick breads"—mixtures that are stirred together lightly, then baked immediately without time for rising—usually called plain muffins, "gems," or nut breads. In future books, recipes for blueberry muffins and sweet potato, peanut, and banana breads appeared regularly, becoming part of our culinary heritage as imaginative cooks added new ingredients from their environments: a handful of nuts or berries gathered in the woods, exotic imports such as bananas and pineapple, or prepared convenience foods like self-rising flour and sweetened condensed milk.

Once I had cooked several different versions of a single dish, I adapted a particular favorite for the modern kitchen, or created a new recipe amalgamated from ones I had found, or created a new recipe, inspired by the original. For *Jubilee*, I focused on the artistry as well as the science of cooking with unfussy food that will make you feel comfortable in the kitchen.

As you cook these recipes, engage all of your senses the way my ancestors did when they cooked. Taste and adjust seasoning according to your own preferences, for example, or calculate the amount of flour to add to bread dough by touch, depending upon the moisture in the air. These skills, often mischaracterized as a mythicized natural-born talent or a culinary "mystique," are acquired by observation and practice and intelligence. As you are guided by your senses, you will feel empowered by the skills you have mastered. You will make these recipes your own.

A historical recipe accompanies many of the recipes in *Jubilee*, as a sidebar just as the author published it, without any changes. This, I think, will help you see some of the ways dishes and styles have evolved over time, spurring your imagination, broadening your perception of the black culinary experience.

With *Jubilee*, we can redeem that can of bacon grease on the back of the stove because it conveys a worldly social and environmental responsibility, not just frugality. We can be proud of classic casseroles that express *ingenuity* with repurposed leftovers, not just filling ourselves with scraps. And we're eager to hand down Grandmother's scratch-cooking recipes to our children.

I thought about labeling this culinary revival "bougie" cooking, but that seemed pretentious, aloof.

Instead, I hope that by the time you finish cooking your way through *Jubilee*, you will think of African American cooking like a sultry gumbo: built, perhaps, on a foundation of humble sustenance, but layered with spice, flavors, and aromas, embellished by the whim and the skills of the cook, served with grace and richness as well as love.

Let's cook.

COOKING IS A GRAND FORM OF GIVING.
—PEARL BAILEY

Food for Company

Pearl Bailey once said the kitchen was her temple—a spiritual space where everything has meaning and serving others is a pleasure. The singer, actress, and entertainer reached audiences through the power of her voice and the sensitivity of her performances, but on the culinary stage, she reached a different kind of audience: "People who could join me happily in a good solid one-pot meal, a full three-course dinner, or just a plain cup of good coffee," Bailey wrote in 1973 in *Pearl's Kitchen, An Extraordinary Cookbook*. "I don't like to say that my kitchen is actually a religious place," she professed, "but I would say that if I were a voodoo priestess, I would conduct my rituals there."

Inexpensive paintings, framed posters, and a calendar with a poem adorned the walls. In the corner, there was a portable radio and a small television playing music or news "once in a while." A telephone? Yes, but sometimes she took it off the hook to keep it from ringing and disturbing her culinary groove.

Kept to a minimum were distractions that might interfere with the main business of Bailey's sanctuary. She found peace and expressed the special warmth of the heart there. Kitchen sounds and aromas had value. For Bailey, a renowned star, "giving from the stage or the kitchen is the same impulse."

Which is why, when it was my turn one year to host an annual Jack and Jill Christmas ornament exchange in my Austin, Texas, home, the writings of Bailey and several other cookbook authors from *The Jemima Code* came to mind. Cooking for others is always an act of giving, but cooking to *entertain*, to celebrate festive occasions, can be seen as another level. Cooking not just for sustenance, to ward off hunger, but to shower your guests with luxurious delights is a kind of performance—a performance black cooks have been in charge of since the beginnings of our country.

I remember fretting as I wondered how I could re-create the magic of my family's intimate holiday parties for fifty business-y women. Because Jack and Jill of America is an international organization dedicated to nurturing African American leadership, I wanted the gathering to be a little Sankofa project, which meant tapping into our African and African American roots to help frame the future. *Sankofa* is a Ghanaian word that means, "Go back and get it."

I came up with an ambitious plan. I would set a communal table that combined the friendliness of Sunday dinners after church with homey yet sophisticated food. It would reflect African rituals of hospitality. And the table would be set with "food for company," a kind of entertaining and cooking practiced in our community: first in aristocratic homes by the enslaved and free chefs of color, then by black food service workers, and then by well-to-do African American hosts and hostesses, like Mamie Cook, who compiled a 1928 cookbook on behalf of the New Jersey State Federation of Colored Women's Clubs.

Easy-peasy.

I was animated by the practices of African hospitality I read about in Bea Sandler's *The African Cookbook*: a Moroccan hostess washing guests' hands from a pitcher of water scented with cologne or a few drops of perfume, the Sudanese slaughtering a sheep for the guest of honor, Kenyans who welcome guests with tea served in small cups with tiny bananas to take the edge off hunger, followed by groundnut soup.

In America, the legacy of enslavement overshadowed notions of African sociability, when in truth, some captive and free chefs should be ranked among this country's culinary royalty; this inheritance is validated consistently by the recipes recorded in black cookbooks over the years, and the notion carries weight.

During "slavery days," enslaved domestic servants and free people of color achieved a kind of elite status in the kitchens of the landed gentry. "They usually ate better and wore better clothes than the field slaves because they received leftovers from the planter's larder and hand-me-downs from his wardrobe," historian John W. Blassingame explained in *The Slave Community: Plantation Life in the Antebellum South*.

Their aristocratic owners hosted elaborate dinner parties and flamboyant balls to flaunt their affluence, characterized by grand food displays, elegant table arrangements, and overflowing sideboards. Slaveholding wives set aside certain recipes from their diaries, the family journal, or cookbook to be prepared for these opulent affairs—stylish dishes "for parties" and those "well-suited to the chafing dish." These special-occasion dishes eventually gave way to predinner nibbles like the potato chips and puffs of the 1850s and the oyster patties that became popular in the early twentieth century. Inevitably, it was black cooks who created these convivial experiences, which began with soup and didn't end until the last crumb of sweet potato pie was eaten.

Legendary chef Sans Foix rose to prominence as the force behind John and Rebecca Couper's merrymaking, seldom serving fewer than twenty-four guests for dinner at their Cannon's Point Plantation on St. Simons Island off the Georgia coast; the record of his mastery is in the memoirs of the Coupers' relative Charles Spalding Wylly.

A free man of color, Sans Foix learned and refined his craft under the tutelage of another black chef, Cupidon, who lived and worked in the home of the Marquis de Montalet, on nearby Sapelo Island.

Cupidon and his students were proficient in the French culinary tradition. Their sensibilities were influenced by Ude's *The French Cook* and the works of the French gastronome Brillat-Savarin, and they cooked extravagant meals served by an army of helpers.

Following Emancipation, cooks like Sans Foix and Cupidon, who sautéed frog legs in butter, deglazed the pan with vermouth, lemon juice, parsley, garlic, and a dash of Worcestershire sauce, became domestic servants or worked in food businesses that served wealthy whites. But some also established thriving catering businesses based on the elegant menus that epitomized the previous generation's fancy cooking, putting their own spin on festive-occasion and cocktail-party foods. These entrepreneurs mastered dishes such as eggs baked in cream or stuffed with crab, cheese wafers, vegetable fritters, crustless finger sandwiches, pâtés and meat spreads, creamed oysters served in toast baskets called vol-au-vents, and almost anything one could "devil."

As black families gained material wealth, they developed a palate for sophisticated dishes with a European taste, influenced by the higher standard of living they experienced in other people's homes. A handful of them memorialized this trend in their cookbooks. In 1910, Bertha Turner whetted the appetites of increasingly affluent African Americans and curious whites with delicate tidbits—such as baked fish timbales, black oyster soup, stuffed dates, and olive sandwiches—in a collection dedicated to "weary housewives." Beatrice Hightower Cates's 1936 collection, *Eliza's Cookbook,* assembled stylish recipes from discriminating members of the Negro Culinary Art Club of Los Angeles. It included mouthwatering hors d'oeuvres, recipes of grand flair seasoned with cultural spices, plus ideas for attractive food arrangements and garnishes that set a party mood. Both authors reject the reasoning that limits black cooking to privation and making do.

I considered recipes from these books and more when I was planning the menu for the ornament exchange, our version of a white elephant gift swap. But, ultimately, I turned to *Cooking with Jack and Jill,* published by the Greensboro, North Carolina, chapter of the organization as my muse when it was time to put the food on the table.

My home was already decked out for the occasion—black Santas in the family room; nutcrackers in the foyer; the fireplace mantel dressed with pine boughs, holly, candles, and tall vases filled with cranberries; a Christmas tree trimmed with African American ornaments.

Channeling the old African American cooks helped me create a stunning buffet of assorted nibbles—a just-right mix of then and now to both educate and allure. The food was delicious, inspired in part by cultural tradition, and also by flavors that reflect the good life: glazed pecans, baked Brie, onion dip with homemade potato chips, marinated and roasted vegetables, honey-glazed chicken wings, Creole jambalaya, Southwest cornbread, chocolate and lemon pound cakes, and Christmas party punch. Not even a sisterly squabble over who would take home the Santa ornament adorned in African kente cloth or the porcelain angel with brown skin dressed in white chiffon could get in the way of our good cheer.

Pearl Bailey would have been proud.

Crackers, Chips, Spreads

At the turn of the twentieth century, the predinner nibbles African American hostesses served were most often bread-based—simple sandwiches made from thin-sliced bread cut into shapes and spread with butter, a cheese-nut mixture, or peppers or olives mixed with mayonnaise. By midcentury, the sandwiches gave way to canapés: basic spreads made by stirring together butter or cream cheese with chicken livers, clams, oysters, ham, or avocado; and puffs—airy, buttered bread rounds topped with crab salad, cheese, and fluffy egg whites, then broiled. Today, assorted chips and crackers fill the bread tray.

Freda DeKnight's 1948 *A Date with a Dish* presented "cosmopolitan" recipes, including dozens for hors d'oeuvres, plus serving suggestions and menu advice from middle-class readers of *Ebony* magazine. Successful cocktail parties, she explained, involved attractive arrangements of "tasty sauces," tiny cheese balls on toothpicks, strips of meat, cooked or marinated vegetables in bowls or trays surrounded by potato chips, rye bread strips, assorted crackers, melba toast, or white bread squares. Her spreads included a basic mix of butter and ketchup, mayonnaise spiked with horseradish, oysters simmered in an herb-based chili sauce, Cheddar cheese mixed with rum, or Roquefort with brandy.

I captured DeKnight's spirit of elegant simplicity in the following recipes adapted for modern tastes. For a welcoming yet hassle-free buffet, I serve a mix of homemade and prepared foods. Among the homemade recipes that follow, benne wafers add a diasporic flair to the cracker basket while homemade chips with avocado dip bring a little African American culinary trivia to the party (see page 28). And among the store-bought, I like to serve an assortment of hard and soft cheeses and bowls of hummus or an onion or spinach dip. Pickled okra, olives, and brightly colored fresh vegetables sit pretty on a relish tray, and warm roasted nuts finish off the display.

BENNE WAFERS

MAKES ABOUT 50 CRACKERS

Before the advent of baking powder and soda, beating biscuit dough with a wooden stick, hammer, or heavy rolling pin with up to one thousand whacks—a *minimum* of half an hour—to tenderize the dense paste was a common pathway to small, crisp "beaten biscuits." Remembered in the Slave Narratives as "the grandfather of all afternoon tea refreshments," beaten biscuits held a place of honor in black cookbooks for generations, presumably because white families in the Old South always considered beaten biscuits a luxury, and a hostess's pride. The historian Arturo Schomburg's list of party dishes included them. Street vendors in New Orleans sold them, and beaten biscuits are the very first recipe in Abby Fisher's dignified collection from 1881, *What Mrs. Fisher Knows about Old Southern Cooking.*

These crackers, perfect for dips and spreads, became easier to make with the introduction of baking soda and baking powder, and took on an African character when cooks stirred in sesame seeds—called *benne* by African slaves—which arrived in the Sea Islands in the early eighteenth century and were cultivated in their hidden gardens for nearly a century. By the time the authors of *Charleston Receipts* published the recipe for the ethereal, seed-studded crackers in the mid-1950s, to which they gave the title Benne (Sesame) Seed "Cocktailers," the *New York Times* assured readers that this cocktail biscuit would "revolutionize cocktail parties."

I serve benne wafers in a sweetgrass basket I purchased from a basket weaver near Boone Hall plantation in Mt. Pleasant, South Carolina. Weaving the baskets is a craft handed down through generations of Gullah/Geechee women that enabled their African ancestors to winnow rice or carry water from a brook, stream, or well

to the kitchen house. It's my way of reconciling our artisanal past with its burdens.

½ cup white sesame seeds

2 cups all-purpose flour, plus more for the work surface

1 teaspoon baking powder

½ teaspoon salt, plus more for finishing

½ cup shortening or lard, cut into ½-inch dice and chilled, plus more for greasing the baking sheet

6 tablespoons cold whole milk, plus more if necessary

1 Preheat the oven to 425°F. Line a rimmed baking sheet with parchment paper.

2 Spread the sesame seeds in an even layer in the pan and toast until lightly browned and fragrant, about 5 minutes, stirring occasionally to prevent scorching. Watch carefully as the seeds burn easily. (The seeds also smoke as they toast.) Remove from the oven to cool completely, but leave the oven on and reduce the temperature to 350°F.

3 When the baking sheet has cooled to room temperature, lightly grease it or line with a clean sheet of parchment paper. Grease or line a second sheet for quick baking.

4 In a medium bowl, whisk together the flour, baking powder, and salt. Sprinkle the shortening pieces over the dry ingredients. Using your fingertips, a pastry blender, or two knives, cut the shortening into the dry ingredients, blending until the mixture resembles coarse crumbs. Sprinkle the toasted seeds over the mixture. Stir with a fork to distribute evenly. Make a well in the center, add the milk, and use a fork to blend the dry ingredients and milk, sprinkling over more milk as needed to make a stiff, rough dough.

RECIPE CONTINUES

5 Scrape the dough onto a lightly floured board. With floured hands, knead the dough 15 to 20 seconds, until smooth. Divide the dough in half. Using a floured rolling pin, roll it out to slightly thinner than a dime. Cut the dough with a 1-inch biscuit cutter and transfer the rounds to the prepared baking sheets with a spatula. Re-roll the scraps, handling as lightly as possible, and cut out more rounds. Prick each round 2 times with a fork and sprinkle with additional salt, if desired.

6 Bake 10 minutes, until the dough rises slightly. Rotate the pans and continue to bake until light brown, 5 to 10 minutes longer. Immediately remove to wire racks to cool. Store the wafers in a tightly covered container for 2 to 3 weeks. Before serving, reheat the wafers 2 to 3 minutes in a 250°F oven.

NOTE: To freeze benne wafer dough, shape it into a log and wrap it in parchment paper. To bake it, thaw slightly, slice it into ⅛-inch rounds and bake as directed.

CHEESE STRAWS

The Federation Cook Book: A Collection of Tested Recipes, Contributed by the Colored Women of the State of California, Bertha L. Turner, 1910

12 tablespoons flour
8 tablespoons butter
6 tablespoons grated cheese
1 and 1 half cups water

Add salt and red pepper. Mix well and roll out thin. Cut in strips and bake quickly.

AVOCADO DIP
WITH SPICED CHIPS
MAKES ABOUT 3 CUPS

Velvety dips made from cooked meat, fish, cheese, and vegetables appear often in our cookbooks, ranging from simple to complex—creamed ham or chicken, chicken liver pâté, cream cheese balls rolled in nuts, a wacky mushroom-collard greens concoction one old cook called "soul food dip," and a West African mashed alligator pear salad similar to guacamole, but chunkier.

I composed this dip to accompany a colorful mix of fresh vegetable crudités; a relish tray of marinated veggies, pickles, and olives; and a basket of Creole-spiced chips. The dip should be seasoned to taste with salt, depending upon whether you'll serve it with veggies or salty chips.

2 large avocados
2 tablespoons fresh lime juice (1 lime)
½ cup minced red onion
½ cup minced tomato (1 medium)
¼ cup minced red bell pepper
1 teaspoon minced garlic
1 teaspoon minced Scotch bonnet pepper or other hot chile, or to taste
2 tablespoons minced fresh cilantro
2 teaspoons minced fresh parsley
½ teaspoon dried oregano
¾ to 1 teaspoon salt, or to taste
1 tablespoon crumbled Cotija or feta cheese (optional)
Spiced Potato and Plantain Chips (page 28), for serving

RECIPE CONTINUES

1 Halve and pit the avocados and scoop the flesh into a bowl (you should have about 2½ cups). With a fork or potato masher, mash the avocado until smooth. Stir in the lime juice to thoroughly mix. Blend in the onion, tomato, bell pepper, garlic, chile pepper, cilantro, parsley, oregano, and salt. Refrigerate until chilled. Taste and adjust seasonings.

2 Sprinkle with the cheese before serving with Spiced Potato and Plantain Chips.

POTATOES "A LA PAULINE"

Pauline's Practical Book of the Culinary Art for Clubs, Home or Hotels,
Carrie Pauline Lynch, 1919

Prepare potatoes and drop in deep hot fat as in a French fry.

SPICED POTATO AND PLANTAIN CHIPS

MAKES ABOUT 3 QUARTS

I serve these russet potato chips seasoned with a southwestern spice blend as a tribute to a fabled African American chef, along with a favorite diasporic snack, fried plantains.

According to legend, George Crum was head chef at Moon's Lake House in Saratoga Springs, New York, in 1853. One evening, a guest complained that Crum's French-fried potatoes were cut too thick, so Crum very thinly sliced another batch, fried them very crisp, and seasoned them with salt: the first potato chips. After that, he served the crunchy snack as an hors d'oeuvre in baskets in his own restaurant for thirty years.

Plantains are an important food in East and West Africa and throughout the Caribbean. They are a member of the banana family but are never eaten raw. In Ghana, vendors sell fried plantains from wooden trays on street corners every evening. "It is one of the very favorite snacks after the cinema," Dinah Ameley Ayensu wrote in 1972 in *The Art of West African Cooking*. At home both firm-ripe and unripe (green) plantains may be fried as chips and served as an appetizer. The riper the plantain, the sweeter and softer the chip.

Peanut oil is mild tasting and has a high smoking point. Use it for deep-frying foods of all kinds.

1 pound russet potatoes, scrubbed

1 pound sweet potatoes, peeled

1 teaspoon salt, or to taste

⅛ teaspoon cayenne pepper, or to taste

½ teaspoon smoked paprika

½ teaspoon chipotle chile powder

½ teaspoon brown sugar

¼ teaspoon onion powder

¼ teaspoon garlic powder

2 ripe but firm plantains

2 teaspoons fresh lemon juice

2 teaspoons ground ginger

Peanut oil, for deep-frying

1 Using a mandoline, a vegetable peeler, or a sharp knife, slice the potatoes into ⅛-inch-thick rounds. Place in a large bowl. Rinse with cold water until the water is clear. Cover the potatoes with ice water and refrigerate for 1 hour. Repeat with the sweet potatoes, placing them in a separate bowl of ice water.

2 Meanwhile, in a small bowl, combine the salt, cayenne, smoked paprika, chipotle powder, brown sugar, onion powder, and garlic powder. Set aside.

3 Place the plantains on a board. Trim the ends and make 4 shallow cuts lengthwise to score the skin of the plantains, then peel. (Scoring makes peeling easier.) Using a mandoline or a sharp knife, slice the plantains into ⅛-inch-thick rounds. In a medium bowl, combine the lemon juice and ground ginger. Add the plantains to the bowl and toss with a rubber spatula to thoroughly coat with the juice mixture.

4 Pour about 2 inches of the oil into a large Dutch oven or deep skillet and heat to 350°F over medium-high heat. (Use a thermometer or flick in a few bread crumbs; if they sizzle almost immediately but don't burn, the oil is ready.) Adjust the heat to maintain this temperature.

5 Working in batches (do not crowd the pan), fry the plantains until golden, 2 to 3 minutes per batch. Use a slotted spoon to remove to paper towels and then transfer to a serving bowl. Toss with one-third of the reserved spice mixture.

6 Return the oil to 350°F. Drain the russet potatoes in a colander. Thoroughly pat dry with paper towels. Fry in batches until golden, 4 to 5 minutes per batch. Use a slotted spoon to remove to paper towels. Season with one-third of the spice mixture while hot. Transfer the potatoes to the bowl with the plantains.

7 Return the oil to 350°F. Drain the sweet potatoes in a colander. Thoroughly pat dry with paper towels. Fry in batches until golden, 3 to 4 minutes per batch. Use a slotted spoon to remove to paper towels. Season with the remaining spice mixture while hot. Let stand at least 10 minutes to allow the chips to firm up. Transfer to the bowl with the plantains and russet potatoes.

For the Chafing Dish

Oklahoma caterer Cleora Butler chronicled the evolution of savory chafing dish hors d'oeuvres in her 1985 cookbook, *Cleora's Kitchens: The Memoir of a Cook & Eight Decades of Great American Food.* The recipes she gave that represented the early 1920s and 1930s were for warm first courses such as thin buckwheat pancakes topped with chicken livers in cream sauce, Mexican Rarebit (a chile-spiced warm cheese dip served with melba toast), oysters or prunes wrapped with bacon, and dried beef and artichoke dip.

By the 1960s and 1970s, she added ideas for warm dishes that reflected the financial security for some at the time—exotic and ethnic flavors took the place of simple ketchup-based or barbecue sauces, duck pâté replaced inexpensive meat spreads, and sophisticated Camembert en Croûte (cheese wrapped in a pastry crust and baked) appeared in place of cheese balls and crackers.

Among the treasures in my mother's vintage cookware collection is a stoneware bean pot that sits on a electric hot plate, which allowed families to serve dishes designed for the elegant chafing dish more casually. (The company that made it, West Bend, did give it the name of "Buffet Patio Server," after all.) It was perfect for saucy recipes like meatballs in a sticky-sweet sauce, which Mom served with decorative cocktail picks for skewering. The crock pot also kept creamy dips made with tuna or mushrooms and chicken dishes hot.

Today, a small slow cooker does the trick.

ORANGE-GLAZED CHICKEN WINGS

SERVES 4 TO 8

The chefs Alexander Smalls and J. J. Johnson take much inspiration from the combination of Asian and African flavors, as they showed us in their James Beard Award–winning cookbook, *Between Harlem and Heaven: Afro-Asian-American Cooking for Big Nights, Weeknights, and Every Day*. This recipe, though, for orange-spiked barbecue wings, is a cousin to a dish they served at Minton's in Harlem, where the talented chefs fried their wings until golden crisp before tossing them in homemade jam. In this case, the wings are roasted with a sweet-savory orange marmalade glaze.

4 pounds chicken wings

3 tablespoons orange marmalade

1 tablespoon light brown sugar

1 tablespoon soy sauce

1 tablespoon fresh lemon juice

1½ teaspoons salt, or to taste

1 teaspoon black pepper

½ teaspoon smoked paprika

¼ teaspoon ground cumin

¼ teaspoon dried oregano

½ teaspoon garlic powder

Cola Barbecue Sauce (optional; page 229), for serving

1 With a sharp knife, separate the wings into 3 pieces by inserting the knife between the drumette and the "flat," and then in between the flat and the tip. Discard the tips, or save them for stock.

2 In a large bowl or plastic zip-top bag, combine the marmalade, brown sugar, soy sauce, lemon juice, salt, pepper, smoked paprika, cumin, oregano, and garlic powder. Add the wings to the marinade. Let stand at least 30 minutes, or ideally refrigerate, covered, up to 8 hours.

3 Preheat the oven to 375°F. Line two 15 × 9-inch rimmed baking sheets with foil. Place a wire rack in each pan.

4 Reserving the marinade, use tongs to place the wings on the racks with a little space between them. Brush them with the marinade and roast until lightly browned, about 30 minutes. Turn and roast for 30 minutes more, then turn again. Roast until the wings are well glazed, 10 to 15 minutes longer. Serve immediately. If desired, pass barbecue sauce on the side.

HONEY-SOY GLAZED CHICKEN WINGS

SERVES 4 TO 8

I found the earliest printed mention of chicken wings as a standalone dish in Freda DeKnight's 1948 collection of the "choicest Negro recipes," *A Date with a Dish*, stewing them in a chile-spiked tomato gravy. Legendary New York chef Princess Pamela revised DeKnight's dish as part of her soul food repertoire, serving the sauced wings over hot rice. And soul cook Kathy Starr combined the best of the old and new worlds, creating a sweet-hot dunking sauce for fried wings with ribbon cane syrup, butter, and hot pepper sauce in *The Soul of Southern Cooking*. These treatments remind me of the Nigerian practice of roasting tough birds with high spice and pepper—a dish called bendel chicken.

When wings come on the restaurant and home entertaining scene in full force, it is Oklahoma caterer extraordinaire Cleora Butler who gives the bony parts a cosmopolitan flair, picking up on the interest in international cuisines dominating the food world during the 1950s. Her Chinese chicken wings infused the sweet-and-sour taste from the ribs at the legendary Los Angeles Polynesian destination, Trader Vic's, with the red peppers and onions that were all the rage.

Taking its cues from Cleora Butler's Afro-Asian pairings, this recipe blends the savory flavors of soy sauce, ginger, and garlic with sweet honey, a classic Chinese combination. Choose dark brown sugar over light to imbue the dish with the subtly rich taste of molasses.

4 pounds chicken wings

¼ cup plus 2 tablespoons soy sauce

2 tablespoons honey

3 tablespoons dark brown sugar

3 tablespoons cider or rice vinegar

**1 tablespoon minced fresh ginger
or 1½ teaspoons ground ginger**

**1 tablespoon minced garlic (3 to 4 cloves)
or 2 teaspoons garlic powder**

4 green onions, thinly sliced

**½ teaspoon minced Scotch bonnet or
habanero pepper**

1 teaspoon black pepper

1 teaspoon salt, or to taste

Sesame seeds, for garnish

1 With a sharp knife, separate the wings into 3 pieces by inserting the knife between the drumette and the "flat," and then in between the flat and the tip. Discard the tips, or save them for stock.

2 In a large bowl or large plastic zip-top bag, combine the soy sauce, honey, brown sugar, vinegar, ginger, garlic, half of the green onions, the Scotch bonnet, black pepper, and salt. Add the wings to the marinade, cover (or close the bag), and refrigerate at least 8 hours.

3 Preheat the oven to 375°F. Line two rimmed baking sheets with foil. Set wire racks in the baking sheets.

4 Reserving the marinade, use tongs to place the chicken pieces on the racks, with some space between each. Roast until lightly browned, about 30 minutes.

5 Meanwhile, in a small saucepan, heat the marinade over medium heat to bring to a simmer.

6 Brush the wings with the marinade, flip and brush again. Roast for 30 minutes more. Brush again and bake until tender, 15 minutes longer. Sprinkle lightly with sesame seeds and remaining green onions before serving.

MEATBALLS IN BARBECUE SAUCE

MAKES ABOUT 50 BITE-SIZE MEATBALLS; SERVES 4 TO 8

Meatballs are the quintessential party food and the variations are endless—from smothered Swedish style in a cream gravy or simmered in sweet-and-sour or barbecue sauce. They were considered important elements of a black caterer's special-occasion repertoire as far back as the late nineteenth century.

A dish called "forced steak" appears in the first recipe collection published by free woman of color Malinda Russell in 1866, *A Domestic Cook Book*. And "beef cakes" are among more than six hundred sophisticated dishes published by S. Thomas Bivins in his 1912 collection, *The Southern Cookbook: A Manual of Cooking and List of Menus, Including Recipes Used by Noted Colored Cooks and Prominent Caterers*.

An *Ebony* magazine reader's recipe for pork balls in 1948 reflected Creole roots, relying upon rice instead of bread and milk as the binding that held together a batch of ground pork balls simmered in tomato soup. And, as African cooking experienced a renaissance in the late 1970s, authors like Dinah Ayensu reminded revelers that the dish (seasoned ground meat, bound with bread and milk) is pure North African fare—known as kofta.

After trying all of these and so many more, I present the classic mix of ground beef and pork, rolled into balls and baked in barbecue sauce, typifying party perfection.

½ pound ground beef

½ pound ground pork

1 cup minced onion

1½ teaspoons minced garlic (about 2 cloves)

1 teaspoon salt, or to taste

½ teaspoon smoked paprika

½ teaspoon black pepper

⅓ cup panko bread crumbs

1 large egg, beaten

1 cup Molasses Barbecue Sauce (page 222) or Cola Barbecue Sauce (page 229), plus more as needed for serving

1 tablespoon honey

1 Preheat the oven to 350°F.

2 In a large bowl, use your hands or a wooden spoon to thoroughly combine the beef, pork, onion, garlic, salt, smoked paprika, pepper, panko, and egg. Quickly pan-cook or microwave a small bit of the mixture to taste for seasoning, and add more salt as desired. Use a tablespoon to divide the mixture into equal portions.

3 Roll the mixture into balls and place them on a rimmed baking sheet. Bake until cooked through, about 15 minutes. Drain any liquid.

4 To serve immediately: Increase the oven temperature to 375°F. Toss the meatballs with 1 cup of desired barbecue sauce and the honey. Bake for 10 minutes more until barbecue sauce glaze is set. Serve hot.

5 To serve on a buffet: Place the partially cooked balls in a slow cooker with the honey and enough barbecue sauce to partially cover the meatballs. (The amount will depend upon the size of the slow cooker.) Simmer on low for up to 3 hours, covered, adding barbecue sauce and honey as needed to keep meatballs moist.

BEEF CAKES FOR SIDE OF DRESSED MEAT

The Southern Cookbook: A Manual of Cooking and List of Menus, Including Recipes Used by Noted Colored Cooks and Prominent Caterers, S. Thomas Bivins, 1912

Pound some beef that is rare-done, with a little fat bacon or ham. Season with pepper, salt, and a little shallot or garlic; mix them well, and make into small cakes three inches long and half as wide and thick; fry them a light brown, and serve them in a good thick gravy.

FORCED STEAK

A Domestic Cook Book, Malinda Russell, 1866

Grind the steak through the mill, then put it out into rolls; put into a saucepan with one tablespoon lard, seasoning the steak with pepper and salt; add a very little water. Simmer until done, turning often; chop onions fine, layering over the meat; baste the meat with the liquid and the onions. When done, make a butter and cream gravy and serve hot.

SWEET POTATO BISCUITS WITH HAM

MAKES 12 BISCUITS

Two recipes for sweet potato biscuits and three for sweet potato bread appear in the fourth edition of *How the Farmer Can Save His Sweet Potatoes: And Ways of Preparing Them for the Table*—one of eight booklets written by George Washington Carver that revealed his experiments with sweet potatoes and the possibilities for their use at table.

Starting in 1898, the innovative scientist educated readers about sweet potato botany, taught the importance of land preparation, explained compost use, offered instruction in home pesticides and remedies for destructive diseases, and shared tips about harvesting, storing, and curing, including the practical uses of the "potato bank." (A potato bank was a hole dug in the ground below slave cabins where root vegetables were stored.)

By 1921, recipes for sweet potato biscuits had become legion throughout the South, and also among African Americans throughout the country. They are the second recipe you'll see in Caroline Pickett's *Aunt Caroline's Dixieland Recipes* (transcribed by Emma and William McKinney), made with fresh-churned butter, tangy buttermilk, and leftover mashed sweet potatoes. Stephanie L. Tyson, the chef, restaurateur, and author of *Well, Shut My Mouth!: The Sweet Potatoes Restaurant Cookbook*, bakes tender sweet potato–buttermilk biscuits in her Winston-Salem restaurant that are fragrant with cinnamon, nutmeg, and cloves and perfect stuffed with sliced ham. Slivers of country ham also bring biscuit sandwiches into the front room of cookbook author, journalist, and editor Eric V. Copage, who served them with honey-mustard as part of a buffet.

All of these recipes descend from the old slave combination of sliced salt pork in biscuits and foreshadowed the salty-sweet formula I have adapted here.

2½ cups all-purpose flour, plus more for the work surface

2 tablespoons light brown sugar

4 teaspoons baking powder

½ teaspoon ground cinnamon

¾ teaspoon salt, or to taste

½ cup (8 tablespoons) butter, shortening, or lard, cut into ½-inch dice and chilled

1 cup cold cooked mashed sweet potatoes

1 cup cold whole milk, or as needed

12 thin slices country ham, as desired

1 Preheat the oven to 400°F.

2 In a bowl, whisk together the flour, brown sugar, baking powder, cinnamon, and salt. Sprinkle the chilled butter over the dry ingredients. Using a pastry blender or two knives, cut the butter into the dry ingredients until the mixture resembles coarse crumbs. In a small bowl, stir together the sweet potatoes and ½ cup of the milk. Add this to the flour mixture and stir lightly with a fork, just until moistened. Add the remaining ½ cup milk, as needed, until the mixture forms a soft dough.

3 Flour a work surface, turn the dough out, and knead lightly for 30 seconds or until the dough is smooth. Roll the dough out ½ inch thick. Cut biscuits with a 2-inch biscuit cutter and place each 1 inch apart on an ungreased baking sheet. Gather the scraps into a ball. Knead 1 to 2 times, re-roll, and cut more biscuits, handling very lightly. Bake until golden brown, 15 to 20 minutes. Split the biscuits open and fill with slivers of country ham. Serve warm.

CURRIED MEAT PIES

MAKES 30 SMALL PIES

Cooked meat or fish enclosed in a thin pastry crust is an adaptation of a colonial dish—British pasties—turned into everyday food that is served throughout the African diaspora. In some regions, stuffed pastries are sold as a snack at street stands. The people of Cape Verde fry a peppery tuna mixture in pockets of coarse pastry dough made from sweet potato and corn flour—"pastry with the devil inside." In Jamaica, the "patty" is a rich, turmeric-laced crust leavened with baking powder, and it cradles a mixture of ground meat and vegetables. Latin Americans trace their love of fillings made of beef, raisins, and olives to a combination that originated with the Moors, as Sandra A. Gutierrez explained in *Empanadas: The Hand-Held Pies of Latin America*. To heighten the island experience, I have also slipped in a little jerk chicken or pork.

During the late eighteenth and early nineteenth centuries, enslaved and free pastry chefs mastered the art of baking with dough, David S. Shields explained in *Southern Provisions: The Creation and Revival of a Cuisine*, especially the puff pastry that cradled savory mixtures such as creamed oysters, sweetbreads, or crab (called patties), and hot meat pies of all kinds.

When the soul cooks of the 1960s adopted hand-held meat pies into their repertoires, the names became Americanized. Inez Yeargan Kaiser called them hamburger turnovers in *Soul Food Cookery*, a collection of "well-seasoned, savory dishes" she believed would "bridge the gap in our society," enable readers to "understand the cultural backgrounds of all people," and provide a "channel for better communication." The year was 1968, and she was using her education in home economics

to heal racial disturbances by developing appreciation for "Negro" cooking.

Serving these tender little packets rekindles that hope. Today, recipes for samosas, samusas, empanadas, meat pies, and zamboosies turn up frequently in black cookbooks, a casual reminder of our international heritage. I adapted this recipe from Eric Copage's curried lamb samosas. He enveloped the spicy filling in wonton wrappers (another nod toward the global pantry). My version maintains the ancestral character of the African diaspora and the Caribbean, cradling a spicy beef filling in curry-scented homemade pastry. I omitted the baking powder some cooks call for, which yields a somewhat sturdier crust, and added more fat to make my pockets flaky. Or, you may opt to use the wonton wrappers (see the Variation, page 40) and fry them until crisp.

1 pound ground beef

1 cup minced onion

¼ cup minced red bell pepper

½ to 1 teaspoon minced chile pepper, such as Scotch bonnet or habanero

1½ teaspoons minced garlic (about 2 cloves)

½ teaspoon salt, or to taste

¼ teaspoon cayenne pepper

2 teaspoons curry powder, preferably Jamaican

½ teaspoon dried thyme

2 tablespoons tomato paste

Oil, for greasing the baking sheet

1 egg

Curried Pastry Crust (page 41)

All-purpose flour, for the work surface

Paprika (optional)

RECIPE CONTINUES

1 Heat a large skillet over medium-high heat until very hot. Add the ground beef and cook, stirring occasionally, until browned, about 5 minutes. Drain all but 1 tablespoon of the drippings from the pan. Add the onion, bell pepper, chile pepper, and garlic to the skillet and sauté over medium heat, stirring occasionally, until lightly browned on the edges, about 5 minutes. Stir in the salt, cayenne, curry powder, thyme, tomato paste, and ¼ cup water. Bring to a low simmer and cook, stirring occasionally, for 7 to 10 minutes to thicken the mixture. Taste and add salt as desired. Set the filling aside to cool completely.

2 Preheat the oven to 400°F. Lightly grease a baking sheet or line with parchment paper.

3 In a small bowl, stir together the egg and 1 tablespoon water. Set the egg wash aside.

4 Divide the pastry into quarters. On a lightly floured board, working with one piece of pastry at a time, roll the pastry ⅛ inch thick. Cut out rounds with a 3-inch cutter. Stack the pastry rounds on a plate and cover with a damp cloth. You should have 30 rounds total. Spoon 1 tablespoon filling onto one side of each round, leaving a ½-inch border around the filling. Brush the edges with a small amount of water to just moisten. Fold the other half of the dough over the filling to create a half-moon shape. Press the edges together with a fork or fingers to seal in filling.

5 Place the meat pies on the baking sheet and brush with the egg wash. Bake until golden, 25 to 30 minutes. Sprinkle with paprika, if desired. Serve warm.

VARIATION

EASY CURRIED MEAT PIES
Make the filling as directed. Have ready thirty 3½-inch round or square wonton wrappers. Place the wrappers on a lightly floured surface and cover them with a damp towel to prevent drying out. Working with 1 wrapper at a time, spoon 1 tablespoon filling just above the center of the wrapper, leaving some room for a border around the filling. Brush the edges with enough water to just moisten. Fold the wrapper over the filling to create a half-moon or triangle shape. Press the edges together with fingers to seal in the filling. Instead of baking, deep-fry the wontons a few at a time in 350°F oil until golden. Drain.

CURRIED PASTRY CRUST

MAKES ENOUGH FOR 30 (3-INCH) PIES

2 cups all-purpose flour
1 teaspoon curry powder
⅛ teaspoon cayenne pepper
1 teaspoon salt
¾ cup shortening, cut into ½-inch dice, chilled
⅓ cup ice-cold water, or as needed

In a large bowl, whisk together the flour, curry powder, cayenne, and salt. Sprinkle the shortening pieces over the dry ingredients. Using your fingertips, a pastry blender, or two knives, cut in the shortening until the mixture resembles coarse crumbs. Sprinkle half of the water over the dough and stir with a fork to mix. Stir in enough additional water, 1 tablespoon at a time, to form a shaggy dough. Scrape the dough onto a floured board. Knead 5 to 10 seconds, until the dough is smooth. Wrap the dough in a large sheet of wax paper or plastic, folding the edges over to completely cover the dough. Press the dough into a flat disc and refrigerate until ready to use.

NOTE: For a sturdier crust, reduce the shortening to ½ cup and increase the water to ⅔ cup.

Seafood Hors d'Oeuvres

I confess that trying to understand the difference between all the fish fritters, patties, croquettes, cutlets, cakes, and balls in African American heritage cooking nearly drove me crazy. It is fascinating, though, to follow the evolution of small fried salt cod batter balls from the African diaspora to its rebirth as a breakfast staple—salmon croquettes—to the plump Maryland crab cakes that grace menus in fine-dining restaurants today.

In her *Caribbean and African Cooking,* Rosamund Grant offered her spin on the linguistic drama: "Cakes are potato-based, whereas fritters are flour-based. The shape and size of saltfish cake may vary from oval rissoles, served as part of a meal, to small round balls for cocktails."

But what about croquettes that are roux based or bread based? Layer onto that the African American tradition of serving these creations made with dried salt cod, fresh poached cod, or any leftover white fish. And then there's Abby Fisher. In 1881, Fisher, a formerly enslaved woman, moved to Northern California with her husband, won awards for her cooking, and published a far-reaching recipe collection, *What Mrs. Fisher Knows About Old Southern Cooking.* She pushed notions about black cooking as an art beyond survival. Her book incorporated an entire section of croquettes, made with lamb, chicken, crab, veal, liver, oysters, and fish.

Regardless of what we call these novelties and what goes in them, though, as the historian Karen Hess explained in the reprint of Fisher's book, "It has generally been accepted that black women were particularly adept at their confection and frying."

What follows are three of my favorite versions: salmon croquettes, tender potato-based codfish balls, and crab cakes. Any of these cakes would be fabulously delicious as hors d'oeuvres. Make them ahead of time, store them covered in the refrigerator, then reheat them gently in a hot oven to recrisp just before your guests arrive.

SALMON CROQUETTES

SERVES 4 TO 8

When I read Beatrice Hightower Cates's 1936 *Eliza's Cook Book*, I was surprised to find a recipe for salmon croquettes that refused to conform to a "heritage" mixture—that is, it didn't have a roux-based white sauce to hold the croquettes together. In her book of recipes, collected from the ladies of the Los Angeles Negro Culinary Art Club, a luxurious combination of eggs and cream kept the fish mixture bound together during cooking. She rolled her flat cakes in crushed cornflakes for extra crunch, called them "salmon patties," and served them perched on a slice of hot toast. Today, salmon croquettes are a staple on soul food breakfast menus.

But Cates wasn't the only cook to take a detour with this beloved dish. Many black cooks who had migrated out of the South learned myriad makeshift ways to hold the canned fish mixture together. Some soaked bread in the salmon liquor from the can; some added mashed boiled potatoes or cheese, or cornmeal, or dried bread or cracker crumbs. The most common method was to simply add enough all-purpose flour to "tighten up" the mixture, as Sheila Ferguson explained in *Soul Food: Classic Cuisine from the Deep South*, "until Dad says, 'it's no longer juicy.'"

I owe inspiration for this modern interpretation to Stephanie L. Tyson, who, along with her partner Vivian Joiner, honored Stephanie's grandmother's memory in two Winston-Salem, North Carolina, restaurants and in the cookbook *Soul Food Odyssey*. The recipe comes together fast, and works well with leftover cooked salmon, poached fresh salmon, or canned salmon. Make the recipe as directed to serve as a first course, or make smaller croquettes and serve them in a chafing dish on the buffet.

1 (14.75-ounce) can pink salmon, or 1 pound cooked salmon

¼ cup finely minced celery

½ cup finely minced onion

1 teaspoon fresh lemon juice

1 teaspoon salt, or to taste

½ teaspoon black pepper

¼ teaspoon cayenne pepper (optional)

2 large eggs, beaten

1½ cups fine dried bread crumbs (preferably homemade, see Note, page 47) or cracker crumbs

Flour, for your hands

Oil, for pan-frying

Tartar sauce or Rémoulade Sauce (recipe follows)

1 In a medium bowl, break up the salmon. If using canned, mix with a fork until the bones and skin are well blended. Stir in the celery, onion, lemon juice, salt, black pepper, cayenne (if using), the eggs, and crumbs.

2 With a ¼-cup measure and lightly floured hands, scoop the salmon mixture, then shape into 8 flat discs. (Or, for bite-size hors d'oeuvres, scoop 2 tablespoons of the mixture and shape into 16 discs.)

3 Pour ½ inch oil into a large skillet and heat to 350°F over medium-high heat. (Use a thermometer, or flick in a few bread crumbs; if they sizzle almost immediately but don't burn, the oil is ready.) Adjust the heat to maintain this temperature.

4 Working in batches (do not crowd the pan), fry the croquettes until golden brown, turning over once, about 3 minutes per side (less if making them small). Using a fork and spatula will help make turning easier and prevent croquettes from breaking. Drain on paper towels. Serve hot with sauce of your choice.

RECIPE CONTINUES

RÉMOULADE SAUCE
MAKES ABOUT 1½ CUPS

¾ cup mayonnaise

½ cup Creole mustard

1 teaspoon minced garlic

¼ cup minced green onion

¼ cup minced celery

¼ cup minced fresh parsley

1 tablespoon Worcestershire sauce

1 tablespoon fresh lemon juice

¼ teaspoon sugar (optional)

Salt and black pepper

In a bowl, combine the mayonnaise, mustard, garlic, green onion, celery, parsley, Worcestershire sauce, lemon juice, sugar (if using), and salt and pepper to taste and mix well. Cover and refrigerate for at least 1 hour before serving.

CODFISH BALLS
MAKES 12 BALLS

These versatile codfish balls call for a cup of flaked white fish, whether you take the authentic route (soaking salt cod in water over a day or two to remove its saltiness) or simply cook up fresh fish of your own. Catfish is a tasty option. If you choose to soak the salt cod, the texture will be a little meatier and chewier, and the flavor more complex. It's up to you how long you'd want to soak the cod—some prefer to soak it for 24 hours, leaving a bit of the salt in the fish, and some like to soak it for 2 or 3 days. Soak it in the refrigerator, changing the water every 6 to 12 hours. Taste the fish for salt before you make the mixture and adjust the seasoning of the mixture accordingly.

2 cups diced (¾-inch) peeled potatoes

Salt

1 teaspoon Dijon mustard

¼ teaspoon black pepper

¼ cup minced onion

1 teaspoon minced garlic (about 1 clove)

1 large egg, separated

1 cup cooked and flaked cod or soaked and drained salt cod

1 cup fine dried bread crumbs (preferably homemade, see Note, page 47) or cracker crumbs

Oil, for deep-frying

1 In a medium saucepan, cook the potatoes in boiling salted water to cover, until fork-tender, about 15 minutes. Drain well and mash until smooth. Stir in the mustard, 1 teaspoon salt (or to taste), the pepper, onion, and garlic and let cool to warm. Beat in the egg yolk, then carefully fold in the cod. Shape the mixture into golf ball–size balls.

2 In a shallow dish, beat together the egg white and 1 tablespoon water. In a second shallow dish, spread out the bread crumbs. Dip the codfish balls in the egg wash, then roll in the crumbs to coat.

3 Pour about 3 inches oil into a large Dutch oven or other wide deep pot and heat to 350°F over medium-high heat. (Use a thermometer or flick in a few bread crumbs; if they sizzle almost immediately but don't burn, the oil is ready.) Adjust the heat to maintain this temperature.

4 Working in small batches (do not crowd the pan), fry the balls, turning occasionally, until golden brown, 4 to 5 minutes per side. Drain on paper towels and serve hot.

CRAB CAKES

SERVES 8

Throughout his career and private life, photographer and author John Pinderhughes, a Baltimore native, dedicated himself to preserving the resilient African American spirit. His advertising images encouraged spontaneity in baking cakes for Pillsbury, emphasized the Thanksgiving communal table for Kraft, captured the good life with model, restaurateur, and author B. Smith for *Essence* magazine, and celebrated chef Leah Chase's "recipe for living" in a Publix supermarket campaign.

I turned to Pinderhughes and his paternal grandmother, Gum Gum, for these crab cakes. In Gum Gum's kitchen, Pinderhughes learned old-fashioned values of love, caring, family, and hard work, along with passion for "a little higher grade of cooking."

Grandpa "would never eat crabs the way most people would. . . . He would sit down with a bowl, a napkin, and a knife and fork, and just pick all the meat out into that bowl. He would season it with a dash of salt, pepper, and mayonnaise, almost like we did the crab cakes," Pinderhughes remembered in the *Family of the Spirit Cookbook* (1990).

Unlike crab croquettes, patties, or cutlets, Gum Gum's crab cakes are not held together with a sturdy cream sauce or mashed potatoes, so you will want to handle them as gently as possible; they are light and delicate and aromatic with the perfume of the sea. I learned from trying out dozens of crab cake recipes that half as much mayonnaise-egg binding and more than double the bread crumbs Gum Gum called for in her classic Maryland-styled crab cakes makes handling easier without compromising taste. But try to buy the best-quality crabmeat you can; the deliciousness of these cakes is all about the quality of the crabmeat you use.

2 tablespoons mayonnaise

2 teaspoons Dijon mustard

1 teaspoon minced fresh parsley

¼ cup finely chopped green onions (optional)

¼ teaspoon cayenne pepper

½ teaspoon salt

2 large eggs, lightly beaten

½ cup fine dried bread crumbs (preferably homemade, see Note, opposite) or cracker crumbs

1 pound lump crabmeat

Oil, for frying

Coarse sea salt, for finishing

Lemon wedges, for serving

Tartar sauce, for serving (optional)

1 In a medium bowl, stir together the mayonnaise, mustard, parsley, green onions (if using), cayenne, salt, and eggs. Mix well. Add ¼ cup of the bread crumbs and stir until the crumbs are moistened. Gently stir in the crab, tossing lightly to just mix. Divide the mixture evenly into 16 golf ball-size portions. Flatten the portions into patties, dredge them in the remaining bread crumbs, and place on a platter. Refrigerate 1 hour.

2 Pour 1 inch of the oil into a large skillet and heat to 350°F over medium-high heat. (Use a thermometer, or flick in a few bread crumbs; if they sizzle almost immediately but don't burn, the oil is ready.) Adjust the heat to maintain this temperature.

3 Working in batches (do not crowd the pan), pan-fry the crab cakes until golden brown, about 2 minutes per side. Drain on paper towels. Repeat with the remaining crab cakes. Serve immediately, sprinkled lightly with coarse salt and garnished with lemon wedges and tartar sauce, if desired.

NOTE: Once you make your own bread crumbs, you will never go back to the inferior variety sold at the supermarket. And it's easy. Simply trim the crusts from a couple of stale slices of bread and process them in the food processor or blender into crumbs. Toast in a 325°F oven until browned and dry. Watch the crumbs closely. They toast quickly.

DEVILED CRAB
SERVES 4 TO 8

Deviled crab is popular in Maryland, the Gulf states, and the Lowcountry, where crabs are plentiful. It has been the star attraction on party menus recorded in early black cookbooks, but the dish also helped enslaved and free cooks in Colonial America earn extra money and gain their independence. Howard Paige recorded a traveler's observation in his 1995 cookbook, *African American Family Cookery*: "Years ago, in Tidewater, Virginia, one could buy the most deliciously cooked deviled crabs from the shellfish vendors. The crabs were carried in wicker baskets slung over the shoulders of an amiable old Southern darky whose melodious voice would sing out his wares: 'Hey, ye! Devilly cra-a-abs, cra-a-abs, cra-a-abs! Hey, ye! Devilly cra-a-abs!'"

Recipes for the dish show up in print sporadically during the early twentieth century in cookbooks from coastal regions. Once we get to the 1950s, caterers, educators, and domestic servants published recipes that are not what you'd expect from a dish named "deviled." While the name may suggest some piquant thing, cooks named their creamy crab recipes—crabmeat stirred into a cream sauce with parsley and minced boiled eggs, topped with buttered bread crumbs, baked in buttered crab shells—"deviled" just the same.

I think I know why.

A creamed crab formula spiked with hot pepper sauce (Tabasco), a staple in African American kitchens, appeared in a volume of Time-Life's Foods of the World series, *American Cooking: Southern Style*, in 1971, attributed to a black woman from Coden, Alabama (see recipe, page 49). My guess is that some black cookbook authors presumed the addition of hot sauce in their upscale recipes would seem a bit too "ethnic," so they left it out of their deviled crab recipes.

Despite all this name-calling, deviled crab is a spectacular first course. When the guest list is short, serve the creamy dip in scallop shells, ramekins, or well-scrubbed crab shells with toasted baguette. For crowd-size dining, I keep the dip warm in a slow cooker set on low and let guests serve themselves. And of course, either way, serve it with a bottle of hot pepper sauce.

4 tablespoons (½ stick) butter
2 teaspoons minced onion
1 teaspoon minced garlic (1 clove)
2 tablespoons all-purpose flour
1 teaspoon Dijon mustard
1 cup whole milk or half-and-half
2 teaspoons Worcestershire sauce
½ teaspoon salt, or to taste
¼ teaspoon black pepper
¼ teaspoon paprika
1 pound lump crabmeat, flaked
½ cup fine dried bread crumbs (preferably homemade, see Note, above)
Fresh dill sprigs, for garnish (optional)
Sliced baguette, toasted, for serving
Hot pepper sauce, for serving

RECIPE CONTINUES

1 Preheat the oven to 400°F.

2 In a medium saucepan, heat 2 tablespoons of the butter over medium heat until foaming. Add the onion and garlic and sauté until softened, about 1 minute. Whisk the flour and mustard in well. Cook and stir 1 minute longer. Whisk in ½ cup of the milk. Cook and stir until thick, about 4 minutes. Whisk in the remaining ½ cup milk, the Worcestershire sauce, salt, pepper, and paprika. Gently stir in the crab. Taste and adjust salt, if desired.

3 Pour the mixture into a shallow baking dish or divide among ramekins or scallop shells (or crab shells if you have them). Melt the remaining 2 tablespoons butter and stir it together with the bread crumbs. Sprinkle this over the crab mixture and bake until heated through and the crumbs are golden, 10 to 20 minutes, depending on the size of the baking dishes. Garnish with dill, if desired, and serve with toasted bread and hot pepper sauce.

MARY BRANCH'S BAKED CRAB

Time-Life Books *American Cooking: Southern Style,* Foods of the World, vol. 8, 1971

After the crabs are boiled and shelled, she mixes the meat with milk-soaked bread, raw egg, bell pepper, onion, celery, garlic, Worcestershire and Louisiana hot sauce [a milder version of Tabasco]. She then spoons this spicy stuffing back into the shells, bakes them briefly and serves the crabs piping hot.

SAVANNAH PICKLED SHRIMP

SERVES 6 TO 8

Escovitch fish is a delicious dish of Spanish origin that is beloved by Jamaicans. Known throughout the Caribbean as escovitch or caveach fish, it is made by cooking any variety of whole, small, or sliced fish, then pickling it in a vinegar sauce and garnishing with julienned vegetables, sliced onion, and lemon. I saw strains of escovitch in recipes for pickled shrimp recipes throughout my research for *The Jemima Code.*

Daisy Redman catered extravagant parties in some of the finest homes in Savannah, Georgia. In 1980, she and three other renowned black caterers and restaurateurs shared favorite party and home-style dishes in *Four Great Southern Cooks,* a romantic collection of traditional and regional recipes from the grand houses of the Lowcountry South.

Redman's pickled shrimp is classic Savannah, marinating shrimp in vinegar overnight with onions, chile peppers, and pickling spices. Texans add cilantro and lime to the dish for Southwestern flair, while Scotch bonnet or habanero peppers make Jamaican "pepper shrimp" fiery.

I asked another celebrated Savannah chef how she adapted her pickled shrimp for guests today.

Mashama Bailey is the creative force behind Savannah's award-winning restaurant The Grey. Located in a formerly segregated Greyhound bus station, the fine-dining eatery built its reputation on Bailey's sophisticated nods to the foods of her childhood, fine foods introduced to her by her grandmother: trout, collard greens, chicken liver mousse, pimento

RECIPE CONTINUES

cheese, chicken schnitzel with white barbecue sauce, and pickled shrimp.

"My grandmother became a nurse and a caretaker who worked for rich families too," Bailey explained in a *Garden & Gun* feature story. "And so she always had this elitism about food. It was a sign of success to her. It gave her great pleasure to have the best ingredients she could afford."

For her restaurant, Bailey wanted to turn a spotlight on Georgia shrimp by incorporating "warm spices, like cinnamon, clove, allspice, star anise and nutmeg. We do toast them to bring out the essential oils. And for vinegar, my favorite is white wine, but a nice apple cider also works."

I experimented with multiple recipes from across the diaspora, including Bailey's, to come up with my own version. This spicy specialty is also delicious served on a bed of salad greens for a first course. Be sure to use a fork to remove the shrimp and a few onion slices from the marinade so you and your guests don't get a mouthful of spice.

1 teaspoon salt, plus more for cooking shrimp

3 celery stalks, diced

1 cup sliced yellow or white onion

2 bay leaves

1 large lemon, sliced

2 pounds shell-on large or jumbo shrimp

¼ cup fresh lemon juice

¾ cup white wine vinegar or apple cider vinegar

1 teaspoon pickling spice, toasted in a pan until fragrant

1 teaspoon dried or 1 tablespoon fresh dill

1 Scotch bonnet pepper, minced, or ½ teaspoon crushed red pepper flakes

1 teaspoon minced garlic (1 clove)

3 sprigs fresh tarragon

¾ cup extra-virgin olive oil

½ cup sliced red onion

1 In a large saucepan, combine 2 quarts well-salted water, the celery, onion, bay leaves, and lemon slices and bring to a boil. Add the shrimp and cook until just pink, 2 to 3 minutes. Drain the shrimp in a colander and rinse under cool running water to stop the cooking. (If you'd like, reserve the liquid and use it as a seafood stock; you can further flavor the stock by simmering the shells from the next step in it for another 20 minutes.)

2 When cool enough to handle, peel the shrimp, devein, and set aside to cool completely.

3 In a glass bowl or a wide-mouthed jar with a tight-fitting lid, whisk or shake together the lemon juice, vinegar, pickling spice, dill, 1 teaspoon salt (or to taste), chile pepper, garlic, tarragon, and oil until well blended. Add the red onion and shrimp. Refrigerate, covered, overnight. Use a slotted spoon or fork to serve.

IS IT ANY WONDER
THAT MANKIND STANDS
OPEN-MOUTHED BEFORE
THE BARTENDER,
CONSIDERING THE
MYSTERIES AND MARVELS
OF AN ART THAT
BORDERS ON MAGIC?
—TOM BULLOCK,
THE IDEAL BARTENDER, 1917

Liquified Soul

"What can I get you?" It is a classic barkeep's greeting, a way of welcoming with an offer to quench your thirst. Liquid refreshment comes in many forms: Water we need to survive. Juice and milk nourish. But spirits manipulate the soul; some soothe, others stimulate.

In the case of Tom Bullock, the invitation to refreshment hinted at something ethereal, transcendent, instinctive. Bullock was in the spirit-satisfying business.

After a quarter century animating members of the Pendennis Club of Louisville and the St. Louis Country Club with his "liquified soul," Bullock published *The Ideal Bartender*, a recipe book that included two testimonials. One was written by former President George W. Bush's grandfather. The other one, an editorial in the *St. Louis Post-Dispatch*, praised the elite bartender's expertise in the "art of the julep." It declared: "There is no greater mixologist of any race, color or condition of servitude."

Bullock certainly earned the accolades. He worked his way up from bellboy to bartender, perfecting the rules and the theater of barkeeping. He knew how to wrap wine with a napkin; the correct temperature for serving ale, beer, stout, red wine, or champagne; the proper way to serve liqueurs—over shaved or cracked ice, with straws, or just before coffee. He taught readers to pour ingredients "with great care to prevent the colors from blending," and shared his techniques for a wide assortment of fancy mixed drinks and punches, including the Blue Blazer, a flaming concoction of sugar, water, lemon, and whiskey poured dramatically from one mug to another.

Even before Bullock, black colonial and late eighteenth-century bartenders, caterers, and owners of grogshops, cookshops, oyster houses, taverns, and restaurants—"Liquotarians," as Arturo Schomburg called them—kept African hospitality rituals alive and promoted cultural unity while shaking and stirring their way to independence. Finding out how they did that captivated me.

Water with honey, fermented palm and fruit wines, corn or ginger beer, tea brewed from kola nuts and hibiscus flowers, and a drink of sour milk thickened with millet or sorghum were some of the "memory dishes" that the enslaved transplanted from Africa to the New World, Judith Carney explained in *In the Shadow of Slavery: Africa's Botanical Legacy in the Atlantic World*.

These drinks soothed the horrors of enslavement and oppression while lubricating spirits during religious acts, then largely disappeared following Emancipation. As Frederick Douglass recounted in *My Bondage and My Freedom*, captives spent holidays "fiddling, dancing and 'jubilee beating'" (both a form of music and a form of dance) anointed by distilled and fermented beverages brewed with native ingredients.

The ring shout was one of the rituals during which food and drink triggered cultural solidarity. Described as a group dance of West African origin, the secret worship ceremony involved counterclockwise movement, call-and-response singing, hand clapping, and foot stomping. It took place around a fire in the woods or in the plantation cookhouse, during "camp meetings," at the climax of the planting season, to celebrate the harvest, or to honor ancestors or village and town founders. It survived openly in the North when the enslaved came into town and commingled with free people of color while making purchases at the market for their masters or selling a few homemade goods for themselves, and it evolved into hybridized ceremonies that intertwined a show of respect for leaders and elders with Christian exaltation rites and other Anglo celebrations. Libations were often involved, according to Jessica B. Harris. The Pinkster Festival, for instance, was a Dutch Protestant celebration of Pentecost that became a parade of black royalty, where gingerbread and rum were served. The old folks danced in costumes, rode around on horseback, held dinner feasts, and drank in taverns. Free blacks owned a few of those taverns, known variously as grogshops or drinking shops.

Catering to elites also afforded black bartenders a somewhat privileged social status and a sense of autonomy, especially in New York.

In the late 1700s, Samuel Fraunces, an exemplary cook nicknamed "Black Sam," owned and operated a New York mansion as a tavern that was a gathering place for revolutionaries, including General George Washington. It was first named Queen Charlotte's Head Tavern, then Queen's Tavern, and ultimately Fraunces Tavern. Washington delivered his farewell address to his officers there, and the popular dining spot was the site of an unsuccessful assassination attempt—the "Poisoned Pea Plot of 1776," as Adrian Miller pointed out in *The President's Kitchen Cabinet: The Story of the African Americans Who Have Fed Our First Families, from the Washingtons to the Obamas.* (A replica of the building stands at its original location in Manhattan's Financial District.)

Thomas Downing was another one of Manhattan's prosperous restaurateurs, celebrated for his culinary skill, professionalism, cultural leadership, and "dignified ethos," David S. Shields explained in *The Culinarians: Lives and Careers from the First Age of American Fine Dining.* Downing's stylish Oyster Saloon catered to an elite clientele. He sold oysters stewed, fried, pickled, and in the shell and boasted of his expertise "in the most modern style boned Turkies, Alamode Beef, Hams, Tongues, jellies, etc." He was so respected by the New York elite that when he died the New York Chamber of Commerce closed to attend his funeral. At the same time that this black man, who came to New York from Virginia in 1819, ran an oyster house that was a landmark for the powerful, he was also an influential activist who championed education, advocated for racial equality, and maintained a stop on the Underground Railroad.

Then there was Cato Alexander, who purchased his freedom and amassed appreciable wealth while bartending. Alexander kept Cato's Tavern for forty-eight years. Poets wrote about him, and at a time when bondsmen didn't even own themselves, an 1829 advertisement listing the contents of Alexander's estate revealed his riches: paintings, prints, and several business establishments. A 1916 feature story in *Americana,* a historical magazine published by the National American Society, described Cato this way: "Those who tasted his okra soup, terrapin, fried chicken, curried oysters, roast duck or drank his New York brandy punch, his Virginia egg-nogg or South Carolina milk punch, wondered how anyone who owned him ever could sell him even to himself. . . . He was a famous man in his generation. A sale son of Africa, he lived and died respected in a community far more aristocratic and exclusive than its more pretentious democratic successors."

That these black entrepreneurs could build such reputations was testament to their skills, yes, but to the traditions of hosting and entertaining throughout African diasporic culture as well. By the early twentieth century, from Seattle and Los Angeles to Atlanta and Clarksdale, Mississippi, the African American–owned grogshops of the Deep South had evolved into bars, jazz clubs, and juke joints where booze, music, and merriment converged.

Black cookbook authors affirmed these distilling, fermenting, and mixology traditions and more when they marketed recipes to upwardly mobile blacks who had access to fine spirits and champagne. Frederick Douglass Opie, who mined many of those cookbooks, has clarified that hosts and hostesses served everything from plantation wines and "bootleg likker" to revitalizing waters and nectars, soothing hot tea and coffee, brightly colored punches, syrups, shrubs and vinegars, and fancy cocktails, "adding their own ideas for making special occasions festive."

I found many of their suggestions worth remembering and emulating in my own home. One of them was a progressive automobile party, outlined by John B. Goins in 1913. On a soggy Saturday morning, after my family moved to Austin, Texas, I rolled my boys in a wagon from house to house inviting my neighbors to a gathering featuring some of the elements outlined in *The American Waiter*: "This party consists of twelve or more ladies who take turns entertaining . . . starting from the residence of Mrs. H., who serves the Martini cocktail, standing. The first stop after leaving Mrs. H. is for beef broth *en tasse* and wafers." Goins included menu and table setting suggestions, the time allowed at each home, the room in which the party should take place, plus driving and conversational instructions designed to keep the party moving on time, such as "re-enter machine and proceed to Mrs. B. . . . retire to parlor for fifteen minutes' chat. Proceed to Mrs. C.'s reception room. Pass 'Lalla Rookh' punch in sherbet glass on six-inch plate with paper doily, vanilla wafer and spoon. Chat a few minutes, proceed to Mrs. D's dining room and be served with salad and brown bread sandwiches. Chat a few minutes and proceed to Mrs. E.'s reception room where after dinner coffee is served. . . . The broth, punch and coffee cake may be taken standing or as hostess desires."

My neighbors and I chose our courses; I served soup—a silky butternut squash bisque garnished with a last-minute splash of sherry. By the time we staggered home after the last stop, where my next-door neighbors passed dessert, coffee, and liqueurs, we had learned a lot about one another, established a bond beyond the concept of "just being neighborly" that still exists, and remembered the dignity associated with the business of serving food and beverages.

Home Brews

Ginger beer is a refreshing, tangy drink. It is one of several African formulas, including palm wine, that enslaved and free black people handed down as part of their homebrewing lineage.

In the New World, these traditions were applied to native, wild, and discarded ingredients. Locust beer, made of the edible pods from locust trees, and beer from persimmons or sweet potato peelings were among the drinks some believed ensured vitality or soothed ailments, while others indulged to stimulate the spirit or simply to celebrate special occasions.

There are many ways to make and serve ginger beer. The documented methods I've seen go all the way back to Robert Roberts, the butler of Gore Place in Massachusetts, who infused water with cinnamon, raisins, berries, cherries, citrus, and aniseed for refreshing drinks. He put forth his recipe for the "best ginger beer" in his 1827 guide to household management, *The House Servant's Directory*.

African and Caribbean recipes rely upon yeast and allow the mixture to stand at room temperature for several days to give ginger beer its fermented tang and effervescence. Ginger punch takes a tamer approach, boiling ginger root with water and sugar and flavoring it with citrus juice. In ginger tea, milk stands in for the citrus.

GINGER PUNCH
MAKES ABOUT 8 CUPS

This is a combination of several ginger beer recipes from the books in *The Jemima Code*. Simply made, it relies upon journalist Eric Copage's steeping method, which yields a sweet-tangy ginger infusion rather than an effervescent beer. With this technique, your beverage will be ready in less than an hour. Add a little rum or vodka for a heady brew.

½ **pound fresh ginger**
1 **cup honey or 1½ cups sugar**
¼ **teaspoon salt**
½ **cup fresh lemon or lime juice**
6 **cups still or sparkling water**
Ice cubes

1 Scrub the ginger with a brush to clean off any dirt and cut into ¼-inch-thick slices. Do not peel. In a small saucepan, combine the ginger and 2 cups water. Bring to a boil over high heat, then reduce the heat to low, cover, and simmer gently until you have a strong infusion, about 20 minutes. You may add water ¼ cup at a time, to keep the ginger covered by water, if needed.

2 Stir in the honey, salt, and lemon juice. Cool completely. Strain and chill.

3 To serve, add the still or sparkling water to the syrup and serve over ice.

ELDERBERRY WINE

Hamilton Hall Cookbook,
Chestnut Street Associates, 1947

1 qt. elderberry juice, 3 lbs granulated sugar and warm water to fill 1 gallon jug. To extract juice easily from berries put them in the sun or warm place until they ferment a little.

Put cork in jug with rubber tubing ½ inch inserted in the cork, have tubing flush with bottom of cork, the other end of tube in bottle of water to exclude air, as too much turns the wine to vinegar.

Do not have the jug so full that it will siphon into bottle of water. Put in warm place to work about 6 months. When it is clear pour off from the dregs.

This can be made in same proportion, using 5 gallons or any size keg.

——*Edward P. Cassell of Salem, Massachusetts*

PERSIMMON BEER

What the Slaves Ate: Recollections of African American Foods and Foodways from the Slave Narratives,
Dwight Eisnach and Herbert C. Covey, 2009

Gather your persimmons, wash and put in a keg, cover well with water and add about two cups of meal to it and let sour about three days. That makes a nice drink. Boil persimmons just as you do prunes now day and they will answer for the same purpose.

——*Millie Evans of Arkansas*

Life Everlasting Tea

Flavorful infusions are an age-old custom, particularly important among diasporic cooks who flavored water to improve its taste and nutrition, and to express hospitality. One only needs to follow the path of the teas brewed across the diaspora—West African *bissap* (also known as sorrel or hibiscus tea), "leopard tongue," and kola tea; the molasses waters of enslavement; the strawberry and cherry cordials crafted by caterers and bartenders; and the pink lemonade, red soda pop, and Kool-Aid memorialized at Emancipation Day picnics—to see how red drinks became the quintessential African American celebration beverage.

Enslaved and free Africans steeped all sorts of plants as medicinal aids for sickly folks and for hot or cold refreshment. The rosy bark from trees, roots, sassafras leaves, even beef soothed everything from cramps to colds. Dried and ground whole nutmeg, fruit leaves from wild blackberries or strawberries, and flowering blossoms such as goldenrod and rose hips quenched thirst, as Ruth L. Gaskins explained in her 1969 soul food cookbook, *A Good Heart and a Light Hand*.

In freedom, families continued to believe in the wisdom of these old ways. In her memoir, *God, Dr. Buzzard, and the Bolito Man*, Cornelia Walker Bailey, a "saltwater geechee" from Sapelo Island, Georgia, shared memories of Life Everlasting tea, a brew her family drank daily for good health: "Papa would come across Life Everlasting growing in the woods . . . and he would bring home these huge bunches of it tied to his knapsack, and hang them outside in the corn house to dry. Life Everlasting's got tiny, little leaves that turn kinda silver-gray in the fall, when it's ready for you to pick it, and little white blossoms on the top. So when he wanted some tea, he'd go out back, break a piece and boil it up."

Among the formerly enslaved, Charles Hayes remembered the tradition in a Federal Writers' Project interview in 1936: "Us useta have all sorts of cures for de sick people, f'rinstance, us used de Jerusalem weed cooked wid molasses into a candy for to give to de chilluns to git rid of worms. Den us'd bile de root an' make a tea for de stomach worms. Horehound, dat growed wild was used for colds. Mullen tea was used for colds en'swollen j'ints. Den dere was de life everlastin' tea dat was also good for colds and horse mint tea dat was good for de chills an' fevers."

Brewed tea didn't just soothe. Caterers and home cooks mixed tea with fresh fruit and juice in refreshing beverages served with meals, on special occasions, and in large quantities for a crowd.

CITRUS-HONEY TEA PUNCH

MAKES ABOUT 11 CUPS

Oklahoma caterer Cleora Butler, author of *Cleora's Kitchens: The Memoir of a Cook & Eight Decades of Great American Food*, intensified the flavor of her tea by allowing the brew to steep for several hours at room temperature. Then she added zesty citrus fruit, honey, and mint to give this punch personality. Honey harvested from nearby beehives guaranteed a refreshing glass of iced tea, even when sugar was limited. Inspired by her, this modern-day punch combines honey, mint tea, fresh citrus, and the effervescence of lemon-lime soda or sparkling water.

1 cup boiling water
4 mint tea bags
½ cup honey
1 cup fresh lemon juice (from about 6 lemons)
1 cup fresh orange juice (from about 3 oranges)
1 (1-liter) bottle or 3 (12-ounce) cans lemon-lime soda or sparkling water, chilled
Ice cubes
Lemon and orange slices, for garnish
Mint sprigs, for garnish

1 In a teapot or heatproof pitcher with a lid, pour the boiling water over the tea bags. Cover and steep for 5 minutes. Remove the tea bags. Stir in the honey, mixing until dissolved. Add 4 cups cold water, the lemon juice, and orange juice and chill.

2 To serve, combine the tea mixture, soda, ice, and lemon and orange slices in a punch bowl. Serve in mason jars or tall glasses garnished with sprigs of mint.

RUSSIAN TEA

Aunt Julia's Cook Book, ca. 1930
[Both Southern Spiced and Russian Tea appear interchangeably in African American cookbooks throughout the years. This recipe booklet, produced by the Standard Oil Company of Pennsylvania during the 1930s, featured recipes for both, with virtually the same ingredients, created by two unnamed black women who appear to have been domestic workers or caterers.]

2 pounds sugar
1½ cups water
30 whole cloves
Grated rind of 3 oranges
2 dozen large oranges
4 large lemons
½ pound Orange Pekoe tea

Boil the sugar, water, cloves and grated orange rind ten minutes, or until it is a thick syrup. This should be done twenty-four hours before serving. Strain the juice of the oranges and lemons, make a very black tea and add the syrup and fruit juices. Bring to the boiling point and serve very hot. This serves about fifty people—the exact amount made depending on how much water is used in making the tea and how much juice the oranges produce.

SORREL (HIBISCUS) TEA
MAKES 2 QUARTS

Sorrel is "the favourite drink of Jamaicans at Christmas time, made from the sorrel plant, a low bushy shrub with red stems and calices, which comes into season toward the end of the year. No Jamaican Christmas is complete without bottles of red drink brewed with rum and ginger," Enid Donaldson wrote in *The Real Taste of Jamaica*. The sorrel is brilliantly red and sweet-tart, with a delicious bite from ginger and aromas of clove and citrus. Note that the "sorrel" here is a Caribbean name for hibiscus flowers, also called *jamaica* in Spanish. When shopping, make sure you are getting that rather than the green herb called sorrel that tastes tartly of lemon.

2 cups dried hibiscus (sorrel) flowers
⅓ cup peeled fresh ginger slices (¼ inch thick)
2- to 3-inch cinnamon stick
6 whole cloves
¼ cup grated orange zest
Grated zest and juice of 1 lemon
Demerara sugar, honey, or agave nectar
Mint leaves, for garnish

In a large saucepan, bring 2 quarts water, the hibiscus, ginger, cinnamon, cloves, and orange and lemon zests to a boil over medium heat. Boil for 5 minutes. Remove from the heat. Add the lemon juice, cover tightly, and let stand for 1 to 2 days at room temperature. Strain and discard the solids. Sweeten to taste with demerara sugar, honey, or agave nectar. Chill thoroughly. Serve over ice and garnish with mint.

Coffee

(or Java, as Edna Lewis Called It)

Coffee is believed to have originated in Ethiopia, where wild trees thrive on the hillsides of Kaffa and Harar; the town of Kaffa may have given coffee its name. Ethiopian coffee is served unsweetened in demitasse cups, poured from the typical black *jebena* (jug), after being spiced, boiled, and reboiled into a concentrated richness that smells faintly of cloves.

In the Americas, however, the African enslaved devised coffee substitutes to supplement diets limited to smoked pork and cornmeal rations. In his 1853 narrative, *Twelve Years a Slave,* Solomon Northrup described cornmeal scorched in a kettle, then boiled and sweetened with molasses, if available. Katie Darling, a nurse and housegirl on a plantation near Marshall, Texas, during the mid-nineteenth century, remembered the parched meal, which she called "Lincoln coffee": "They'd parch [corn] meal in the oven, bile [boil] it and drink the liquor . . . dat 'Lincoln' coffee was sumpin' to us. . . ."

During the Civil War, when Southerners generally struggled to obtain coffee, sugar, rum, and other luxuries, the practice spread. Cooks brewed parched bran, sweet potatoes, acorns, grains, okra, and the seeds of persimmons and watermelon. Dr. George Washington Carver's peanut coffee was another coffee substitute.

But then Carrie Alberta Lyford, director of the Home Economics School at Hampton Normal and Agricultural Institute in Virginia in the early twentieth century, opened a whole new window for students at freedmen's schools. She instructed on the art of proper, true coffee and focused attention on transitioning cooks from "cooking coffee" over an open fire to more gently steeping the grounds, in terms that modern-day baristas would appreciate.

The luxury of coffee was never lost. Creole (French) coffee, coffee with milk, and coffee drinks spiked with booze were pure Louisiana at the turn of the twentieth century. And Edna Lewis recalled in *The Taste of Country Cooking* that morning was "incomplete without that cup of well-boiled coffee with cream from overnight milk, which was stirred in to make a mocha-colored kind of coffee syllabub." In Freetown, the Virginia town where she grew up among the formerly enslaved, the froth on top "signified unexpected money coming to the one who drank the coffee." Some cooks added salt, some eggshells, and some others egg whites or yolks to the boiling pot, but "all were divine," Lewis wrote.

CALYPSO COFFEE

SERVES 2

~~~~~~

Two after-dinner drinks come together in one, with inspiration from Africans in the West Indies who creatively blended coffee, fruit, sugar, and alcoholic beverages into tasty drinks. Sparked by Helen Willinsky's *Jerk from Jamaica: Barbecue Caribbean Style*, I replaced the coffee liqueur in this island treat with hot chocolate, which mellows the strong coffee.

½ **cup heavy whipping cream**

5 **tablespoons sugar**

6 **ounces semisweet chocolate, chopped**

1 **cup strong-brewed coffee, such as Cuban or Jamaican Blue Mountain**

1 **to 2 tablespoons dark rum, to taste**

Chocolate shavings, for garnish

1 In a bowl with an electric mixer, beat the cream on high speed until soft peaks form. Reduce the speed to low. With the machine running, sprinkle 1 tablespoon sugar over the cream. Increase the speed and continue to whip to stiff peaks. Do not overwhip.

2 In a saucepan, combine the chocolate and ¼ cup water and stir over low heat until melted. When smooth, add the remaining 4 tablespoons sugar and bring to a boil over medium heat, stirring. Reduce the heat to a simmer and allow to bubble gently for 5 minutes, stirring constantly and scraping the pan bottom to keep the mixture from sticking. Stir in the coffee a little at a time and continue to heat until just boiling. Remove from the heat. Stir in the rum and pour into coffee cups. Top with dollops of whipped cream and chocolate shavings and serve.

HOMEMADE COFFEE

Cotton Patch Cooking, Esther Nelson, 1981

~~~~~~

$^2\!/_3$ cup cornmeal

$^1\!/_3$ cup molasses

2 cups bran

$^1\!/_2$ cup boiling water

Mix dry ingredients in a bowl. Add the boiling water to molasses and mix well. Pour over the bran and meal. Mix thoroughly. Pour into a baking pan and bake in oven at moderate temperature until desired color.

To make coffee, remove from oven and cool. Grind through a food mill until fine. Use in the same manner as ordinary coffee. Adding boiling water, bring to a boil, and let stand on the edge of stove under cover for 10 minutes; strain.

TATER COFFEE

~~~~~~

Wash raw potatoes. Do not peel. Chop into small pieces about the size of an almond. Place in a small pan; place in oven 300 degrees. Stir frequently to prevent sticking together. When dry, place in a box or bag. When used they must be roasted the same as coffee beans and then ground in a mill.

CAFÉ BRÛLOT

SERVES 8

For generations, this flaming, spiced Cognac-coffee cocktail has been the "grand finale" in a cup and on a pedestal at the end of a fabulous Creole meal in legendary New Orleans restaurants, such as Arnaud's, Antoine's, Brennan's, and Galatoire's.

I adapted this recipe, which re-creates the spectacle at home, from Rudy Lombard and Nathaniel Burton's 1978 cookbook, *Creole Feast: Fifteen Master Chefs of New Orleans Reveal Their Secrets*. You can make it with or without the flameproof brûlot bowl.

1 orange
4 (2- to 3-inch) cinnamon sticks
12 whole cloves
¼ cup sugar
6 ounces Cognac, rum, or good whiskey
4 cups hot strong-brewed coffee

With a sharp knife or vegetable peeler, remove the orange peel. Use a knife to cut off as much white pith as possible from the orange peel. Thinly slice the peel and place it in a medium heatproof bowl or saucepan with the cinnamon, cloves, and sugar. In a separate small saucepan, gently warm the Cognac over low heat, until steaming. Pour the hot Cognac over the orange peel mixture and ignite with a long match. Use a ladle to stir in the coffee to extinguish the flames. Stir until the sugar dissolves. Serve in brûlot or demitasse cups.

CREOLE CAFÉ AU LAIT

SERVES 2

Creole coffee, the beloved elixir of the French Market in New Orleans, served alongside warm beignets, is a very strong coffee accented with a subtle taste of the woods, from chicory. The demitasse contains a potent beverage, served as the famous "small black" or "*café noir*," or poured over hot milk and cream and called *café au lait*—French for "coffee with milk." Most Creole recipes call for half coffee and half milk or cream, but this version of *New Orleans Cookbook* author Lena Richard's recipe is uber-rich, a bit like hot milk and cream with a splash of coffee.

1 cup whole milk
1 cup heavy whipping cream
½ cup strong-brewed coffee (with chicory, such as Café du Monde brand, if you like)
Sugar or sweetener of choice (optional)

In a small saucepan, combine the milk, cream, and coffee and bring to a boil over medium-low heat. Immediately remove from heat, pour into coffee mugs and serve with sweetener, if desired.

Fruit Punch for Grown-ups

Planter's Punch and mixes named by region—like Mississippi Planter's Punch and Whiskey Punch St. Louis Style—are boozy beverages that stir together rum, whiskey, brandy, wine, and citrus juice in varying proportions.

During the mid- to late-nineteenth century, black bartenders like Jasper Crouch concocted and served these punches at country clubs and gentlemen's private gathering places (and should not be confused with the sweet, fizzy, fruity beverages served in teacups at ladies' luncheons). These potent drinks took their cues from rum libations served all across the Caribbean. By midcentury, caterers and bartenders alike were adapting single-serve cocktails to crowd-size punch bowl proportions, with libations such as Tom Bullock's Pineapple Julep, fruit shrubs mixed with soda water, and an assortment of mixtures simply called "cup."

Whimsical shrub- and fruit-based cocktails crafted by skilled mixologists and cookbook authors have been making a comeback since the soul era.

Back then, the beverage section in black cookbooks featured drinks to be served during special gatherings, such as this alluring array mentioned in Ruth Gaskins's *A Good Heart and a Light Hand*: Punch for 100, Cider Punch, Fruit Punch, Mint Julep Punch, Rhubarb Punch, and Wine Punch (see page 73)—the latter a recipe Gaskins offered with gendered variations: "The women prefer the first three ingredients mixed with ginger ale; the men, the first three mixed with nothing."

CHAMPAGNE COCKTAIL

MAKES 8 COCKTAILS

The bartender Tom Bullock (see page 53) published two recipes for champagne punch, made with oranges, pineapple, maraschino cherries, maraschino liqueur, Curaçao, and brandy.

This beautiful cocktail is my own special-occasion tribute to his sweet country club libation. I also took my cue from home cooks who adapted the punch as a cocktail by replacing French Champagne with American sparkling wine. Prosecco works too. Think of it as a dressed-up mimosa, prepared in small batches and served regally in flutes. Keep in mind that champagne glasses vary in size (mine hold about 4 ounces), so the number of servings in this recipe may vary, and you may have a bit of sparkling wine left over. To serve the drink in a wineglass, prepare as directed, then top off each serving with the remaining wine.

8 maraschino cherries, with stems
8 teaspoons grenadine
West Indian orange bitters
2 cups Ruby Red grapefruit juice
1 (750 ml) bottle chilled sparkling wine, brut or extra dry

Place champagne flutes in the refrigerator to chill. Add 1 cherry, 1 teaspoon grenadine, 2 dashes bitters, ¼ cup grapefruit juice, and 2 to 3 ounces of sparkling wine to each chilled flute, depending upon the size of the glass. Add any remaining sparkling wine to fill the glasses.

PLANTER'S PUNCH

MAKES 1 DRINK

Tiffanie Barriere, Atlanta mixologist extraordinaire, re-created Jasper Crouch's Quoit Club Punch as an homage for the 2012 Southern Foodways Alliance symposium. This is my rendition, but you may increase the proportions to serve in pitchers or a punch bowl at larger gatherings.

1 ounce rum
1 ounce bourbon or good-quality whiskey
1 ounce brandy
1 ounce fresh lemon juice
1 tablespoon Simple Syrup (recipe follows)
½ cup crushed ice
¼ to ½ cup club soda or sparkling water
Lemon twist

In a shaker, combine the rum, bourbon, brandy, lemon juice, simple syrup, and crushed ice. Shake to mix well. Fill a tall Collins glass with club soda and pour the punch over. Serve with a lemon twist.

SIMPLE SYRUP

MAKES ABOUT 3 CUPS

3 cups water
2½ cups granulated or demerara sugar

In a heavy saucepan, stir together the water and sugar. Bring to a boil over high heat, then reduce the heat to medium-high and simmer until clear, thickened and reduced by about one-third, about 10 minutes. Cool and store refrigerated in a jar with a tight-fitting lid.

RUM PUNCH

SERVES 10 TO 12

Rum Punch is a Caribbean cocktail with a rhyming recipe that helps the barkeep remember how to make it: One of sour, two of sweet, three of strong, four of weak. The "measures" can be tablespoons, cups, or gallons, but are always in the same ratio.

Dunston Harris, author of *Island Cooking: Recipes from the Caribbean*, helped me fill in the classic memory verse, using a variety of sweeteners and spices to develop complex flavor, and substituting light rum for dark. Feel free to experiment with the measures yourself, trying various proportions of light and dark rum, flavored or simple syrup, your favorite fruit juice, such as pineapple or orange, and sparkling water in place of some or all of the still water.

1 cup fresh lime juice
1 cup sugar
½ cup grenadine
½ cup Orange Syrup (recipe follows)
3 cups light rum
4 cups water (see Note)
1 teaspoon ground or grated nutmeg
6 allspice berries, cracked
Ice
Orange slices, for garnish

1 In a pitcher, combine the lime juice, sugar, grenadine, orange syrup, rum, water, nutmeg, and allspice. Refrigerate 1 hour.

2 Strain the mixture into a punch bowl. Fill the bowl with ice and orange slices. Serve in old fashioned glasses.

NOTE: If substituting cold sparkling water for the still water, add it to the punch bowl after the chilled juice mixture to preserve its effervescence.

ORANGE SYRUP

MAKES ABOUT 2 CUPS

2 tablespoons grated orange zest
1 cup fresh orange juice
2 cups sugar

In a heavy saucepan, combine the orange zest, orange juice, and sugar. Stir over low heat until dissolved. Bring to a boil over medium-high heat, reduce the heat to a simmer, and cook until the syrup is thick, about 5 minutes. Cool and store in the refrigerator in a jar with a tight-fitting lid.

WINE PUNCH

A Good Heart and a Light Hand,
Ruth L. Gaskins, 1968

1 bottle apricot brandy
1 bottle of Sauterne
1 bottle of dry Champagne
1 quart of soda water

Mix all ingredients and chill. Serves 12.

Cocktails and Libations

I have to give Jack Daniel's credit: The Lynchburg, Tennessee, distillery celebrated its 150th anniversary admirably—with a public telling of Nearest Green's previously obscured role in establishing Jack Daniel's lucrative whiskey-making process. Green, a black master distiller, was Jack's right hand and, it's thought, the man who devised the whiskey that bears Daniel's name.

African Americans have a peculiar connection to whiskey making, moonshining, and bootlegging. Although most planters forbade the enslaved from distilling and consuming alcohol, African Americans enjoyed illicitly made corn liquor simmered in stills hidden in the woods, rye grain sprouted in crock jars, and pumpkin whiskey left to ferment under the bed, Jacqueline Jones divulged in *Labor of Love, Labor of Sorrow: Black Women, Work, and the Family, from Slavery to the Present.* Some did receive strong drink from planters as an incentive to work hard during the harvest season, while others were allowed to make liquor as compensation for their unpaid labor, as Rebecca Hooks, a ninety-year-old woman of mixed white, Cherokee, and black heritage, explained in 1936. Her father purchased books for her with money he earned by selling corn whiskey. Esther Nelson's 1981 collection of Kentucky folk traditions celebrated this heritage with a thirty-eight-step recipe for corn liquor that included a detailed drawing of an old-fashioned still and began with this important instruction: "Find a hideout in the woods."

Today, we can get bourbon and whiskey distilled in single barrels and small batches, with ice or "neat," straight up or mixed in sweet cocktails, such as the toddy, julep, and festive punches appreciated at special occasions of all kinds.

QUICK EGGNOG

SERVES 12 TO 15

Everywhere you look in our history, sweetened milk imbued with alcohol has sparked the imagination. Rum has infused milk punch, the holiday brunch drink, with a hint of molasses and the taste of the Caribbean. Brandy and bourbon hint at French New Orleans. And in Martinique, creamy coconut milk makes milk punch taste like a tropical dessert.

Former bondservants interviewed for the Federal Writers' Project expressed fond memories of indulging in eggnog during holiday celebrations in the homes of the landed gentry. Maybe that's why African Americans of means favored eggnog at Christmastime—a symbol of conviviality in the midst of tribulation.

Flossie Morris's "Very, Very Unusual Egg Nog" is indeed very unusual—and decadent. I adapted her recipe but kept the accompanying warning: "After you serve this to your guests, they will want to spend the night."

4 large eggs, separated
1½ cups sugar
1 quart whole milk
1 cup half-and-half
1 pint eggnog ice cream, softened
1 quart prepared eggnog, chilled
¾ cup bourbon or good-quality whiskey
½ cup rum
½ cup brandy
Pinch of salt
1 cup heavy whipping cream, whipped
Ground or freshly grated nutmeg

1 In a large heatproof bowl set over a pan of boiling water (make sure the bowl doesn't touch the water), whisk the egg yolks while gradually adding the sugar, stirring constantly until thick and creamy. Whisk in the milk and half-and-half. Continue to cook and stir until the mixture thickens again, then remove the bowl from the pan.

2 In a separate bowl, with an electric mixer (or in a stand mixer), beat the egg whites to stiff peaks. Fold the beaten whites into the egg-milk mixture. Return the bowl to the pan of boiling water and cook and stir until slightly thickened and the egg whites are cooked, about 5 minutes. Remove from the heat and let cool.

3 Refrigerate until completely cold, then stir in the softened ice cream, prepared eggnog, bourbon, rum, brandy, and salt. Fold in the whipped cream and serve or store covered in the refrigerator. Sprinkle with nutmeg before serving. It will keep 4 to 5 days and it improves as it sits.

ICE MILK PUNCH [W]

Colorful Louisiana Cuisine in Black and White,
Ethel Dixon and Bibby Tate, 1990
[This recipe is marked with a "W" for white and their eggnog is marked with a "B" for black, presumably because black cooks were associated with the hard work in the kitchen; milk punch is easier to make.]

1½ cups bourbon
2 quarts vanilla ice milk
2 cups milk
3 tablespoons sugar
1 teaspoon vanilla

Add bourbon to ice milk, sugar and vanilla, then add milk. Fill tall glasses with mixture and sprinkle with nutmeg on top. This can be mixed in blender.

APPLE HOT TODDIES

SERVES 4

I had never heard of making hot toddies for a crowd before Jesse Lewis. The caterer from Bay St. Louis, Mississippi, claimed his recipe for this soothing hot tea served over slices of unpeeled apple and lemon, topped off with rum, came from a band of Spanish gypsies. The convivial potion he re-created is remarkably good on a cold winter's night and excellent for Thanksgiving, Christmas, or New Year's parties, "guaranteed to give a party twice the sparkle on half the rum," Lewis assured in *Jesse's Book of Creole and Deep South Recipes*.

I've taken a few liberties with Jesse's version, as I am a bourbon drinker, after all.

1 teaspoon whole cloves
3 lemons, cut into ¼-inch-thick slices
4 medium apples, cored and cut into 8 slices
3 to 4 tablespoons dark brown sugar, to taste
4 ginger or apple-flavored tea bags
4 (2- to 3-inch) cinnamon sticks
Whole nutmeg
Bourbon, whiskey, or rum

1 Insert the cloves into the centers of the lemon slices (this makes it easier to manage the cloves). In a medium saucepan, combine the clove-studded lemons, apples, brown sugar, and 1 quart water. Bring to a boil over medium-high heat, then reduce the heat to medium and simmer, covered, until the apples are tender and the mixture thickens, about 15 minutes.

2 Remove the saucepan from the heat. Add the tea bags and cinnamon sticks and let steep for 5 minutes.

3 Discard the tea bags and cinnamon sticks. Carefully spoon some of the fruit into mugs and pour in about ¾ cup of the tea. Top off each mug with a grating of nutmeg and liquor of your choice and serve.

JOHN TODDY

Rebecca's Cookbook, Rebecca West, 1942
[West grew up in a family that was "strictly temprunce," so when her "lady" suggested she include recipes for cocktails in her collection, she turned to her country club chef friends for help.]

Use an 8-ounce glass, and into it put a half teaspoonful of sugar and a drink of whisky. Keep a spoon in the glass to keep it from breaking while you fill it two-thirds full of hot water.

MINT JULEPS

MAKES 2 COCKTAILS

Tom Bullock spent a quarter century as the "ideal bartender" who "refreshed and delighted" the members and their friends at the Pendennis Club in Louisville, Kentucky, and the St. Louis Country Club of St. Louis, Missouri. But the recipe for his distinctive mint julep was incorrectly attributed to a "well-known member" of the Pendennis Club in the 1904 collection of recipes from the fine families of Lexington, *The Blue Grass Cook Book* by Minnie C. Fox.

Bullock reclaimed his creations—brandy juleps, champagne juleps, pineapple juleps, and mint juleps in both the Kentucky and St. Louis style—in a recipe book he titled *The Ideal Bartender*.

The version of the recipe presented here is classic, but for variety, you can follow Bullock's lead by substituting one part brandy and two parts rum for the whiskey.

6 mint leaves, plus 2 sprigs fresh mint for garnish
2 tablespoons Simple Syrup (page 72)
4 ounces bourbon, whiskey, brandy, or rum
Crushed ice

Refrigerate 2 tumblers until thoroughly chilled. Combine the mint leaves and syrup in each glass. Stir well with a muddler or long-handled bar spoon to extract the oils from the mint. Do not crush the leaves. Remove the mint from the glass and discard. Stir in the whiskey. Mix well. Fill each glass with ice, mounding above the rim into a pyramid shape. Insert a straw and garnish with a mint sprig.

PENDENNIS CLUB MINT JULEP

The Blue Grass Cook Book, Minnie C. Fox, 1904

These are some essentials:

1st. Fine, straight, old Kentucky Bourbon whisky—blended whiskies do not give good results.
2d. An abundant supply of freshly cut sprigs of mint—preferably young shoots— no portion of which has been bruised.
3d. Dry, cracked flint ice. A glass will answer the purpose, but a silver mug is preferable. At this club, silver cups are kept on ice. A syrup of sugar and water is also kept on hand.

The silver cup is first filled with the ice, and then the desired quantity of fine whisky poured in and thoroughly shaken with a spoon or shaker until a heavy frost forms on the mug. The desired amount of syrup is then poured in and stirred enough to be mixed. The mint is then carefully placed in the mugs with the stems barely sticking in the ice and the tops projecting 2 inches above the top of the cup. Straws are then placed in the cup, reaching from the bottom to about 1 inch above the top, and the sooner one sticks one's nose in the mint and begins drinking through the straws the better. There is no flavor of mint, merely the odor.

Any stinting in quality or quantity materially affects the result.

—Tom Bullock, Louisville, Kentucky

GOOD BREAD MAKES THE
HOMELIEST MEAL ACCEPTABLE.
—CARRIE PAULINE LYNCH,
*PAULINE'S PRACTICAL BOOK
OF THE CULINARY ART FOR CLUBS,
HOME OR HOTELS,* 1919

The Staff of Life

Harriet Jacobs was the enslaved daughter of a South Carolina planter who published an 1861 memoir, *Incidents in the Life of a Slave Girl, Seven Years Concealed,* in which she reminisced about, among other things, her devotion to her Aunt Marthy, the benevolent grandmother who made crackers at night to sell.

Aunt Marthy was "much praised for her cooking," Jacobs mused, "and her nice crackers became so famous in the neighborhood that many people were desirous of obtaining them. She asked permission of her mistress to bake crackers at night, after all the household work was done; and she obtained leave to do it . . . after working hard all day for her mistress, she began her midnight baking assisted by her oldest children. The business proved profitable; and each year she laid by a little, which was saved for a fund to purchase her children." Baking mattered.

The relationship between plantation cooks like Aunt Marthy, house servants, free people of mixed race, and the black privileged class was dynamic. House servants, having had exposure to white practices in the big house, used these as pathways for creating their own opportunities and autonomy. Steeped in West African cooking techniques, such as steaming pudding in banana leaves, baking pones in hot ashes, or frying pounded dough in deep oil, they "arrived without material possessions but equipped with sensibilities of marketing and trading foodstuffs into other consumer goods," Psyche Williams-Forson observed in *Building Houses Out of Chicken Legs: Black Women, Food, and Power*. They maintained these culinary habits in the privacy of the slave village and in the isolated neighborhoods where free people of color lived and worked. They developed new skills in landowners' kitchens, taverns, restaurants, inns, and hotels. And they combined the two in food service businesses—some became street vendors who dominated the marketplace, and others established bakeshops that enriched their families for years.

In the years following the Civil War and Emancipation, many in this group went on to pursue educations to enhance skills of personal service at schools for the newly freed, such as Hampton Normal and Agricultural School, not far from where the first Africans landed in Virginia in 1619. Learning to cook "scientifically" improved a black woman's social status. It helped her obtain a degree of independence, provided food, clothes, and education for her children, and allowed her to participate in community work.

I looked in history books for evidence of the knowledge and skills achieved by these new "domestic science" students, but their accomplishments were generally overshadowed by the black bourgeoisie, a small group of African Americans who established their livelihoods in education, business, ministry, and medicine. *A Book of Recipes for the Cooking School,* published in 1921 by Hampton's director of the Home Economics School, Carrie Alberta Lyford, changed that, and opened a path of stories for me to explore.

Lyford established herself as a font of baking wisdom. Her book featured tested recipes from cooking schools across the country. She offered succinct lessons on baking chemistry that covered subjects like the "methods of entangling air or gas in a batter" and "the thickness of batters and doughs."

African American cooking school teachers in the private sector, including Mrs. T. P. (Sarah Helen) Mahammitt and caterer Cleora Butler, transferred baking competencies in their writings as well.

Mahammitt's *Recipes and Domestic Service,* published in 1939, was the textbook for the Mahammitt School of Cookery in Omaha, Nebraska. In it, she introduced basic recipes, such as baking powder biscuits, plain muffins, "hot roll foundation," and popovers, then she advanced the reader to more complex variations: Danish pastry, flavored biscuits, strudel, and quick breads.

Butler traced her family history, then published the stories in *Cleora's Kitchens: The Memoir of a Cook & Eight Decades of Great American Food* in 1985. Her mother, Maggie, was an excellent baker. She baked bread "so highly esteemed in Muskogee that she could charge twenty-five cents a loaf when the going rate for bread was a nickel." Cleora studied Maggie like a book. By age ten, Cleora had made her first batch of biscuits, using a new baking powder and cookbook supplied by Calumet. She went on to become a successful caterer and pastry shop owner, baking sourdough French bread and inventing new dishes from native ingredients and Southwestern cooking techniques—like other migrating African American families, Cleora's people were lured to the West, to Indian Country, by the promise of free land, liberty, and self-sufficiency.

With so much knowledge and experience in the community, it's no surprise that black inventors developed ways to turn out perfect loaves, rolls, muffins, and cakes without all the strenuous and time-consuming effort. In 1875, Alexander P. Ashbourne devised a spring-loaded die cutter that cut biscuits into a variety of thin, uniform shapes. Two years later, Joseph Lee, known as the "bread specialist," designed a bread crumb machine to reuse stale bread. In 1884, Willis Johnson of Cincinnati patented an improved mechanical egg beater with two chambers that allowed a cook to beat eggs in one section and mix batter in the other, and Judy Reed patented a hand-operated dough kneader and roller. And in the mid-twentieth century, Lucille Bishop Smith, a chef, home economist, entrepreneur, and author, developed and sold the first packaged hot roll mix—a commercial product that was a boon to housewives.

Lucille's All-Purpose Hot Roll Mix, begun as a fundraiser for Smith's church in the mid-1940s, promised convenience and effortless results. Its premeasured ingredients saved time and reduced the guesswork ordinarily associated with homemade bread, while its moist, easy-to-handle dough yielded fine-textured dinner rolls, sweet and cinnamon rolls, doughnuts, and pizza crust that made baking a joy. She continued to excite bakers with the versatility of yeast breads in a recipe card collection, *Lucille's Treasure Chest of Fine Foods* published in 1945. (Among the suggestions for turning hot rolls into special occasion fare were tea rolls flecked with parsley and sweet rolls drenched in preserves.)

Distinctively endowed. Professionally grounded. Supremely industrious. The recipes in this chapter memorialize these innovators as role models, equipped as they were with an inheritance from ancestors who fashioned flatware from oyster shells, carved mortars and pestles from tree logs, sewed baskets for winnowing rice using bones and sweetgrass, burned corncobs to make baking soda, and distilled salt from the soil under a smokehouse.

Through them, I discovered my inner baker. When I'm happy, I bake; when I'm blue, I bake. For me, it is fun and relaxing, the ultimate expression of cooking with joy. The main requirement you'll need is, as 1960s soul-era cookbook author Ruth Gaskins puts it, "a light hand and a good heart."

Biscuits

White flour biscuits were once considered a delicacy, a Sunday treat, something special on Christmas morning. Made with what the enslaved called "seconds," or "shorts," meaning the coarsest leavings from processing wheat into white flour, and a little pig fat, this crude fare still reveals the delight African captives took in simple pleasures like hot bread for breakfast.

Millie Williams remembered the experience this way: "Heep o' times we'd eat coffee grounds fo' bread. Sometimes we'd have biscuits made out o' what was called de 2nd's. De white folks allus got de 1st's."

The story was different if you were a free person of color operating a baking business. Access to white flour and new technologies such as baking powder made it possible to produce biscuits of fine quality. In 1866, if you wanted to make biscuits similar to what we know now—light and fluffy—you would have to be a baker proficient in the chemical reactions of multiple leaveners. For instance, Malinda Russell's recipe for biscuits got its lift from a balanced mix of egg, yeast, and baking soda. But with the popularization of new baking powder brands like Calumet and Rumford, and with white flour being made inexpensive by industrial mills, "baking powder biscuits" start showing up in black cookbooks in the early twentieth century. By midcentury, the biscuits that once were a special-occasion food, treasured on weekends, were everywhere.

Whenever I look to experienced cooks for lessons about biscuit making, though, the story is usually about the same: The recipe is plain and simple, too easy to write down.

But to tell you the truth, good biscuit making is a science and an art. And it takes practice, however you do it and whatever you use—shortening, lard, or butter; more or less baking powder; buttermilk or milk.

The science lies in keeping the mixture cool, blending the flour and fat well, and adding just enough liquid to moisten and make a soft, somewhat sticky dough. The amount of milk you'll need varies, depending upon the density of your flour and, believe it or not, the humidity in the air.

The art is in your hands—in the motion of your fingers during mixing and your unique way of kneading the dough.

BAKING POWDER BISCUITS

MAKES 12 BISCUITS

This Sunday morning, conduct your own experiment. Bake this recipe as it is here, then, the next time, give your biscuits a rich flavor by mixing half butter and half shortening. See which one you prefer. Serve it with my family's favorite spread, honey butter—or with home-made jam, or a mix of molasses and butter.

2 cups all-purpose flour
4 teaspoons baking powder
¾ teaspoon salt
¼ cup shortening, cut into pieces and chilled
⅔ cup whole milk, or as needed

1 Preheat the oven to 450°F.

2 In a bowl, whisk together the flour, baking powder, and salt. Sprinkle the shortening over the dry ingredients. Using your fingertips, a pastry blender, or two knives, cut in the shortening until the mixture resembles coarse crumbs. Using a fork, blend in enough milk to make a slightly sticky dough that pulls away from the sides of the bowl. Turn the dough out onto a lightly floured surface. (Keep two things in mind: Add as little flour to the kneading board as possible. And the less you handle the dough, the better.)

3 To knead properly, use only the heel of your hand to push the dough away from you so that the heat from your hands does not warm up the dough. Then, working quickly, pick up the dough, sprinkle the board with a little flour and return the dough to the board. Fold the dough in half and push it away from you again. Repeat this technique several times for biscuits that are light and airy. Ruth Gaskins recommends kneading the dough just 6 to 8 times; Edna Lewis prefers 8 to 10. Knead the dough just until the dough comes together and is smooth. Do not overwork.

4 Roll or pat the dough to a ½-inch thickness. Cut with a floured 2-inch round biscuit cutter, pressing down firmly and pulling the cutter straight out of the dough. Do not twist. Cut the biscuits close together, leaving no space between. (After rolling and cutting my biscuits, I gather the leftover dough on the board and lightly pinch together the scraps into a scraggly shaped biscuit that I reserve for myself rather than re-rolling and cutting the dough.)

5 Place the biscuits on an ungreased baking sheet. Bake until puffed and golden brown, 12 to 15 minutes, rotating the sheet halfway through the baking time for even baking.

VARIATION

CREAM BISCUITS
Substitute chilled heavy whipping cream for the milk.

ANOTHER SORT OF BISCUIT

The Southern Cookbook: A Manual of Cooking and List of Menus, Including Recipes Used by Noted Colored Cooks and Prominent Caterers, S. Thomas Bivins, 1912

Rub into a pound of flour six ounces of butter, and three large spoonfuls of yeast, and make into a paste with a sufficient quantity of new milk, make into biscuit and prick them with a clean fork.

Another Sort: Melt six or seven ounces of butter with a sufficiency of flour into a stiff paste, roll thin, and make into biscuits.

BUTTERMILK BISCUITS

MAKES 12 BISCUITS

The difference between these biscuits and those leavened with baking powder alone is the addition of baking soda, which you'll need to stabilize the dough. Do this when you introduce any type of acid, whether that's buttermilk, yogurt, sour cream, molasses, vinegar, or lemon juice. The reaction between the acidic ingredient and the baking soda produces more lift in the dough, and a lighter biscuit.

2 cups all-purpose flour, plus more for the work surface

1 tablespoon baking powder

½ teaspoon baking soda

½ teaspoon salt

¼ cup shortening, cut into pieces and chilled

¾ to 1 cup buttermilk

Melted salted butter (optional)

Honey butter, jam, or molasses and butter, for serving

1 Preheat the oven to 450°F.

2 In a bowl, whisk together the flour, baking powder, soda, and salt. Sprinkle the shortening over the dry ingredients. Using your fingertips, a pastry blender, or two knives, cut in the shortening until the mixture resembles coarse crumbs. Using a fork, blend in enough buttermilk to make a slightly sticky dough that pulls away from the sides of the bowl. Turn the dough out onto a lightly floured surface.

3 It's time to knead the dough. Keep two things in mind: You should add as little extra flour to the kneading board as possible, just enough to let you handle the dough. And the less you handle the dough, the better.

4 To knead properly, use only the heel of your hand to push the dough away from you so that the heat from your hands does not warm up the dough. Then, working quickly, pick up the dough, sprinkle the board with a little flour, and return the dough to the board. Fold the dough in half and push it away from you again. Repeat this technique several times for biscuits that are light and airy. Ruth Gaskins recommends kneading the dough just 6 to 8 times; Edna Lewis prefers 8 to 10. Knead the dough just until the dough comes together and is smooth. Do not overwork, which makes it tough.

5 Roll or pat the dough to a ½-inch thickness. Cut with a floured 2-inch round biscuit cutter, pressing down firmly and pulling the cutter straight out of the dough. Do not twist. Cut biscuits close together, leaving no space between. (After rolling and cutting my biscuits, I gather the leftover dough on the board and lightly pinch together the scraps into a scraggly shaped biscuit that I reserve for myself rather than re-rolling and cutting the dough.)

6 Place the biscuits on an ungreased baking sheet. Bake until puffed and golden brown, 12 to 15 minutes, rotating the sheet halfway through baking time for even baking.

7 Brush with melted butter after baking, if desired. Serve immediately with honey butter, jam, or molasses and butter.

Biscuits for Teatime

I have a theory that the sweet biscuits in black cookbooks generally evolved from the British practice of afternoon tea; enslaved and free people would have observed this habit.

While studying recipes, I found lush formulas for biscuits laced with fresh herbs, lemon juice, cinnamon, and raisins; spread with raspberry jam; or garnished with a fruit juice–soaked sugar cube tucked in the center—with pineapple juice as Sallie Miller did it in *Mammy's Cook Book* in 1927, or with orange juice as Lucille Bishop Smith did it in midcentury. Miniature sweet biscuits are still an afternoon tea tradition. Today we call them scones.

ORANGE BISCUITS

MAKES 12 BISCUITS

Of all the flavors of sweet biscuit I have found in African American cookbooks, orange biscuits particularly can be traced to the Brits' fondness for orange marmalade. But it surprised me to learn that it was the Moors who, in the tenth century, introduced bitter oranges, the basis of orange marmalade, to Europe in the first place.

That North African heritage gives new meaning to the black penchant for a citrus fruit that was once considered exotic, expensive, and out of reach for cooks.

For biscuits with a delightful flavor of orange, author Dorothy Shanklin Russey in the book *Forty Years in the Kitchen: A Collection of Recipes,* rolled her dough ¾ inch thick and spooned marmalade into a little dip she pressed into the center with her finger. I roll the marmalade inside the biscuit dough, jelly-roll fashion, and add orange zest and a touch of juice to the dough itself. A brush of melted butter and the richness of heavy cream takes these dainties right over the top.

Butter, for the baking pan

2 cups all-purpose flour, plus more for the work surface

4 teaspoons baking powder

1 teaspoon salt

⅓ cup butter or shortening, chilled and cut into pieces

⅔ cup heavy whipping cream

2 teaspoons grated orange zest

2 teaspoons fresh orange juice

½ cup orange marmalade

1 tablespoon butter, melted

1 Preheat the oven to 400°F. Lightly butter a 9-inch baking pan.

2 In a large bowl, whisk together the flour, baking powder, and salt. Sprinkle the butter pieces over the dry ingredients. Using your fingertips, a pastry blender, or two knives, cut in the butter pieces until the mixture resembles coarse crumbs. Set aside.

3 In a small bowl, combine the cream, orange zest, and orange juice. Using a fork, gradually blend three-quarters of the cream-juice mixture into the flour mixture, stirring gently. Stir in enough of the remaining cream-juice mixture to make a slightly sticky dough that pulls away from the sides of the bowl. Depending upon your flour, you may have a couple of teaspoons of the liquid left over.

4 Turn the dough out onto a lightly floured surface. Knead 8 to 10 times, just until the dough comes together and is smooth. (See page 85 for more detail on my preferred technique, or let your hands guide you.)

5 Roll or pat the dough into a rectangle about 12 inches long and ¼ inch thick. Spoon the marmalade over the dough, spreading it to the edges. Starting with a long side, roll up the dough, jelly-roll fashion, and cut the roll crosswise into 1-inch slices. Place the biscuits in the prepared baking pan, leaving no space in between. Brush with melted butter.

6 Bake for 10 minutes. Reduce the oven temperature to 375°F and bake until puffed and golden brown, about 10 minutes longer. Serve warm.

QUICK CINNAMON ROLLS

MAKES **12 ROLLS**

In 1931, a new time-saving baking mix came to market as an inexpensive solution to the "slavery of housework." What the manufacturer of Bisquick neglected to mention was the catalyst behind the product was an African American chef who, in 1919, composed a baking mix to help him crank out hot biscuits fast, as Linda Civitello divulged in *Baking Powder Wars: The Cutthroat Food Fight That Revolutionized Cooking*. Unfortunately, the chef's name has so far been lost to history.

Decades later, Vera Beck—my first test kitchen cook at the Cleveland *Plain Dealer*—devised her own biscuit mix recipe, which appeared in the *PD* Food Section, along with instructions for baking variations, so that fresh breads could be prepared in an instant.

You can make these cinnamon pinwheels as I do, from scratch, or use my adaptation of Vera's Master Mix (see Note, opposite).

Butter, for the muffin tin

2 cups bread flour, plus more for the work surface

4 teaspoons baking powder

1 teaspoon salt

2 tablespoons shortening, cut into pieces and chilled

4 tablespoons (½ stick) butter, cut into pieces and chilled

¾ to 1 cup whole milk

¼ cup sugar

1½ teaspoons ground cinnamon

FROSTING

1 tablespoon butter, softened

¼ cup powdered sugar

1 tablespoon whole milk

1 Preheat the oven to 425°F. Butter a 12-cup muffin tin or a baking sheet.

2 In a bowl, whisk together the flour, baking powder, and salt. Sprinkle the shortening and 2 tablespoons of the butter pieces over the dry ingredients. Using your fingertips, a pastry blender, or two knives, cut the shortening and butter into the flour mixture until the mixture resembles coarse crumbs.

3 Using a fork, blend in ¾ cup milk to make a slightly sticky dough. Stir in enough of the remaining ¼ cup milk until the dough pulls away from the sides of the bowl. Turn the dough out onto a lightly floured surface. Knead 8 to 10 times, just until the dough comes together and is smooth. (See page 85 for my preferred kneading technique, or let your hands guide you.)

4 Roll the dough into a rectangle about 12 inches long and ¼ inch thick. In a bowl, combine the sugar and the cinnamon.

5 Sprinkle the dough with the cinnamon sugar and dot with the remaining 2 tablespoons butter. Starting with a long side, roll it up, jelly-roll fashion, and cut crosswise into 1-inch slices. Place the pinwheels in the prepared muffin cups or on the greased baking sheet, about 1 inch apart. Bake until golden brown, 15 to 20 minutes.

6 Meanwhile, make the frosting: In a small bowl, combine the softened butter, powdered sugar, and milk and stir with a spoon until smooth.

7 Let the rolls cool in the pan for 5 minutes, then transfer to a wire rack. Spoon frosting onto the rolls.

NOTE: You may use 2 cups Country-Style Master Biscuit Mix (recipe follows) in place of the flour, baking powder, salt, shortening, and 2 tablespoons of the butter. Place the baking mix in a bowl and proceed with the recipe, starting with adding the milk.

COUNTRY-STYLE MASTER BISCUIT MIX

MAKES ABOUT 12 CUPS

Adapted from Vera Beck and Mildred Council

10 cups sifted all-purpose flour
5 tablespoons baking powder
1 tablespoon salt
1½ cups shortening, cut into pieces and chilled

In a large bowl, combine the flour, baking powder, and salt. Sprinkle the shortening over the dry ingredients. With a pastry blender or 2 knives, cut in the shortening until the mixture resembles coarse crumbs. Store in an airtight container in the refrigerator or freezer.

Batter Cakes

A batter of flour, eggs, milk, and leavening cooked on an iron griddle or waffle iron is everywhere on Southern menus and in African American cookbooks, variously titled Flannel Cakes, Griddle Cakes, Hotcakes, Pancakes, or Flapjacks, and adapted from the Dutch, according to food historian Frederick Douglass Opie.

On occasion, when flour supplies were exhausted, the enslaved fashioned breads from dried beans, rice, potatoes, or mashed peas, making batters out of these ingredients—just as they would have before captivity—or from starchy fruits and vegetables such as cassava and plantain. The dough was shaped into cakes, flat loaves, or pones that were fried or baked, as Dwight Eisnach and Herbert C. Covey documented in their study, *What the Slaves Ate: Recollections of African American Foods and Foodways from the Slave Narratives.*

Since then, black cooks have been inextricably associated with expertly prepared batter cakes, whether characterized in literature by the Old South's plantation mammy, in advertising trademarks such as Aunt Jemima, or in any one of many fictionalized maids, including Delilah in Fannie Hurst's 1933 novel and its follow-up film, *Imitation of Life.*

From America's Colonial days to the present, an assortment of tricks have earned black cooks this great legacy. One doubled the eggs in the recipe to substitute for baking powder. Another mixed in sour cream or buttermilk instead of whole milk to give the waffles a subtle tang. For texture, cornmeal or crisp, cooked bacon might be stirred into the recipe. The type of fat could vary from rendered salt pork or chicken fat to butter, depending upon the pantry of the cook, while the choice of grain changed according to the region of the country the cook was in. Wheat, buckwheat, or rice flour; leftover cooked rice; hominy grits; and cornmeal all made appearances in black cookbooks. And the secret to the commercial success of Aunt Jemima pancake mix, according to the marketing legend, was a delicate balance of wheat, corn, rye, and rice, attributed to a mythical black cook.

GINGERBREAD WAFFLES AND CREAM

MAKES 6 WAFFLES

Who can resist rich, golden waffles? Few, including Thomas Jefferson, who first enjoyed the crisp batter cakes in France, bought a waffle iron, and returned to the States with a new recipe for his enslaved French-trained chef, James Hemings, to perfect. Since then, African Americans have enjoyed plain waffles made slightly tangy with sour milk, stretched for a crowd (when white flour was scarce) with sweet potato flour, and lightened, in the rice-growing regions of South Carolina, with cooked rice instead of yeast.

Spiced gingerbread waffles are one version of the honeycombed cakes that endured tests of locale and economy. I experimented with Nebraska cooking teacher Sarah Helen Mahammitt's way of cutting together the flour and fat as for biscuits and sweetening the waffles with blackstrap and sorghum molasses. But for this recipe, I mixed Lucille Bishop Smith's Recipe #15 with Norma Jean and Carole Darden's family formula, folding in stiffly beaten egg whites for waffles that are light and sweet. The waffles will be soft when you remove them from the iron, but crisp up a bit after a few minutes.

2 cups all-purpose flour

¼ cup packed dark brown sugar

1 teaspoon ground ginger

¼ teaspoon ground cinnamon

1 teaspoon baking powder

1 teaspoon baking soda

¼ teaspoon salt

⅓ cup butter, melted and cooled

½ cup molasses (blackstrap, sorghum, or a blend of both)

1 cup buttermilk

2 large eggs, separated

Oil, for greasing the waffle iron

Freshly grated nutmeg, for finishing (optional)

1 Preheat a waffle iron.

2 In a bowl, whisk together the flour, brown sugar, ginger, cinnamon, baking powder, baking soda, and salt. In a separate bowl, combine the melted butter, molasses, and buttermilk, stirring until smooth. Beat the egg yolks together and stir them into the liquid mixture. In a third bowl, beat the egg whites to stiff peaks using a whisk, hand mixer, or stand mixer. Stir together the flour mixture and buttermilk mixture, then gently fold the whipped whites into the batter.

3 Grease the heated waffle iron and bake the waffles, following the waffle iron's instructions, to desired doneness. Sprinkle with nutmeg, if desired.

WAFFLES FOR BREAKFAST

What Mrs. Fisher Knows About Old Southern Cooking,
Abby Fisher, 1881

Two eggs beat light, one pint of sour milk, to one and a half pint of flour, one teaspoonful of soda sifted with the flour, one tablespoonful of butter, teaspoonful of salt, mixed well, and then add the eggs. Always have your irons perfectly hot and well greased. In baking, melt butter before mixing in flour. Place them in a covered dish and butter them on sending to the table.

BUCKWHEAT CAKES

Farmer Jones Cook Book, The Fort Scott Sorghum
Syrup Company, 1914

*Mix at night one pint of pure buckwheat flour, with
enough warm water to make a thick batter.
Add yeast, using one-half cake of dry yeast dissolved
in warm water. Stand this batter in warm place over
night and next morning add one tablespoonful Farmer
Jones' Sorghum, soda size of a pea, dissolved in little
water, one teaspoonful salt and enough milk to make
batter as thin as cream. Bake on hot griddle.*
[Use left-over batter to start the next cakes.]

OLD-FASHIONED PANCAKES
WITH BERRY SYRUP

SERVES 4 TO 6

In Colonial America, pancakes were made with buckwheat or cornmeal. Another type of griddle cake, made from stale, leftover bread crumbs and served with homemade syrup, epitomized the kind of economical scratch cooking old-time cooks perfected before packaged mixes became affordable. Soul cooks celebrated both during the 1960s, adding recipes for homemade brown sugar syrup, flavored with maple or wild berries, honoring their ancestors' ingenuity when maple syrup was out of reach.

Here, I combine an homage to those cooks and Edna Lewis's way with the breakfast dish, from her acclaimed cookbook, *The Taste of Country Cooking.*

2 cups all-purpose flour

4 teaspoons baking powder

2 teaspoons sugar

½ teaspoon salt

2 to 2½ cups whole milk

2 tablespoons butter, melted and cooled, plus 3 tablespoons room-temperature butter (or oil), for the griddle or skillet, plus more for serving

2 large eggs, beaten

Warm Berry Syrup or Homemade Pancake Syrup, for serving (recipes follow)

1 In a bowl, whisk together the flour, baking powder, sugar, and salt. In a separate bowl, stir together 2 cups milk, the melted butter, and eggs. Add the milk mixture to the flour mixture, stirring just until the batter is smooth enough to pour, but a few small lumps still remain. Stir in additional milk, as needed, for thinner cakes.

2 Heat a griddle or a large skillet over medium-high heat and lightly grease with the softened butter. Spoon ⅓ cup batter for each pancake onto the griddle or skillet and cook until bubbles begin to form on the surface and the edges look dry. Flip and cook on the other side until golden brown. Do not turn again. Serve the pancakes with butter and syrup.

WARM BERRY SYRUP

MAKES ABOUT 1½ CUPS

½ cup sugar

1½ cups blueberries or blackberries

½ teaspoon fresh lemon juice

In a heavy saucepan, combine the sugar and ½ cup water and bring to a boil. Reduce the heat, add the berries and lemon juice, and simmer until the berries are tender, 8 to 10 minutes. Use a wooden spoon to mash half of the berries against the side of the pot. Simmer a few minutes, until the syrup thickens to desired consistency. Serve warm.

HOMEMADE PANCAKE SYRUP

MAKES ABOUT 1 CUP

1 cup packed light brown sugar

Pinch of salt

¼ teaspoon vanilla extract or ⅛ teaspoon maple flavoring

In a heavy saucepan, combine the brown sugar, salt, and ½ cup water and bring to a boil. Reduce the heat and simmer until the mixture thickens to your desired consistency, 10 to 12 minutes. Stir in the vanilla. The syrup keeps, covered and refrigerated, for about 1 month.

Soul Bread—The Cornbread Flight

Thin, light cornmeal cakes, baked on a hot cast-iron "spider"—an old-fashioned skillet with three short legs—hold a special place in the hearts and minds of Southern cooks. They trigger memories of Mother stirring and tasting her cornmeal mush as it bubbled on top of the stove; of African bondswomen who "took Indian maize and turned it into hoe cakes, mush, and dumplings akin to African Fufu and Kenkey," as scholar John W. Blassingame explained in *The Slave Community: Plantation Life in the Antebellum South*.

Eliza Leslie, the nineteenth-century cookbook author who penned household management and etiquette books for white women, attributed the recipe for Aunt Lydia's Corn Cake to a "Southern colored woman" and affirmed it "the very best preparation of Indian cakes" in 1857 in *Miss Leslie's New Cookery Book*.

Aunt Lydia and cooks like her perfected one of the enduring symbols of Southern cuisine: cornbread, in all its forms. "Cornbread has been called the staff of life in the South, and it comes in a real conglomeration of shapes, sizes, mixtures and names. There's corn cake, corn pone, corn dodgers, batter cake, spoon bread, corn muffins, hoecake, hushpuppies—plus the varied combinations of corn meal and flour, corn meal and rice, corn meal and hominy," chef Jimmy Lee said in the *Soul Food Cook Book*.

And the variations on these themes have seemed endless.

I marveled at the attention to detail and skill associated with the creation of one notable form: cornbread cooked directly in hot ashes. There is a narrative, recorded for the Federal Writers' Project of 1936 by Austin Pen Parnell of Arkansas, who recalls his grandmother's "art" of making ash or hoe cakes in the years following the Civil War:

> "My father rented it from the big man named Alf George for whom he worked. Mr. George used to come out and eat breakfast with us. We'd get that hoecake out of the ashes and wash it off until it looked like it was

as clean as bread cooked in a skillet. I have seen my grandmother cook a many a one in the fire. We didn't use no skillet for corn bread. The bread would have a good firm crust on it. But it didn't get too hard to eat and enjoy. Two-thirds of the water used in the ash cake was hot water, and that made the batter stick together like it was biscuit dough. She could put it together and take it in her hand and pat it out flat and lay it on the hearth. It would be just as round! That was the art of it!"

Aleck Woodward, a formerly enslaved man from South Carolina, also fondly remembered cracklin' bread—cornbread baked with crumbled fried pork skin: "De cracklin' bread was called on our place, 'de sweet savor of life.'" African captives also pounded sweet potato into pones to serve with pigeon and stretched cornmeal batter with persimmon pulp, inspiring home economics teacher Ethel Brown Hearon, author of *Cooking with Soul: Favorite Recipes of Negro Homemakers,* to mix sweet potato and cornmeal together. She called the concoction "soul bread."

With all of these variations in mind, I bundled recipes here in a "cornbread flight." Think of the grouping as a timeline, or a family tree. First, a coarse mix of meal, lard, and water was baked in the ashes of a roaring fire or cooked on a flat surface above a fire—what the authors of *The Picayune's Creole Cook Book* called "Southern darky cake," and what is more commonly known as ashcake, hoecake, or hot water cornbread. That mush was improved with egg and milk and fried into golden brown griddle cakes, or turned into a cake-like cornbread when leavened with eggs, baking powder, and buttermilk. Cornbread also traveled out of the South, taking on flavors from other regions, like the chiles and cheese of the Southwest. And other cooks delighted special-occasion diners with cornmeal soufflés, otherwise known as spoonbread.

HOT WATER CORNBREAD

SERVES 4 TO 6

Whether shaped into small pones, dropped by the spoonful onto a hot griddle, or baked into one large cake in a skillet, hot water cornbread is likely the original form of cornbread—a simple, unleavened corn batter that historian Fred Opie described as "a facsimile" of the cornbread that African women in Angola and São Tomé had wrapped in banana leaves and baked in the "cinders of fires."

1 cup cornmeal

½ teaspoon salt

¾ teaspoon sugar (optional)

1½ cups boiling water or scalded whole milk

2 tablespoons melted butter, shortening, lard, or bacon drippings

1 In a small bowl, stir together the cornmeal, salt, and sugar (if using). Stir in the hot water and let stand 1 hour.

2 Heat a cast-iron griddle or skillet over medium heat and grease well with the butter. Drop the batter by rounded tablespoonful onto the cooking surface. Smooth with the back of the spoon, if needed, to make disc-like cakes. Cook until golden, 1 to 2 minutes, then turn and brown the other side.

CORNMEAL GRIDDLE CAKES

MAKES 20 SMALL PANCAKES

Visitors to Thomas Jefferson's Monticello praised his enslaved French-trained chef, James Hemings, for a special meal of fried chicken with corn cakes and cream gravy. In early twentieth-century Charleston, gubernatorial butler William Deas was honored for the identical meal. And the recipe for cornmeal batter cakes earned a cook named Marcellus star status in Minnie C. Fox's *Blue Grass Cook Book*. I brought the 1904 edition of *Blue Grass* back to life, publishing a facsimile edition in 2005, because of its tributes to the black cooks of the region. Marcellus followed a recipe for cornbread, stirring in less milk to make cakes that were just thick enough to drop from a spoon and cook on a hot surface rather than in an oven.

After tasting dozens of updated and classic versions to compose this recipe, I am convinced that finely milled or medium-grind cornmeal is a fine alternative to the stone-ground variety that would have originally been called for. These cakes cook up light, making them a surprising alternative to plain bread at any meal. If you lean more toward the authentic, you can make a more rustic, textured version with coarser stone-ground cornmeal (see Note, opposite).

1 cup cornmeal (see Note)

1 tablespoon sugar

½ teaspoon baking soda

1 teaspoon baking powder

½ teaspoon salt

2 large eggs

1 tablespoon melted butter, shortening, lard, or bacon drippings, cooled, plus more for greasing the pan

1 cup buttermilk

1 In a bowl, whisk together the cornmeal, sugar, baking soda, baking powder, and salt. In a separate bowl, combine the eggs, melted butter, and buttermilk. Mix the buttermilk mixture into the cornmeal mixture and stir just until blended.

2 Heat a lightly greased griddle or skillet over medium-high heat. Drop the batter by tablespoon onto the hot pan. Cook until bubbles form on the surface and the edges are set, then flip and cook another 30 seconds to 1 minute.

NOTE: To substitute stone-ground cornmeal in the recipe above, stir together ½ cup water and 1 cup stone-ground cornmeal and let stand for 10 minutes for the cornmeal to soften and the water to be absorbed. Proceed with the remaining ingredients.

PLANTATION CORN BREAD OR HOE CAKE

What Mrs. Fisher Knows About Old Southern Cooking,
Abby Fisher, 1881

Half tablespoonful of lard to a pint of meal, one teacup of boiling water; stir well and bake on a hot griddle. Sift in meal one teaspoonful of soda.

EXTRA-LIGHT BUTTERMILK CORNBREAD

SERVES 8 TO 10

Asking a Southern cook whether sugar belongs in cornbread is like pouring gasoline on a smoldering fire. I was there once when the embers ignited. It happened the year that corn was the topic of the Southern Foodways Alliance's annual symposium at the University of Mississippi. Ronni Lundy, the beloved Appalachian cookbook author, declared that anyone who put sugar in their cornbread batter might as well go ahead and call that dish cake.

I sat meekly in the back of Barnard Observatory, thinking, "If you are African American and you don't put sugar in the batter, it isn't cornbread." But I waited until Ronni and I were alone to share my thoughts. After much theorizing, we agreed that recipes for classic "Southern" cornbread seldom, if ever, call for adding sugar to the batter, and that sugar in cornbread was probably a regional habit—a response to cornmeal ground outside of the South, which could be less sweet.

Our assumptions went up in smoke when I discovered that sweeteners have appeared in cookbooks written by African Americans since Tunis Campbell added molasses to the mix in 1848, in the book *Hotel Keepers, Head Waiters, and Housekeepers' Guide*. And there was a plantation habit of pouring sorghum molasses over cornmeal mush in a West African dish the Cajuns adapted for breakfast that they called coosh-coosh. Obviously, there are more connections between black folks and sweet cornbread than we know.

By the time Arturo Schomburg compiled his list of African American recipes during the 1930s, unsweetened cornbread was set off by

RECIPE CONTINUES

the modifier: "Southern." Today, with so many writers investigating the distinctions between Southern and soul food, that modifier has changed to "skillet," as in skillet cornbread.

But just to show you how far some cooks have gone to impart their own sense of cornbread flair, Joyce White explained in *Soul Food: Recipes and Reflections from African-American Churches* that a Mrs. Esther Mae Archie followed a classic recipe, then stirred in fresh fruit and sugar. I call that cake.

This recipe, adapted from Mrs. Archie's formula, tones the sugar way down, but if sweet is the way you like it, double the sugar.

Heating the butter in the pan until sizzling will ensure your cornbread has a crisp, crusty edge. Fruit, of course, is optional.

1 cup cornmeal
1 cup all-purpose flour
2 tablespoons sugar
1 tablespoon baking powder
½ teaspoon baking soda
1 teaspoon salt
1 large egg, beaten
1 cup buttermilk
6 tablespoons butter

1 Preheat the oven to 425°F.

2 In a large bowl, whisk together the cornmeal, flour, sugar, baking powder, baking soda, and salt. Stir in the egg and buttermilk until just mixed.

3 Place the butter in a 9-inch cast-iron skillet and heat in the oven until the butter is foamy. Swirl the butter around to coat the bottom and insides of the hot pan, then pour the hot butter into the batter and stir until well mixed. The batter will be thick. Immediately pour the batter into the hot buttered pan and return to the oven. Bake until golden, about 20 minutes.

SPANISH CORNBREAD
SERVES 12

Black authors living and publishing in the Southwest and West developed a fondness for including ingredients associated with Mexican cooking, such as tomatoes and hot chile peppers, and calling them "Spanish." Here, cheese and canned corn give the bread its moist character.

1¼ cups yellow cornmeal
1¼ cups all-purpose flour
¼ cup sugar
2 teaspoons baking powder
½ teaspoon baking soda
1 teaspoon salt
1 cup cream-style corn
1 cup buttermilk
1 (4-ounce) can diced green chiles
½ cup minced onion
1 egg, lightly beaten
1 cup shredded sharp Cheddar cheese
4 tablespoons butter, cut into pieces

1 Preheat the oven to 400°F.

2 In a large mixing bowl, whisk together the cornmeal, flour, sugar, baking powder, baking soda, and salt.

3 In a separate bowl, combine the corn, buttermilk, chiles, onion, and egg, and mix well. Stir in the cheese.

4 Pour the liquid ingredients into the dry and stir together just until combined. Heat the butter in a 10-inch cast-iron skillet in the oven until foamy. Swirl the butter to coat the pan, then stir the hot butter into the batter, and then immediately pour the batter into the hot skillet. Bake for 30 minutes, or until golden brown.

SPOONBREAD

SERVES 6 TO 8

In 1927, Katharin Bell published a collection of Southern recipes with a Virginia flavor, *Mammy's Cook Book*. The dishes were created and perfected by her mammy, Sallie Miller, a "famous cook" whose memory and culinary lore Bell was determined to preserve. Of all the recipes enshrined in the collection, Virginia Spoon Bread stands out for its unique combination of white cornmeal and cooked hominy grits; another white author who recorded black recipes called that "Batter Bread Mulatto Style."

I have presented here the classic recipe for spoonbread, which resembles an airy pudding or a soufflé more than a traditional cornbread. To achieve this soft texture, some authors stir the cornmeal into scalded liquid and let it stand a few minutes. Others cook the mixture 5 minutes or so before baking.

1 cup boiling water

1 cup cornmeal

2 tablespoons butter, plus more for the baking dish and for finishing (optional)

1 cup whole milk

1 teaspoon sugar

1 teaspoon salt

2 large eggs, separated

1 teaspoon baking powder

1 Preheat the oven to 350°F. Butter a shallow 2-quart baking dish.

2 Pour the boiling water into a heatproof medium bowl. Pour the cornmeal in a thin stream into the hot water, whisking constantly until smooth. With a wooden spoon, stir in the butter until incorporated. Slowly beat in the milk, sugar, and salt until smooth and no longer thick. Let cool slightly. Beat in the egg yolks and baking powder. In a separate bowl, with a whisk or hand mixer (or in a stand mixer), beat the egg whites to stiff peaks, then gently fold them into the batter.

3 Pour the batter into the prepared baking dish. Bake until puffy and browned, 35 to 45 minutes. To serve, spoon onto serving plates and top with a pat of butter, if desired.

VIRGINIA SPOON BREAD

Mammy's Cook Book, Katharin Bell
[for Sallie Miller], 1927

$^{1}/_{2}$ cup white cornmeal

$^{1}/_{2}$ cup cooked hominy grits

$1^{1}/_{2}$ cup water

1 cup milk

1 tb. shortening

1 egg

1 t. salt

$^{1}/_{2}$ t. sugar

Heat water to boiling point, stir in cornmeal, and cook about 3 minutes, stirring smooth. Add shortening and grits while hot. Beat smooth, adding half of the quantity of milk. Add sugar, salt, and well beaten egg, and gradually beat in remaining milk. Put mixture in buttered pan, and bake about 40 minutes. This serves about 4 persons.

Quick Breads and Muffins

It might seem strange now, but in the days before supermarket shelves were lined with enough bread to feed an army, cooks relied upon both simple and complex breads that could be stirred together fast to bring variety to mealtime.

Quick breads are economical batters leavened without yeast, sometimes called tea breads. The name derives from the fact that you can mix and bake the bread immediately without setting aside time for it to rise—perfect for last-minute preparation when a neighbor stops by.

It's hard to imagine serving plain, sweet batter bread as is, without any added ingredients, but that's just how cooks did it for generations. Plain muffins, made from just white flour, sugar, butter, baking powder, eggs, and milk before baking in a special "gem" pan, resemble quick Sally Lunn, a light, sweet batter bread that is cut into squares after baking. The batter is easy to make and versatile; the long list of quick breads and muffins testifies to that virtue.

In time, cooks embellished ordinary muffins with ingredients harvested from the nearby woods or their own backyard—a handful of wild hickory nuts or berries carted home in an apron, fruits they dried themselves, fragrant spices. In another version, boiled hominy was part of the mix.

In those parts of the Old South where sugar cane was king, molasses, a by-product of the refining process, was known as the sweetener of poverty. Despite its reputation as a lowly ingredient, molasses tastes richer than sugar. It turns ordinary sweet batter bread into something luxurious when mixed with cooked, mashed sweet potatoes, pumpkin, or bananas. Sorghum, which Africans and the enslaved grew and stewed into a porridge, also was savored as a heritage sweetener for quick breads.

During the early years of the twentieth century, a handful of nut bread recipes appears in our cookbooks; one was a lean batter, made without eggs or sugar, found in *The Federation Cook Book: A Collection of Tested Recipes, Contributed by the Colored Women of the State of California*. Another, from 1912, was a less austere, grainy loaf, perfect hot from the oven with coffee or tea for breakfast, or sliced and toasted the following day. Tender cakes dotted with nutmeats occur more consistently until midcentury. With almost interchangeable recipes, both nut breads and nut cakes were made tame with pecans or walnuts, or, for a seductive taste of the wild, with black walnuts or hickory nuts in the batter.

BLUEBERRY MUFFINS

MAKES 8 MUFFINS

I've reworked several versions of blueberry breakfast cake, including the one baked in a hot gem or muffin pan, published in 1912 in *Kentucky Cook Book: Easy and Simple for Any Cook, by a Colored Woman*. The hint of orange or lemon is what makes these blueberry muffins so delightful. The addition of whole wheat flour, which used to also be called graham flour, reflects early twentieth-century health food cooking trends. For muffins that are a touch lighter, substitute whole wheat pastry flour or all-purpose white flour for half of the whole wheat flour.

Softened butter, for the muffin tin
1 cup whole wheat flour
½ cup cornmeal
1½ teaspoons baking powder
½ teaspoon salt
4 tablespoons (½ stick) butter, cut into chunks
¼ cup sugar
1 large egg
⅔ cup whole milk
1 teaspoon grated lemon or orange zest
1½ teaspoons fresh lemon or orange juice
1 cup blueberries

1 Preheat the oven to 400°F. Grease 8 cups of a muffin tin or line with paper liners.

2 In a medium bowl, whisk together the flour, cornmeal, baking powder, and salt. In a medium bowl, with an electric mixer, cream together the butter and sugar until light. In a small bowl, whisk together the egg, milk, lemon zest, and lemon juice. Beat the flour mixture into the butter-sugar mixture in three additions, alternating with the egg-milk mixture, beginning and ending with the flour. Carefully fold in the blueberries.

3 Pour the batter into the muffin cups and bake until golden, about 20 minutes.

GRAHAM MUFFINS

Pauline's Practical Book of the Culinary Art for Clubs, Home or Hotels, Carrie Pauline Lynch, 1919

2 cups Graham flour
1 tablespoon butter
1 tablespoon sugar
½ cup white flour
1 teaspoon baking powder
1 egg
½ teaspoon salt
1½ cups milk

Mix all to make a batter as thick as for griddle cakes, bake in pans in muffin rings about 20 minutes in a quick oven.

RICE MUFFINS

MAKES 12 MUFFINS

~~~~~~

Lessie Bowers's grandmother was born into slavery in South Carolina, where she was recognized as refined, beloved, and wise—the best midwife and cook the community knew. She learned early in life that health and good food are closely related. By the age of twelve, she was alone in the kitchen preparing Sunday dinner for her family of eleven, the minister, his wife, and guests. As a college student at Claflin University in Orangeburg, South Carolina, she proposed, planned, and partnered with the Rosenwald Fund to build a community school.

Like her grandmother, Bowers baked her muffins in a "gem pan" until golden, and added hot cooked rice to the mixture, a reflection of her Carolina roots. In the rice-growing region of South Carolina and parts of North Carolina, rice, grits, and sweet potatoes extended slave rations of salt pork, cornmeal, and molasses.

The gems, inspired by a recipe in Bowers's *Plantation Recipes* (1959), are a great alternative to biscuits, a good use of leftover rice, delicious with meat and gravy—not too sweet, crisp on the outside, and pillowy inside. Preheating the pan adds an extra boost of heat at the start of baking time, which is what gives these muffins their crunch.

1⅓ cups whole milk
½ cup white cornmeal
1 cup hot cooked rice
1 cup all-purpose flour
1 tablespoon sugar (optional)
1 teaspoon salt
1 teaspoon baking powder
2 large eggs, separated
2 tablespoons melted butter, plus more
   for the pan
Softened butter, for serving (optional)

1 Preheat the oven to 400°F.

2 In a bowl, whisk together the milk and cornmeal. Let stand 5 minutes. In a separate bowl, use a fork to fluff the rice and separate the grains. Use a wooden spoon to stir the rice into the milk and cornmeal mixture. Whisk in the flour, sugar (if using), salt, and baking powder. Whisk in the egg yolks and melted butter and stir until the batter is smooth. Place a 12-cup muffin tin in the preheated oven and heat until hot.

3 Meanwhile, in a bowl, with a whisk or hand mixer (or in a stand mixer), whisk the egg whites until stiff peaks form. Carefully fold the whites into the batter.

4 Remove the hot tin from the oven. Carefully brush with butter and return to the oven until the butter is sizzling hot. Pour the batter into the muffin cups. Bake until the muffins are lightly browned, 20 to 25 minutes. Serve immediately with softened butter, if desired.

SWEET POTATO BREAD

SERVES 8 TO 10

The sweet potato batter bread featured in Mildred Council's *Mama Dip's Family Cookbook* is the pumpkin bread of yesterday. Inspired by that recipe, and chock-full of dried cranberries and pecans, this loaf is sweet, with a firm crumb that tastes like Thanksgiving. I toss the fruit and nuts with a bit of the flour to prevent them from sinking to the bottom of the pan during baking.

Softened butter and flour, for the loaf pan
½ **cup chopped pecans**
½ **cup dried cranberries**
1½ **cups all-purpose flour**
2 **teaspoons baking powder**
½ **teaspoon salt**
1 **cup packed light brown sugar**
1 **teaspoon ground cinnamon**
1 **teaspoon ground or freshly grated nutmeg**
¼ **teaspoon ground ginger**
1 **cup mashed cooked sweet potatoes, at room temperature**
2 **large eggs, beaten**
1 **stick (4 ounces) butter, melted**
½ **cup whole milk**

1 Preheat the oven to 350°F. Butter and flour a 9 × 5-inch loaf pan, and tap out any excess flour.

2 In a small bowl, toss together the pecans, cranberries, and 2 tablespoons of the flour and set aside. In a large bowl, whisk together the remaining 1 cup plus 6 tablespoons flour, the baking powder, salt, brown sugar, cinnamon, nutmeg, and ginger. Make a well in the center and add the sweet potatoes, eggs, melted butter, and milk. With a wooden spoon, stir the batter until lightly mixed. Gently fold in the nut mixture.

3 Spoon the batter evenly into the loaf pan. Bake until a toothpick inserted in the center comes out clean, 50 to 60 minutes. Let cool for 5 minutes in the pan, then turn out of the pan onto a wire rack to cool slightly. Serve warm.

VARIATION

SWEET POTATO MUFFINS
To make muffins, pour the batter into 12 greased or paper-lined muffin cups, filling each cup three-quarters full. Bake until the muffins spring back when lightly touched, about 20 minutes.

ISLAND BANANA BREAD

SERVES 8 TO 10

The sweet ripe bananas that grow all over the Caribbean islands, pecans, and molasses are the secret to this alluring dark breakfast cake, adapted from *B. Smith's Entertaining and Cooking for Friends.* For the best banana flavor, be sure to use very ripe, nearly black bananas. I stash peeled whole ripe bananas in the freezer so I can bake this bread anytime I need a hostess gift. Thaw the bananas just before using.

Softened butter and flour, for the loaf pan
½ **cup chopped pecans**
½ **cup chopped dried Medjool dates**
1¾ **cups all-purpose flour**
1 **teaspoon baking soda**
½ **teaspoon salt**
½ **teaspoon ground cinnamon**
½ **teaspoon ground or freshly grated nutmeg**
¼ **teaspoon ground allspice or ginger**
1 **stick (4 ounces) butter, at room temperature**
1 **cup packed dark brown sugar**
2 **large eggs**
1¼ **cups mashed very ripe bananas**
2 **tablespoons molasses**
⅓ **cup buttermilk**
1 **teaspoon vanilla extract**

1 Preheat the oven to 350°F. Grease and flour a 9 × 5-inch loaf pan, and tap out any excess flour.

2 In a small bowl, toss together the pecans, dates, and 2 tablespoons of the flour and set aside. In a large bowl, whisk together the remaining 1½ cups plus 2 tablespoons flour, the baking soda, salt, cinnamon, nutmeg, and allspice. In a bowl, with an electric mixer, beat the butter and brown sugar until light. Beat in the eggs, one at a time, beating well after each addition. In a third bowl, combine the bananas, molasses, buttermilk, and vanilla. Beat the flour mixture into the butter-sugar mixture in three additions, alternating with the banana mixture, and beginning and ending with the flour. Gently fold in the nut and date mixture.

3 Pour the batter into the loaf pan. Bake until a wood skewer inserted in the center comes out clean, about 1 hour. Transfer to a wire rack to cool for 10 minutes. Invert onto a wire rack and cool to room temperature before serving.

PAULINE'S NUT BREAD

Pauline's Practical Book of the Culinary Art for Clubs, Home or Hotels, Carrie Pauline Lynch, 1919

One egg beaten in cup, fill same cup with milk, add another cup milk, 1½ cups sugar, 4 cups flour, 4 teaspoons baking powder, 1 teaspoon salt, stir well, add 1 cup slightly chopped nuts and 1 of raisins, grease pans, pour in dough, let stand 20 minutes, then bake slowly 1 hour.

Hot Dinner Rolls

So many hot roll recipes, so little time. Black cooks have been proficient yeast bread bakers since way, way back, despite limited access to ingredients. "Light bread" was mentioned often in the Slave Narratives, a special-occasion treat baked in a skillet with coals on top, and the form continued to evolve from then.

Potato rolls trace their heritage to the days before commercial leavening agents, when cooks baked bread with a fermented potato starter. In the early years of the twentieth century, for instance, Carrie Alberta Lyford taught students her method for making a liquid yeast starter from hops, sugar, and potatoes in *A Book of Recipes for the Cooking School*. The practice produced rolls that were light and airy, so that even with the advent of yeast, a variation of the recipe lives on. From there, novelist and cookbook author Dori Sanders wrote a recipe using sweet potatoes instead of white; the resulting rolls have a moister texture, a touch of sweetness, and are delicious served with roast beef and grilled vegetables.

Icebox rolls are another iteration of hot yeast bread and rolls. Taking advantage of the technical innovations that made commercial yeast and refrigeration commonplace, caterer Herman Clark's popular rolls were so easy to make they didn't require kneading and rose slowly in the refrigerator. Shortening appeared regularly in the dough, too, proof that some black cooks were excited by the versatile, less expensive fat; others, of course, preferred the luxurious richness contributed by butter alone.

How rolls are shaped is a matter of style, whether the choice is for Parker House rolls that are shaped simply, the more elegant cloverleaf rolls for special occasions, or monkey bread, a sweet yeast loaf that is just plain fun.

When I was growing up, monkey bread was a layered loaf of rich, buttered bread that was perched like an edible centerpiece on the dinner table. It was made by rolling yeast dough into balls, or rolling and cutting it into shapes, then layering the pieces in a tube pan and brushing each layer generously with butter. Since then, I have tasted a sweet bubble loaf made by sprinkling the layers with cinnamon sugar, and a savory pull-apart that seasons the layers with garlic, herbs, and cheese—both sharing the name of monkey bread. The "monkey" part comes, possibly, from the idea that, since the bread is made up of buttery bites stuck together, bites may be snatched off the loaf with the fingers, like a monkey would.

Today, I double either of the recipes that follow and bake them in these shapes to add variety and grace to my Thanksgiving table.

SWEETENED POTATO ROLLS

**MAKES ABOUT 12 SERVINGS
(2 DOZEN PARKER HOUSE ROLLS OR
1 DOZEN CLOVERLEAF ROLLS)**

Carolyn Quick Tillery collected recipes and remembrances from three historically black colleges: Alabama's renowned Tuskegee Institute, the Hampton Institute in Virginia, and Howard University in Washington, DC. She included potato rolls in all three of them. While fermented potatoes are no longer required to raise these rolls—commercial yeast takes care of that—the use of potato harkens back to the past and provides moisture and lightness. The dough can be a little sticky, which produces a slightly dense crumb. The first time you make this sweet dough you may need a bit more flour to help you through the kneading, rolling, and cutting, but once you get the hang of it, you will love the results.

1 medium russet potato (6 to 8 ounces), peeled and diced

1 (¼-ounce) package active dry yeast (2¼ teaspoons)

¼ cup warm water (110°F to 115°F)

⅓ cup shortening, plus more for greasing

⅓ cup sugar

¼ teaspoon salt, plus more for pot

1 large egg

½ cup whole milk, lukewarm

3½ to 4 cups bread flour, plus more for the work surface

Melted salted butter, for brushing the pan and the rolls

Coarse salt (optional)

1 In a small pot, cover the potato with lightly salted water. Bring to a boil over medium-high heat. Reduce the heat to a simmer and cook until tender, about 20 minutes. Drain, reserving ½ cup of the cooking water. Mash the potatoes until completely smooth. Measure out ½ cup of mashed potatoes (reserve leftover potatoes for another use). Let the mashed potatoes cool.

2 In a small bowl, sprinkle the yeast into the warm water and whisk until dissolved. Let stand 5 minutes.

3 In a large bowl, with an electric mixer, beat the shortening, sugar, and salt until smooth. Add the cooled mashed potatoes and egg and mix on medium speed about 1 minute, scraping the sides of the bowl halfway through the beating time. Scrape the bowl again. Add the milk, reserved potato water, and the yeast mixture and continue to blend until thoroughly mixed.

4 Gradually add 3½ cups of the flour to the mixture, 1 cup at a time, adding additional flour, if necessary, to make a stiff tacky dough. Scrape the bowl between additions. Flour your work surface and turn the dough out. Knead until the dough is elastic and smooth, sprinkling with additional flour, 1 teaspoon at a time, as needed to keep the dough from sticking. Grease a large bowl and place the dough in it. Turn the dough over to lightly coat all sides with shortening. Cover it with wax paper, a bowl lid, or a damp towel. Let it rise in a warm place until doubled, about 1 hour. (After this rise, the dough may be refrigerated overnight, but allow it to come to room temperature and rise again before rolling and shaping.)

5 For Parker House rolls: Lightly brush a 15 × 9-inch rimmed baking sheet with butter. Divide the dough in half. Working with one half at a time, roll the dough on a lightly floured surface to ¼ inch thick and cut with a floured 3-inch round cutter or floured glass. Brush each roll with melted butter and fold in half. Place the rolls ½ inch apart on the greased baking sheet. Gather, re-roll, and cut scraps. Place on the baking sheet. Brush with additional butter, if desired. Cover loosely with a clean towel. Allow to stand until doubled in size, about 1 hour.

6 For Cloverleaf rolls: Lightly brush 12 cups of a muffin tin with butter. Divide the risen dough into 12 pieces of equal size. Divide each piece into 3 smaller pieces. Roll them between the palms of your hands into round balls. Place 3 small balls close together in each muffin cup. Brush with melted butter, cover loosely with a clean towel, and allow to rise until doubled in size, about 1 hour.

7 Preheat the oven to 350°F.

8 Bake the rolls until golden, about 30 minutes. Brush with additional melted butter and sprinkle with a pinch of coarse salt, if desired.

NO-KNEAD ICEBOX ROLLS

MAKES 2 DOZEN ROLLS

In *Uncle Herman's Soul Food Cookbook*, Herman Clark's dough is so forgiving it doesn't require kneading. It is firm and easier to handle than most, resulting in rolls that are airy and light with a tender crust.

¼ cup shortening, cut into 4 pieces
2 tablespoons sugar or honey
1 teaspoon salt
1 cup boiling water
1 (¼-ounce) package active dry yeast (2¼ teaspoons)
¼ cup warm water (110° to 115°F)
1 large egg, lightly beaten
4 cups all-purpose flour
Softened butter, for the baking pan
⅔ cup salted butter, melted
Coarse salt (optional)

1 In a large bowl, combine the shortening, sugar, and salt. Pour the boiling water over and stir until the shortening is melted. Set aside to cool until lukewarm.

2 In a small bowl, sprinkle the yeast over the warm water and whisk until dissolved. Let stand 5 minutes. With a wooden spoon, stir the yeast mixture into the cooled shortening mixture, until combined.

3 Stir in the egg, mixing well. Add the flour, 1 cup at a time, stirring after each addition until well blended. Cover tightly and refrigerate overnight.

4 The next day, remove the dough from the refrigerator and cover loosely with a damp towel. Place in a warm place and allow to rise until doubled in bulk, 2 to 4 hours.

5 Butter two 9-inch baking pans, a 13 × 9-inch baking pan, or muffin tins. Divide the dough in half. On a lightly floured surface, roll the dough into 2 logs 12 inches long. Pinch off 12 pieces of equal size from each log for a total of 24. Roll into balls, then place ½ inch apart in the baking pan(s) or in the muffin tin. Brush with melted butter. Cover loosely with a clean towel and let rise in a warm place until they reach the top of the pan, about 1 hour.

6 Preheat the oven to 375°F.

7 Bake the rolls until lightly browned, 25 to 30 minutes. Brush with melted butter immediately and sprinkle with coarse salt.

VARIATION

Edna Lewis substitutes half lard and half butter for the shortening.

HAMPTON UNIVERSITY'S LIQUID YEAST

A Book of Recipes for the Cooking School,
Carrie Alberta Lyford, 1921

2 ounces hops
2 quarts water
½ pound brown sugar
2 teaspoons salt
1 pound flour
3 pounds potatoes

Boil the hops and water 1 hour. Add the sugar, salt, and flour. Let stand for three days in a warm place. If it foams over the top of the jar stir it well. On the third day add the potatoes, boiled and mashed. On the fourth day strain, bottle, and keep in a cool place. Use one cup of yeast to one quart of liquid when starting bread.

Fritters

Fried dough? Yes, that's what we have here.

"Frying in deep oil is one of western Africa's gifts," Jessica B. Harris wrote in *The Africa Cookbook: Tastes of a Continent.* It's a technique that has produced great pleasures all over the continent, and therefore throughout the African diaspora. We're frying pounded cassava, yams, or plantains mixed with water for West African *fufu* and *cou cou*; little doughnuts known as "sweet balls" in Ghana; Nigerian bean balls (*akara*) and Senegalese *pastel*; *maasa*, the sweet millet and brown rice fritters of Mali; Creole rice fritters (calas) that black street vendors once sold on street corners in New Orleans to buy back their own freedom; long pones sweetened with sugar and served with jerk pork that the Jamaicans call "festival"; hushpuppies (also remembered by some old cooks as hominy puffs) and corn fritters from the Old South; and Caribbean fruit fritters with chopped mango or mashed banana. Recipes for fried dough abound in black cookbooks.

FRUIT FRITTERS

SERVES 4 TO 6

Georgia caterer William Mann Jr. kept a handwritten book of his best recipes since the 1920s. A few of them appeared in a spiral-bound collection, *Four Great Southern Cooks*, including a light, sweet batter studded with spiced apples and deep-fried to golden brown.

This is a flexible batter recipe with which you can make fritters like Mann's, with apples, or go farther afield and take inspiration from chefs like Jeanne Louise Duzant Chance, author of *Ma Chance's French Caribbean Creole Cooking*, who bakes banana fritter batter like little pancakes on a griddle so they are crisp, with lacy edges on the outside, and sweet and chewy on the inside. (You can certainly use this batter that way.) Or do like contemporary Senegalese chef and cookbook author Pierre Thiam, who dips banana slices in a coconut-infused batter before frying them. This batter recipe also works wonderfully with pears, mangoes, or other firm-fleshed fruit.

They are a sweet ending to any meal, dusted simply with powdered sugar. Rum in the batter is the secret ingredient.

1½ cups all-purpose flour
3 tablespoons granulated sugar
2 teaspoons baking powder
½ teaspoon salt
¼ teaspoon ground cinnamon
¼ teaspoon ground mace
¼ teaspoon ground or grated nutmeg
2 large eggs, beaten
⅔ cup whole milk
1 tablespoon rum (optional)
2 tablespoons butter, melted
1 teaspoon vanilla extract
2 cups peeled and diced Granny Smith apples, mangoes, diced bananas, or other firm-fleshed fruit
Peanut oil, for deep-frying
Powdered sugar or maple syrup, for serving

1 In a large bowl, whisk together the flour, granulated sugar, baking powder, salt, cinnamon, mace, and nutmeg. Make a well in the center of the dry ingredients. Add the eggs, milk, rum (if using), melted butter, and vanilla to the well. Stir the mixtures together until just combined. Fold in the diced fruit.

2 Pour a few inches of oil into a large Dutch oven or other wide deep pot (making sure you have plenty of clearance to prevent the oil from bubbling over) and heat to 375°F over medium-high heat. Drop the batter by rounded tablespoon into the hot oil. (A small cookie dough scoop also may be used; it helps the fritters maintain their shape when dropped in the hot fat.) Deep-fry until the fritters are golden brown, 3 to 4 minutes. Remove them with a slotted spoon and drain on paper towels.

3 Sprinkle with powdered sugar or drizzle with maple syrup to serve.

NIGERIAN BLACK-EYED PEA FRITTERS

(AKARA)

SERVES 4 TO 6

In the early 1970s, African idealists Monica Odinchezo Oka, Helen Mendes, Dinah Ayensu, and Bea Moten wrote books about heritage cuisine, treating audiences to authentic African recipes adapted to American cooking methods and ingredients. They also spread knowledge about African nations, each country's unique culture, and the ways that the African diaspora paved the way for Southern cooking.

From them, we learn that the rich, savory fritters called *akara* may have inspired the cornmeal fritters Southerners know as hushpuppies. *Akara* can be made from black-eyed peas, red peas, or navy beans, depending upon the cultural tradition of the cook; they may contain a variety of optional ingredients, such as okra, cheese, diced tomatoes, or *egusi* (West African gourd seeds); and in Brazil, women vendors sell *akara* with shrimp sauce.

Traditionalists separate the fleshy pulp of the peas from the skins by rubbing a few peas between the palms of the hands. I save time and effort by pressing small amounts of the peas with the back of a wooden spoon through a fine-mesh sieve.

Here is a recipe for a foundational *akara*, which you can personalize by adding minced hot chile peppers, sweet or roasted bell peppers, ground cumin, chili powder, or smoked paprika to serve as a side dish. For a surprise on your appetizer buffet, accompany with pico de gallo, salsa, or chutney.

1 pound dried black-eyed peas, picked over for stones and rinsed
1 cup minced onion
1 tablespoon minced garlic (about 3 cloves)
1 teaspoon cayenne pepper
1 teaspoon salt, or to taste
Peanut oil, for deep-frying

1 Soak the peas overnight in enough water to cover. Drain them in a colander and discard the soaking water. Working with about ¼ cup at a time, rub the peas between the palms of your hands or press with the back of a wooden spoon in a fine-mesh sieve to remove the skins (discard the skins).

2 Transfer the peas to a food processor. With the machine running, gradually add enough water (about ¼ cup) so the mixture forms a stiff paste. Press the pulse button 2 or 3 times to mix in the onion, garlic, cayenne, and salt.

3 Pour a few inches of oil into a large Dutch oven or other wide deep pot (making sure you have plenty of clearance to prevent the oil from bubbling over) and heat the oil to 375°F over medium-high heat. Scoop the mixture by the tablespoon and drop into the hot fat. (Using a small cookie dough scoop will help the *akara* maintain its shape.) Deep-fry until golden, turning occasionally to ensure even cooking, 2 to 3 minutes per side. Drain on paper towels before serving.

I'VE SEEN SOUP MADE FROM COSTLY DELICACIES, AND IT WAS "SCRUMPTIOUS." I'VE TASTED SOUP MADE FROM LEFTOVERS BY THE POOR, AND IT WAS BREATH-TAKINGLY GOOD. WHETHER IT'S SERVED IN A PALACE OR A SHACK, IT'S GOOD FOR US.
—FREDA DEKNIGHT, *A DATE WITH A DISH*, 1948

For the Welcome Table

With just a few exceptions, African American cooks' passion for leafy salads tossed with dressings, sauces, and spices does not trace as neatly as soup does from the African continent or the antebellum kitchen to the present. In fact, the idea of salad as we know it today has meant different things at different times. American salad could have been a congealed or molded concoction of fruit or vegetables suspended in gelatin, an ethnic mixture inspired by Germans and Italians, or any cooked poultry or seafood surrounded by a few lettuce leaves, John F. Mariani tells us in the *Dictionary of American Food and Drink*. African American cookbook author Abby Fisher's 1881 collection, *What Mrs. Fisher Knows About Old Southern Cooking*, reflected her Alabama roots with just six salad recipes—chicken, veal, lamb, shrimp, crab, and meat.

After World War I, "women were looking for ways to save time in their cooking, and home economists, scientists, and the growing food-processing industry went to work to help them," Sylvia Lovegren explained in *Fashionable Food: Seven Decades of Food Fads*. "Salads in which the ingredients were unrecognizable, masked, or masquerading as something else were the idea."

African American women reaching for affluence noted the trend. Service workers who had fought for social status during the post–Civil War years by continuing to work in "every day" careers gradually moved into the privileged class. Culinary arts helped them resist illiterate servant stereotypes, such as Mammy and Aunt Jemima, the way that the creative, visual, musical, theatrical, and cultural arts promoted notions of the "New Negro" during the Harlem Renaissance.

New social standing enabled early twentieth-century food industry professionals to join black women's benevolent clubs and social organizations dedicated to community uplift, such as the Fannie Jackson Coppin Club and the National Association of Colored Women's Clubs. Gladys Kidd, an educator, nutritionist, mentor, philanthropist, and granddaughter of bondservants, devoted her career and research to improving health through nutrition and safe food. Sarah Massey Overton ran a catering business, supported women's suffrage, and was a charter member of San Jose's Garden City Women's Club. Some of these groups published cookbooks to fundraise for their activities. Fanciful salads and luscious soups caught on.

California state superintendent of domestic science, caterer, and member of the Federation of Negro Women's Clubs Bertha L. Turner published *The Federation Cook Book: A Collection of Tested Recipes, Contributed by the Colored Women of the State of California*, a book that mirrored trends in the salad arts. Her 1910 collection of breads, meats, soups, and preserves featured a whopping twenty-six formulas for modest salads—such as Cherry Salad, Marshmallow Salad, and Chicken Salad—more than any other food category except cakes and desserts.

"The presence of salad on a menu became an effective way to distinguish the meal as one meant for the wealthy, or at least the ambitious middle class, which could afford relatively expensive ingredients wrought into a cajoling design," Laura Shapiro explained in *Perfection Salad: Women and Cooking at the Turn of the Century*.

(For a taste of how elaborate and artful this kind of salad making was, refer to the book *Good Things to Eat, as Suggested by Rufus* by chef Rufus Estes, who cooked for Pullman Private Car travelers. Published a year after Turner's book, it featured rococo and skillful concoctions like Birds Nest Salad, which involved lettuce leaves curled into a "dainty little nest," topped with a tiny speckled egg made by rolling cream cheese into an egg shape and sprinkling with parsley, the dressing hidden under the leaves, or Cauliflower Mayonnaise, which heaped seasoned florets on a platter, arranging them like a flower and surrounding them with carrots, turnips, and green peas.)

In the mid-twentieth century, with an emphasis on wholesome cooking, food editor Freda DeKnight steered readers of *Ebony* magazine and her cookbook, *A Date with a Dish,* back to salads that were "simple, vital to good health, not expensive, chock-full of vitamins and minerals, part of the roughage that our diets require."

My own mother got into the salad spirit during my school-age years, tossing together a "chef's salad" of julienned cold cuts, cheese, tomatoes, cucumbers, and lettuce with Thousand Island dressing for an easy after-work meal.

Vertamae Smart-Grosvenor, on the other hand, used the concept of salad to express aggravation and contempt during the Black Power movement of the 1960s. The story in her 1971 memoir/cookbook, *Vibration Cooking: Or, The Travel Notes of a Geechee Girl,* takes place after a particularly stressful day, and involves a nosy white woman who inquires about collard greens:

"How do you people fix those?"
"Salad," I said.
"Salad?"
"Yeah, salad."
"But I was sure You People cooked them."
"No, never . . . salad."
"What kind of dressing?"
"Italian!"

African American soup history is another matter, remembered reverentially in 1988 by author Dunstan A. Harris in *Island Cooking: Recipes from the Caribbean,* this way: "Agricultural workers—slaves and indentured servants—began their long shifts on the sugar cane and banana plantations in the pre-dawn darkness. It was their custom to pool together each day a variety of vegetables raised from their subsistence garden plots, any scraps of meat that were available, as well as their rations of flour and salted meats. At that very hour, the designated cook would create a soup in a huge wrought-iron cauldron placed over a coal fire to slowly cook for several hours. At mid-day, when the workers broke for lunch, soup, perhaps the day's most complete and nutritious meal, was served."

From these humble beginnings, many soup recipes have become vital parts of Caribbean cuisine, Harris continued. Soups offered to visitors were usually strained and the broth served as an appetizer. At home, with family, soup might be a main course, rich in meat and hearty vegetables.

This is a tradition that spanned the Caribbean and beyond, throughout the African diaspora. Ruth Gaskins explained how this habit of soup making survived poor cabin cooking through the generations in her 1968 collection of "Traditional

Negro Recipes," titled *A Good Heart and a Light Hand*. She tells the story behind "the Negro Welcome," hospitality symbolized by a pot of something wonderful to eat that is never empty, always waiting, with comfort for the soul. Gaskins recalled: "The Welcome comes from back in the days when we were slaves. For over 200 years we were told where to live and where to work. We were given husbands, and we made children, and all these things could be taken away from us. The only real comfort came at the end of the day, when we took either the food that we were given, or the food that we raised, or the food that we had caught, and we put it in the pot, and we sat with our own kind and talked and sang and ate."

In freedom, Gaskins went on to say, the Welcome was evident especially in special times: church dinners and homecoming events, family reunions, and club activities—the Woman's Burial Society, a Savings Club, and her mama's ladies' Luncheon Club among them. The Welcome meant she would see a dozen or so women dressed in their Sunday best—hats and good dresses and gloves—for lunch. "The hostess would really get away from the traditional foods. The menus always sounded like something out of the Thursday food page in the newspaper . . . creamed chicken in patty shells [puff pastry shells] or crab salad with all the little decorations around it. They'd sit at the dining room table which was set with all the best linen and every piece of silver that the hostess owned."

The soups and salads collected here speak to that spirit of power, hope, and abundance—the Welcome's ancestral call to hospitality, inspired by abundant fruits, vegetables, other rich ingredients, and a sense of joy in cooking that nurtures community.

CORN AND POTATO CHOWDER WITH CRAB

SERVES 4 TO 6

William Deas was South Carolina First Lady Blanche Rhett's "able butler" and "one of the greatest cooks of the world," wrote Rhett, Lettie Gay, and Helen Woodward in *Two Hundred Years of Charleston Cooking*. Many of the recipes in the 1930 cookbook are attributed to Deas and his "skilled hand." The historian Arturo Schomburg listed several of Deas's recipes, including his She-Crab Soup, in his unpublished outline for a Negro cookbook that would tell the full tale of black excellence in cooking.

She-crabs, when prepared with their eggs, give this soup a "delicious, glutinous quality" that is very different from standard crab soup. She-crab soup is a coastal Carolina staple and sees many cooks' personal innovations: Charlotte Jenkins's version in her cookbook *Gullah Cuisine: By Land and By Sea* enhances the flavor of lump crabmeat with cloves, mace, and Gullah Seafood Seasoning; Edna Lewis's recipe calls for marinating the crabmeat in cream. But she-crabs are difficult to acquire outside of the Lowcountry, where they are trapped during laying season.

To enjoy crab soup even if you can't get she-crabs at your local market, this mash-up, inspired by a recipe in *My Life on a Plate* by the singer Kelis, brings together the flavors of three popular soups into one: crab soup, potato soup, and corn chowder.

2 cups fresh or frozen corn kernels
(about 4 ears)

5 cups Vegetable Stock (recipe follows)

4 tablespoons butter, or ¼ pound salt pork,
or 8 slices bacon

⅔ cup diced onion

2½ teaspoons minced garlic (about 3 cloves)

2 cups peeled and diced russet potato (1 large)

¾ cup diced carrot

1 tablespoon fresh thyme leaves, minced

1½ teaspoons salt, or to taste

1 cup heavy whipping cream

½ teaspoon black pepper

½ pound lump crabmeat

Paprika, for garnish

1 In a blender or food processor, puree 1 cup of the corn kernels with 1 cup of the vegetable stock.

2 In a large saucepan, melt the butter over medium heat until sizzling. (Alternatively, cook the salt pork or bacon over medium heat until crisp and fat is rendered. Remove the pork to paper towels to drain.) Add the onion, stirring occasionally, then more frequently as it cooks, until softened but not browned, 8 to 10 minutes.

3 Stir in the garlic and cook, stirring constantly, until softened, about 30 seconds. Stir in the potato, carrot, thyme, and salt. Sauté for 2 minutes, stirring. Stir in the remaining 4 cups of stock, the remaining 1 cup of corn kernels, and the reserved corn puree. Bring to a boil, then reduce the heat to a gentle simmer. Cook until the potato is tender and the soup has thickened slightly, 20 to 30 minutes.

4 Stir in the cream, pepper, and crab and cook for about 2 minutes longer to just heat the soup through. Adjust seasoning with salt and pepper.

5 Divide the soup into the bowls, sprinkle with paprika, and serve immediately.

RECIPE CONTINUES

OCHRA GUMBO

What Mrs. Fisher Knows About Old Southern Cooking,
Abby Fisher, 1881

Get a beef shank, have it cracked and put to boil in one
gallon of water. Boil to half a gallon, then strain and
put back on fire. Cut ochra in small pieces and put in
soup; don't put in any ends of ochra. Season with salt
and pepper while cooking. Stir it occasionally
and keep it from burning. To be sent to table with
dry boiled rice. Never stir rice while boiling. Season
rice always with salt when it is first put on to cook, and
do not have too much water in rice while boiling.

SEAFOOD GUMBO

SERVES 10

When making Louisiana's famed thick, murky stew, remember that there are several types of gumbo, based on the ingredient that thickens the broth: okra, filé powder (ground sassafras leaves), or a smooth brown roux. You may choose any of these, or a combination, but okra and filé are seldom used together.

I adapted this recipe from Leroy's Catering in Miami, as printed in K. Kofi Moyo's *Real Men Cook*, because it so closely resembles the way I make mine at home. Stirring the medium-brown roux for gumbo requires patience, but the silky broth that results is well worth the time and effort.

½ cup vegetable oil

½ cup all-purpose flour (or ¾ cup, if you like a thicker gumbo)

1 cup chopped onion

1 cup chopped green onions (about 8)

¾ cup chopped green bell pepper

¾ cup chopped celery

1 tablespoon minced garlic (3 to 4 cloves)

½ teaspoon minced Scotch Bonnet pepper, or to taste

1 teaspoon dried thyme

2 teaspoons salt, or to taste

½ teaspoon black pepper

½ teaspoon cayenne pepper

2½ quarts Chicken Stock (recipe follows) or Fish Stock (page 136), or a combination, warmed

1 bay leaf

1 pound fresh or frozen okra, sliced ¼ inch thick

1 pound shrimp, peeled and deveined

1 pint shucked oysters

1 pound claw crabmeat, picked over

Plenty of hot cooked rice, for serving

¼ cup minced fresh parsley

1 In a large Dutch oven or heavy soup pot, heat the oil over medium-high heat until hot, almost smoking. Gradually whisk in the flour, being careful not to splash the mixture so you don't get burned. Reduce the heat to low and cook and stir the roux continuously until medium brown and smooth, 20 to 30 minutes.

2 Increase heat to medium-high. Add the onion, green onions, bell pepper, and celery and stir until the vegetables are wilted but not browned, about 7 minutes. Add the garlic, chile pepper, thyme, salt, black pepper, and cayenne. Reduce the heat to low and cook to allow the flavors to marry, about 20 minutes.

3 Whisk in the warm stock in batches to prevent splattering. Add the bay leaf, then bring back to a boil over high heat. Reduce the heat to medium-low and simmer for 30 minutes. Taste and add salt as desired. Add the okra, shrimp, oysters, and crab and simmer until just cooked, another few minutes. Taste and adjust seasonings with salt and pepper. Remove from the heat and let stand for 1 hour for the flavors to mingle. Remove and discard the bay leaf.

4 Return the pot to medium-low heat just until the soup is hot again. Spoon into serving bowls, add hot rice as desired, and sprinkle with parsley.

CHICKEN STOCK

MAKES ABOUT 3½ QUARTS

1 (5- to 6-pound) stewing hen or 3 pounds
   chicken bones (backs, necks, etc.)
1 medium onion, quartered
3 celery stalks, with leaves, ends trimmed
3 bay leaves
¼ teaspoon black peppercorns
2 sprigs thyme or ¼ teaspoon dried thyme
3 sprigs parsley

In a large heavy stockpot, combine
5 quarts water, the chicken or bones, and
onion. Cut the celery stalks in half and
add them to the pot. Add the bay leaves,
peppercorns, thyme, and parsley. Bring
the stock to just under a boil over high
heat, then reduce the heat to low, partially
cover, and simmer until the chicken is
very tender and the broth is rich-tasting,
2 to 3 hours. The broth develops stronger
flavor the longer you let it simmer. If using
a whole chicken, remove the chicken from
the broth, and when it's cool enough to
handle, pull off the meat and reserve it
for another use. Strain the stock, let cool,
and refrigerate until the fat floats to the
top. Use a slotted spoon to skim off the fat
and discard. Store tightly covered for up to
1 week in the refrigerator, or freeze.

NOTE: To ensure you always have
homemade stock on hand, freeze cooled
stock in ice cube trays. Pop out the cubes
and store them in heavy-duty freezer bags.
Thaw them as needed.

GUMBO FILÉ

New Orleans Cookbook, Lena Richard, 1939

1 cup chopped chicken meat
2½ quarts chicken stock
½ dozen crabs
1 pound lake shrimp
½ pound or 1 slice raw ham
1 bay leaf
3 teaspoons filé
1 medium sized onion
1 clove of garlic
3 tablespoons flour
4 tablespoons cooking oil
Salt and pepper to taste

*Fry ham and shrimp in cooking oil until ham is a golden
brown. Remove ham and shrimp from fat. Make a roux
with flour and fat, add onions and cook until a golden
brown. Add crabs, chicken, ham and shrimp, stock and
all seasonings except salt and pepper. Cook over a slow
fire until liquid has reduced to about 1½ quarts. Season
with salt and pepper and, just before serving, stir in filé.
It is customary to serve Gumbo Filé with rice.*

CRAWFISH BISQUE

SERVES 4

Order crawfish bisque in a restaurant, and what you really get is crawfish soup. African American cooks have been making this dish, under both these names—and others, fancy-sounding or not—for a long, long time.

Bisque means "thick soup" in French, usually made rich by the addition of cream. Over the years, our cooks used the term to refer to cream soup or "cream of" soup, and they relied on various techniques to give the soup body—from egg yolks to a simple white sauce to the classic French mixture beurre manié. (*Beurre manié* translates to rubbed or kneaded butter. The practice requires a light twist of the fingers—imagine you're snapping your fingers to knead together little cubes of butter with flour, which you can stir into a soup or sauce at the end of the cooking time to add body.)

In 1932, a white author named Mary Moore Bremer featured *potage d'écrevisses* (crayfish soup) in her collection of "proven recipes of New Orleans' most favored dishes." A black cook in a bandanna graced the cover of the spiral-bound collection. Inside, Bremer explained that the cooking of the region owed its allure to the flavors of France, Spain, and Italy, and to the fact that "the negro woman, who reigned in the kitchen, had inherited from her ancestors in Africa, as well as in America, a knowledge of herbs that made her skill look like magic."

The essence of that kitchen prowess isn't wizardry; it is more likely a lifetime of hard work, skills learned, and usage of the "holy trinity," a mix of pungent onion, bright green bell pepper, and crisp celery. This recipe is an adaptation of Leah Chase's springtime crawfish soup from *The Dooky Chase Cookbook*.

4 tablespoons (½ stick) butter
2 tablespoons all-purpose flour
¼ cup chopped onion
⅓ cup chopped celery
⅓ cup chopped green bell pepper
1 teaspoon minced garlic
1 tablespoon paprika
1 teaspoon salt, or to taste
1 teaspoon cayenne pepper
3 cups Fish Stock (recipe follows)
¼ teaspoon dried thyme
1 bay leaf
1 pound cooked crawfish tails
1 cup half-and-half
1 tablespoon minced fresh parsley

1 In a large Dutch oven or heavy soup pot, heat the butter and flour over medium heat. Cook, stirring, about 5 minutes to make a light blonde roux. Stir in the onion, celery, and bell pepper and cook until the vegetables are starting to soften, about 2 minutes. Stir in the garlic and cook 1 minute longer. Stir in the paprika, salt, and cayenne. Add the fish stock, thyme, and bay leaf. Bring to a boil over medium-high heat, then reduce the heat, cover, and simmer for 20 minutes, until the vegetables are tender and the soup has thickened.

2 Remove the soup from the heat. Remove and discard the bay leaf and puree the soup in batches in a blender. Return the soup to the pot. Add the crawfish tails and half-and-half and simmer for 15 minutes to marry the flavors. Taste and adjust seasoning with salt if desired. Garnish with parsley.

RECIPE CONTINUES

FISH STOCK

MAKES ABOUT 3½ QUARTS

Boiled fish heads, bones, or shrimp shells (or a combination) are the basis of this rich cooking stock, but do not use the heads of fatty fish that have strong tastes of their own, like salmon. Among the many pictures Vertamae Smart-Grosvenor painted of her Lowcountry upbringing in *Vibration Cooking: Or the Travel Notes of a Geechee Girl* was one of an "epicurean delight"—a stew her mother made by long-simmering onions and green pepper with fish heads she bought for five cents a pound. The brew, known as fish head stew, was served over grits.

5 pounds fish heads, bones, and/or shrimp shells
2 cups large chunks celery, including leaves
2 medium onions, peeled and quartered
2 bay leaves
1 sprig parsley
¼ teaspoon whole black peppercorns

In a large heavy saucepan, combine 4 quarts water, the bones, celery, and onions. Add the bay leaves, parsley, and peppercorns. Bring to a boil over medium-low heat (it will take a while, but gentle heat is what keeps this stock clear and fresh tasting), then reduce the heat to low and gently simmer, uncovered, 1 to 2 hours, skimming off any foam that rises to the top of the pot. The broth develops stronger flavor the longer you let it simmer. Strain the broth through a colander to remove the bones and vegetables. Then strain it again through a fine-mesh sieve and discard any solids. Refrigerate the broth until fat floats to the top. Use a slotted spoon to skim fat and discard. Store tightly covered for up to 3 days in the refrigerator, or freeze.

POTAGE D'ECREVISSES

New Orleans Creole Recipes,
Mary Moore Bremer, 1932

Wash four dozen crayfish in several waters to get the mud off. Boil in plain water and save this. When cold, take meat out of shells, just as with shrimp, saving two dozen shells, or heads, as they are called.

To make the bisque: Use half the meat and the remaining shells. Chop one half pound of ham, one pound of veal, one large carrot, two parsnips, one large onion. Put one rounded tablespoon of lard into a saucepan; when hot, add one large onion and four shallots, minced. When onion commences to brown, add the chopped vegetables and meat. Now stir in two tablespoons of flour, one tablespoon of butter, and brown, to make roux. Add a small can of tomatoes and let simmer for five minutes; add twelve allspice, six cloves, one clove of garlic, two bay leaves, one tablespoon of chopped celery leaves, one tablespoon of minced parsley, one teaspoon thyme, salt and pepper to taste. Pour from saucepan into the hot water in which the crayfish were boiled. Add the meat and shells and a small can of mushrooms. Let simmer for about two hours, then mash and strain and thin with water to the consistency of thick cream.

Stuffing the heads: Chop an onion very fine and let brown, slightly, in a tablespoon of butter. Squeeze a cup of bread which has been soaked in water, or a cup of cooked rice, and add to the reserved crayfish meat, well seasoned with pepper and salt. Chop another onion and put in melted butter and fry for about 10 minutes; season with parsley and thyme. Take off fire and stuff the reserved heads with this. Put on each head a dot of butter and place in oven to bake for a few minutes.

Put stuffed heads in tureen and pour bisque over. Serve hot with buttered croutons in a separate dish.

Groundnut Soup

William Ed Grimé wanted the world to appreciate African expertise that existed before enslavement, so he assembled quotations from botanists and naturalists as objective testimony about the Old World foods that the enslaved brought with them and the native plants they employed in bondage. He published in 1979 the *Ethno-Botany of the Black Americans*, a book dedicated in memory of Quassi, a servant with "exceptional knowledge of the therapeutic value of plants."

Peanuts were among them, to the point where slavers took advantage of Africans' knowledge of them. Grimé offered these observations by H. Barham and J. Lunan, travelers to Jamaica in 1794 and 1814, respectively: "Some say, if eaten much, they cause the head-ache; but I never knew any such effect, even by those who chiefly lived upon them; for masters of ships often feed negroes with them all their voyage. They may be eaten raw, roasted, or boiled. The oil drawn from them by expression is as good as oil of almonds."

Known commonly then as "American groundnut, earth-nuts, gub-a-gubs, peanut, pindals, and pindars," these edible seeds are actually legumes—not nuts—and they are the foundation of a variety of soups, stews, breads, and sauces in Africa.

Reclaiming that expertise for his community, Dr. George Washington Carver offered five versions of peanut soup in his *Bulletin No. 31, How to Grow the Peanut and 105 Ways of Preparing It for Human Consumption*, a 1925 collection of recipes, nutrition tips, and farm practices.

PEANUT SOUP

SERVES 6 TO 8

This luxurious soup, which makes a decadent first course, brings to mind one of Dr. George Washington Carver's recipes for peanut soup. I adapted the recipe from a French Caribbean Creole soup created by Jeanne Louise Duzant "Ma" Chance for her 1985 recipe collection, *Ma Chance's French Caribbean Creole Cooking*. I enriched it, doubling the peanut butter and substituting cream for milk.

While Dr. Carver, and the West African cooks before him, would have cooked raw peanuts, removed their skins, and mashed, ground, or pounded them until smooth, there is no need to do so in your kitchen. Natural peanut butter, without added sugar, is your friend.

4 tablespoons (½ stick) butter

½ cup minced onion

1 teaspoon minced garlic (about 1 clove)

1 tablespoon all-purpose flour

1 cup natural peanut butter (unsweetened)

1 quart Chicken Stock (page 133)

1 cup heavy whipping cream

Salt and black pepper

Hot pepper sauce (optional)

Crushed roasted peanuts, for garnish
  (optional)

1 In a medium saucepan, heat the butter over medium heat until it is sizzling. Add the onion and garlic and sauté until translucent but not browned, about 3 minutes. Sprinkle the flour over the mixture and use a whisk to stir it together, about 30 seconds. Whisk in the peanut butter until softened and smooth.

2 Gradually whisk in the chicken stock and bring it to a very gentle simmer. Reduce the heat to low and cook it very gently for 20 minutes to thicken and marry the flavors, stirring occasionally to prevent sticking.

3 Stir in the cream and let it gently heat up to your desired serving temperature. Do not overheat, or the oil might separate. Season to taste with plenty of salt, black pepper, and hot pepper sauce (if using). Serve sprinkled with crushed peanuts as a garnish, if desired.

WEST AFRICAN GROUNDNUT STEW

SERVES 6

In 1985, the Africa News Service of Durham, North Carolina, tasked Tami Hultman with compiling a book of recipes to acknowledge the popular and nutritious peanut and other ingredients and culinary techniques that enslaved Africans had reimagined in the American South. *The Africa News Cookbook: African Cooking for Western Kitchens* showed off three varieties of chicken and groundnut stew, each made unique by the addition of local vegetables. This quintessential blend is strikingly similar to the Senegalese peanut stew called *mafé* (see page 214).

1 (4-pound) chicken, cut into parts
2 cups chopped onion (about 2 medium)
2 garlic cloves, minced
1 cup diced carrots
2 teaspoons salt, or to taste
6 whole black peppercorns
1 bay leaf
½ cup natural peanut butter
4 cups undrained chopped canned tomatoes
½ teaspoon minced fresh ginger
½ teaspoon curry powder
¼ teaspoon cayenne pepper
¼ teaspoon crushed red pepper flakes
¼ cup dry white wine (optional)
Freshly cooked rice, for serving

1 In a soup pot or Dutch oven, combine 1 quart water, the chicken, onion, garlic, carrots, salt, peppercorns, and bay leaf. Bring to a boil over medium-high heat, then reduce the heat to medium-low and simmer, covered, until the chicken is cooked through, about 45 minutes. Strain the broth and return the liquid to the pot. When cool enough to handle, separate the chicken meat from the skin and bones, bay leaf, and other solids. Discard the skin and bones. Dice the chicken and set aside.

2 In a small bowl, stir about ½ cup of the hot broth into the peanut butter and mix until smooth. Return the peanut butter mixture to the pot along with the tomatoes, ginger, curry powder, cayenne, pepper flakes, and the white wine, if desired. Bring to a boil over medium-high heat, then reduce the heat to medium-low and simmer 20 minutes to allow the flavors to marry, skimming the fat with a spoon if necessary.

3 Return the chicken to the pot and heat through. Taste, adding salt to adjust the seasoning, and serve with rice.

Green Gumbo

Green gumbo, or gumbo z'herbes, is Louisiana's translation of the tradition of stewed greens. It's a mixture of seven or more greens, often with smoked meats and poultry, associated with Holy Thursday and considered the "Queen of all Gumbos." I also saw strains of the dish in the old plantation habit of consuming the "treasured water" reserved from cooking greens, known as potlikker, with cornmeal dumplings. (Mary Mac's Tea Room in Atlanta still expresses hospitality to first-time guests with a complimentary cup of potlikker and a side of corn-bread, to be crumbled into the smoky broth.)

All of this can be traced to the West African way with greens and to West Indian callaloo. Throughout West Africa, women and children gathered "bush greens," which were simmered with oil, peppers, and seasonings or added to soups. These broad-leafed spinach-like plants accompanied Africans to the West Indies, where the thick green leaves were bundled and sold in open markets as callaloo. Dried okra gave the soup body.

West Indian pepperpot simmers callaloo greens with an assortment of salted or fresh fish, meats, and vegetables in a gumbo-like stew that is served with a starch—sweet potatoes or yams, cornmeal or flour dumplings—Heidi Haughy Cusick wrote in *Soul and Spice: African Cooking in the Americas*. Many West Indian cooks have a pepperpot kettle bubbling on the stove daily, "with the end of the previous day's pepperpot forming the beginning of the next day's stew. Some pepperpots have been simmering for generations," Cusick quipped.

GUMBO Z'HERBES

SERVES 10 TO 12

All kinds of techniques give this dish body: Leah Chase's version calls for a mix of roux and pureed vegetables to thicken; Nathaniel Burton, coauthor of *Creole Feast: Fifteen Master Chefs of New Orleans Reveal Their Secrets*, thickens his green gumbo with a low, slow simmer, not a roux. This version leans Burton's way, making it more like a dense stew, rather than a classic brown gumbo.

1 pound collard greens

3 pounds greens (such as mustard, collard, turnip greens, watercress, kale, chard, beet and carrot tops, spinach), washed, stemmed, and coarsely chopped

¼ head cabbage, coarsely chopped

1 tablespoon plus 2 teaspoons salt, plus more to taste

½ pound beef brisket or veal, cut into ¼-inch dice

¾ teaspoon black pepper, plus more to taste

2 tablespoons bacon drippings or vegetable oil

½ pound smoked sausage, sliced into thick coins

½ pound ham, cut into ¼-inch dice

2 cups chopped onions

½ cup chopped green onions

1 cup chopped green bell pepper

1½ cups chopped celery

1 tablespoon minced chile pepper

1 tablespoon minced garlic (2 to 3 cloves)

1 teaspoon dried thyme

¼ teaspoon cayenne pepper

2 bay leaves

1 quart Chicken Stock (page 133)

2 tablespoons minced fresh parsley

1 tablespoon fresh thyme leaves, minced

Freshly cooked rice, for serving

1 In a large Dutch oven or heavy soup pot, combine the collards and 4 cups water. Bring to a boil, then reduce the heat to medium and simmer until the collards are tender, about 30 minutes. Add the greens, cabbage, and 1 tablespoon salt to the pot. Return to a boil, then reduce the heat to a gentle simmer and cook, covered, until the greens are very tender. (Depending upon the greens you choose, this could be over an hour.) Drain the greens in a colander, reserving the cooking liquid (the "potlikker"). Coarsely chop the greens. Measure out 2 cups of the potlikker and set aside. (Save the remainder in the refrigerator for another use; it has a lot of natural flavor, sweetness, and nutrition.)

2 Season the brisket with ½ teaspoon of salt and ¼ teaspoon of black pepper. In a large skillet, heat the bacon fat over medium-high heat. Add the brisket, sausage, and ham and cook for 10 minutes, stirring occasionally, to render the fat and brown the meats. Stir in the onions, green onions, bell pepper, celery, chile pepper, and garlic and sauté until the vegetables are tender-crisp, 3 to 5 minutes. Stir in the dried thyme, 1½ teaspoons salt, ½ teaspoon black pepper, and the cayenne and cook until fragrant, 2 to 3 minutes longer.

3 In the Dutch oven or soup pot, combine the cooked greens, the reserved 2 cups potlikker, and the browned meat and vegetables. Cook for 15 minutes to concentrate the flavors. Stir in the bay leaves and chicken stock. Bring to a boil, then reduce the heat to a simmer and cook until the meats are tender, about 45 minutes. Remove and discard the bay leaves. After 30 minutes, taste and adjust the seasoning with a generous amount of salt and pepper. Stir in the parsley and fresh thyme. Serve over hot cooked rice.

PEPPERPOT

SERVES 6 TO 8

This recipe is a soup of tender-cooked greens made intensely hot, with Scotch bonnets as the eponymous pepper, and enriched with okra and a splash of coconut milk, which gives it an island character.

1 pound callaloo (see Note) or a mix of cooking greens, washed, stem ends trimmed

¼ pound salt pork or slab bacon, finely chopped (or 3 to 4 tablespoons oil)

1 cup chopped onion

½ cup chopped celery

1 Scotch bonnet pepper, minced

3 garlic cloves, minced

¼ teaspoon dried thyme

6 cups Chicken Stock (page 133)

½ cup coconut milk

1 large sweet potato, peeled and cut into ½-inch dice

½ pound fresh okra, trimmed and cut into ½-inch slices

½ pound crabmeat, picked over

Salt and black pepper

Chopped fresh parsley, for garnish

1 Coarsely chop the greens into 1-inch pieces and set aside.

2 In a Dutch oven or large soup pot, cook the pork over medium-low heat until browned and the fat is rendered, stirring occasionally, about 15 minutes. Use a slotted spoon to remove the browned bits from the pan and drain on paper towels.

3 Stir the onion, celery, and chile pepper into the pot and cook, stirring occasionally, over medium-high heat until the vegetables are tender, 5 to 7 minutes. Stir in the garlic and thyme and cook until fragrant, about 30 seconds. Stir in the chicken stock and reserved browned pork. Bring to a boil over high heat, then reduce the heat to low and simmer for 15 minutes. Stir in the chopped greens, coconut milk, and sweet potato. Return to a boil, then simmer until the greens and sweet potato are tender, about 15 minutes (it may be longer, depending upon the greens you use). Stir in the okra and cook for 10 minutes. Add the crab during the last 5 minutes of cooking time. Season to taste with a generous amount of salt and black pepper. Sprinkle with parsley to serve.

NOTE: Look for callaloo in African and Latin grocery stores, or substitute a mix of Swiss chard, kale, collard greens, and spinach.

Layered and Tossed Salads

Over time, black cookbooks have presented the pageantry of black salad-making through recipes that often identify aspects of culture (techniques rooted in diasporic or Southern cooking and local ingredients), and some cooks fused their salads with trendy elements. African and West Indian cooks mention fruit combinations most often when salad is the subject, perhaps explaining the spell cast by ambrosia, the fruit and coconut combination. Rural country cooks like Mildred Council, Dori Sanders, and Edna Lewis remembered salads of thinly sliced cucumber and onions marinated in vinegar and pickled farm-fresh vegetables dressed with vinegar to cool the heat of summertime. Caterers Cleora Butler and the bourgeois ladies of the Negro Culinary Arts Club of Los Angeles assembled "dainty delights" like tomato aspic made with Knox Sparkling Granulated Gelatine or cherries suspended in cola-laced Jell-O to flaunt their access to new or exotic ingredients. And there were the fibrous raw combinations that home economists including Freda DeKnight and Carrie Alberta Lyford adapted, salads from global cultures that promote good health, such as Middle Eastern tabbouleh, the French Salade Niçoise, and a dish simply entitled Mexican Salad. By the 1980s, these cooling mixtures reflected simplicity, balance, and good taste.

Mrs. Artaway Fillmore was famous for the "fine salads" she created for guests at the Hotel Lubbock in West Texas and as a Dallas caterer. Two elaborate creations in the *Lone Star Cook Book and Meat Special: From the Slaughter Pen to the Dining Room* (1929) reveal her layered salad–making supremacy: lettuce arranged with pineapple and tomato slices on top, and lettuce shreds topped with seasoned sweet potato mash and crowned with mashed russet potatoes that were piped on with a pastry bag—a study in exuberance.

BROCCOLI AND CAULIFLOWER SALAD
WITH CURRIED DRESSING

SERVES 8 TO 10

This version of the layered salad elevates mayonnaise dressing with a taste of spice. It was enlivened by cooking school teacher Sarah Helen Mahammitt, who in 1939 sweetened mayonnaise and spiked it with curry powder. You can make the dressing the night before and assemble the salad later, but the salad should rest at least 8 hours before serving so the flavors can mingle. Curry—the mixture of ground and toasted spices such as turmeric, anise, coriander, cloves, cumin, and fenugreek—is most often associated with India, but cooks along trade and slavery routes invented variations of their own, marrying migrating aromatic seeds and berries with local ingredients throughout Africa and the Caribbean—especially in Trinidad, Guadeloupe, and Martinique.

8 slices bacon

1 cup mayonnaise

½ cup sugar

2 tablespoons cider vinegar

¼ to ½ teaspoon curry powder, to taste

Salt

4 cups broccoli florets, trimmed and cut into bite-size pieces

½ cup sliced celery

4 cups cauliflower florets, trimmed and cut into bite-size pieces

¾ cup raisins

¾ cup toasted slivered almonds

1 In a medium skillet, cook the bacon over medium-high heat until crisp, about 7 minutes. Drain on paper towels and crumble when cool enough to handle. Reserve the fat for another use.

2 In a small bowl, mix together the mayonnaise, sugar, vinegar, curry powder, and salt to taste.

3 In a serving bowl, layer the broccoli florets, celery, and cauliflower. Pour on all of the dressing. Add a layer of raisins, then almonds, then top with the bacon. Cover with a tight-fitting lid or plastic wrap. Refrigerate for at least 8 hours or overnight. Toss before serving.

COOKED SALAD DRESSING

A Date with a Dish, Freda DeKnight, 1948

2 eggs

1 tablespoon flour

2 tablespoons sugar

¼ teaspoon cayenne

¼ teaspoon paprika

1 teaspoon salt

½ cup vinegar

1 cup milk

1 teaspoon dry mustard

Mix together all dry ingredients. Add to slightly beaten eggs. Beat until smooth. Add milk and vinegar. Cook in double boiler 20 minutes. Yield: 1½ cups.

WILTED MIXED GREENS WITH BACON

SERVES 8 TO 10

The dish we've come to know as warm spinach salad—greens tossed with a hot bacon dressing—wasn't really a salad at all, to hear the black cookbook authors tell it through the years. Survey the vegetables section of soul food and early twentieth-century black cookbooks and look for this uberpopular combination with titles like "wilted" or "killed" lettuce or spinach, or you might miss it.

Back in the day, farm folks tossed combinations of bitter greens and herbs, such as escarole, chicory, purslane, and watercress, with a warm dressing they stirred together right in a hot skillet after cooking bacon. In harder times, wild weeds like dandelion and poke, as in "poke sallet," answered the call. Soul cooks carried on the tradition of wilting lettuce leaves instead of spinach. Harmony McCoy, resident chef at Murietta Hot Springs Resort in California, tried to slim down the dish for waistline watchers by topping watercress with a dusting of crumbled bacon and bottled low-cal dressing.

I returned to the wilted lettuce tradition here with so-called power greens. These greens are dark and rich in vitamins and minerals and taste delicious. Try it my way, then experiment with your favorite combination of tender baby greens and herbs.

2 pounds mixed tender greens (spinach, arugula, chard, baby kale, watercress)
4 radishes, thinly sliced
½ cup thinly sliced red onion
2 hard-boiled eggs, sliced
1 cup grape tomatoes, cut into halves
8 slices bacon
⅔ cup cider vinegar
1 tablespoon sugar
2 teaspoons salt
¼ teaspoon black pepper
⅓ cup crumbled blue cheese (optional)

1 In a large salad bowl, toss together the greens, radishes, onion, eggs, and tomatoes.

2 In a large skillet, cook the bacon over medium heat until crisp, about 7 minutes. Leaving the rendered bacon fat in the skillet, remove the bacon to drain on paper towels and crumble when cool enough to handle.

3 Heat the bacon fat in the skillet over medium-high heat. Stir in the vinegar, sugar, salt, and pepper. Swirl the pan over the heat for 1 to 2 minutes to concentrate the flavors and slightly thicken the dressing. Pour the hot dressing over the greens and toss quickly to coat. Sprinkle the greens with the crumbled bacon and blue cheese (if using).

OKRA SALAD

SERVES 4 TO 6

Salada de quiabo is a Brazilian salad that is a classic example of a migrating African ingredient adapting to its new home and making its way onto everyday and fancy menus.

In the early twentieth century, several authors, including Mrs. W. T. Hayes and Carrie Pauline Lynch, carried on the Afro-Brazilian custom; both layered boiled okra with lettuce, onion, and a hot pepper with tomatoes, grated horseradish, and a vinaigrette. In modern times, Afro-Vegan chef Bryant Terry keeps the diasporic tradition alive, grilling the okra and finishing with corn kernels and fresh basil.

My interpretation piggybacks on all of these. A tangy lemon dressing is tossed with quintessential salad bowl ingredients. Fried okra is perched on top, a recipe that comes by way of Maum Chrish'—a fictitious Gullah cook patterned after a real Charleston woman who shared her recipes in Virginia Mixson Geraty's 1992 cookbook, *Bittle en' T'ing': Gullah Cooking with Maum Chrish'.*

Peanut oil, for shallow-frying

1 cup cornmeal

¼ cup all-purpose flour

1 teaspoon salt

½ teaspoon garlic powder

½ teaspoon black pepper

½ teaspoon cayenne pepper

1 pound fresh okra, trimmed and cut into ½-inch slices

2 cups buttermilk

1 head Bibb lettuce, torn into bite-size pieces

1 cup chopped tomato

¾ cup minced red onion

¾ cup minced green bell pepper

Lemon Dressing (recipe follows)

3 slices bacon, cooked crisp and crumbled

1 Pour 1 inch oil into a deep heavy skillet and heat to 375°F over medium-high heat.

2 In a shallow dish, combine the cornmeal, flour, salt, garlic powder, black pepper, and cayenne. In a separate bowl, carefully toss the okra with the buttermilk. Use a slotted spoon to remove the okra from the buttermilk, allowing the excess milk to drain. Dredge the okra in the cornmeal mixture. Carefully spoon the dry ingredients over the okra to coat thoroughly.

3 Working in batches, lift the okra from the cornmeal with a slotted spoon, shaking to remove excess, and add to the hot oil. Cook 1½ to 2 minutes, then turn and cook on the other side until browned, about 1 minute more. Use a slotted spoon to transfer the okra to paper towels to drain.

4 In a large salad bowl, combine the lettuce, tomato, onion, bell pepper, and lemon dressing, to taste. Toss to mix well. Spoon the okra on top of the salad. Garnish with the crumbled bacon.

LEMON DRESSING

MAKES ABOUT 1 CUP

½ cup fresh lemon juice

1 tablespoon Dijon mustard

1 tablespoon minced shallots

1 teaspoon honey

½ cup extra-virgin olive oil

Salt and black pepper

In a small bowl, combine the lemon juice, mustard, shallots, and honey. Gradually whisk in the oil in a slow steady stream, whisking constantly until the mixture is thick and emulsified. Season to taste with salt and pepper. Stir before using.

FRIED OKRA

Bittle en' T'ing': Gullah Cooking with Maum Chrish', Virginia Mixson Geraty, 1992

According to the legend, Maum Chrish' was the granddaughter of slaves and learned to cook from her mother. She believed fried okra was *"Buckruh ok'ry* [white people's okra]," because Gullah-Geechee people prefer the vegetable stewed and viscous, served with rice, hominy, or cornbread. Here is her fried okra recipe in the Gullah language, followed by the translation.

Count de buckruh, en' cut one han' fuh eb'ry head. Wash de ok'ry en' cut'um een leetle slice.

Mekace en' dus'um wid flowuh so dem ent hab chance fuh leak tummuch. Seaz'n'um wid salt en'peppuh en'mekace en'fry'um een berry hot greese. Tek' um out de greese soon ez'e tu'n brong. Tek cya' 'e yent bu'n.

Mis' Ginia lub 'e ok'ry stan'so. Uh tell'um ok'ry ent mek fuh chew.

Translation:

Count the number of people who will be eating and cut a handful of okra for each one. Wash the okra pods and cut them into slices.

Quickly dust them with flour, or the flavorful juices will be lost. Season with salt and pepper, and fry the slices in very hot cooking oil until they are browned. Be careful or they will burn.

Miss Ginia likes okra cooked this way. I told her okra is not supposed to be chewed.

LAYERED GARDEN SALAD WITH GARLIC AND HERB DRESSING

SERVES 6

Restaurateur and author Mildred "Mama Dip" Council adapted the classic seven-layer salad with her own mix of shredded fresh spinach and lettuce, chopped celery, green onions, green peas, ham, and hard-boiled eggs, spread with a buttermilk–sour cream dressing, and topped with cheese. Assembling the salad ahead was a timesaver and made it easy to transport to summer barbecues and picnics. This colorful eight-layer salad modifies that dish. My thick and creamy garlic and herb dressing is a wonderful stand-in for the boiled dressing that once saturated garden salad, or for bottled ranch dressing.

1 cup sliced cucumber
1 large tomato, cut into eighths
5 radishes, sliced
¼ cup sliced red onion
1 celery stalk, sliced
¼ cup shredded carrots
1 hard-boiled egg, sliced
1 cup sweet green peas, blanched and chilled
8 cups mixed chopped greens (such as romaine lettuce, endive, leaf lettuce, and watercress)
1 tablespoon chopped fresh parsley
Garlic and Herb Dressing (recipe follows)

In a salad bowl, layer the cucumber, tomatoes, radishes, red onion, celery, carrots, egg slices, peas, greens, and parsley. Top with the garlic and herb dressing. Cover with plastic wrap and refrigerate until ready to serve. Toss before serving.

GARLIC AND HERB DRESSING

MAKES ¾ CUP

This dressing is light and refreshing on crisp lettuces and assorted veggies, but it also makes a fine dip for parties. It will remind you of bottled ranch dressing, only better.

¼ cup mayonnaise
¼ cup sour cream
3 tablespoons buttermilk
1 teaspoon fresh lemon juice
½ teaspoon tarragon vinegar
1 tablespoon chopped fresh chives
1 tablespoon minced fresh parsley
1½ teaspoons minced fresh dill
¼ teaspoon minced garlic
⅛ teaspoon onion salt
¼ teaspoon celery salt
¼ teaspoon salt
⅛ teaspoon garlic salt
Pinch of black pepper

In a small bowl or jar with a tight-fitting lid, whisk or shake together the mayonnaise, sour cream, buttermilk, lemon juice, vinegar, chives, parsley, dill, garlic, onion salt, celery salt, salt, garlic salt, and pepper. Store in the refrigerator tightly covered. Shake well before using.

NOTE: To serve as a dip, add equal amounts of mayonnaise and sour cream, 1 tablespoon at a time, until it reaches your desired thickness.

Potato Salad

The August Quarterly, also known as the Big Quarterly, is an African American freedom festival held annually in Delaware since the early 1800s to celebrate unity, religious freedom, freedom of speech, and the right of assembly. The event provided an opportunity for enslaved and free peoples of African descent from neighboring states to gather quarterly for worship, socializing, and sharing cultural traditions. Festival-goers danced, told stories, and shared African music, good humor, and home-style cooking, according to a story in *America Eats!*, the Works Progress Administration's unpublished manuscript of regional food profiles.

Potato salad was right there at the top of the menu; it is one of those standard-issue picnic dishes that seems to be everyone's favorite. Yes, there are myriad recipes that claim to wear the mantle of "best potato salad EVER." And, yes, it is possible to be a fan of mustard-based, mayonnaise-based, or some combination of both all at the same time.

If you want to stay close to the classic preparation, Maya Angelou's garnish of extra egg slices around the edge of the bowl will take you straight back to summer family reunions and holiday gatherings like the Quarterly. You can peel and cut the potatoes before cooking, but if you leave them whole they will retain more of their flavor.

Potato salad also gets more "dope" the more you experiment. You can show off your cultural flair with aromatic African spices, go uptown with a little Creole lagniappe—Creole mustard and spicy seasoning—or feed the soul with the addition of cooked shrimp, as Sallie Ann Robinson does with her Sea Islands Sunday dinner favorite—"Tada" Salad, in *Gullah Home Cooking the Daufuskie Way*.

West African yam salad is one of my newest discoveries, a colorful and chic variation of a Nigerian standby. Simply toss together honey vinaigrette, thinly sliced sweet onion, colorful bell peppers, and cooked, diced yams or sweet potatoes, and chill overnight in the refrigerator to let the flavors develop. Or, for a stateside side dish that pairs well with pork, give my interpretation of B. Smith's sweet potato salad a try.

COUNTRY-STYLE POTATO SALAD

SERVES 10 TO 12

There was a time when russet potatoes were standard issue for potato salad. Not today. Creative cooks like former *Top Chef* contender Tanya Holland have upgraded the picnic staple. The owner of Oakland's once very popular restaurant, Brown Sugar Kitchen, Holland tossed fingerling potatoes with a red wine vinaigrette, herbs, and watercress in her restaurant's eponymous cookbook. You might also up your potato salad game with waxy red or Yukon Gold potatoes, but any potatoes will be delicious in this classic mayo-and-mustard–based recipe.

5 cups peeled and cut-up potatoes, in 1-inch cubes (about 2 pounds)

Salt

½ cup diced celery

½ cup sliced green onions

4 hard-boiled eggs, coarsely chopped

3 tablespoons sweet pickle relish

2 tablespoons yellow, Creole, or Dijon mustard

¾ cup mayonnaise

½ teaspoon black pepper

Paprika, for finishing

1 In a large saucepan, combine the potatoes with salted water to cover. Bring to a boil over high heat. Reduce the heat to medium and simmer until fork-tender, 30 to 40 minutes. Drain and cool.

2 In a large bowl, combine the potatoes, celery, green onions, eggs, and relish. In a small bowl, stir together mustard, mayonnaise, pepper, and salt to taste. Gently fold this into the potato mixture, until well mixed. Cover and refrigerate several hours or overnight to allow flavors to marry.

3 Sprinkle the potato salad with paprika before serving.

SWEET POTATO SALAD
WITH ORANGE-MAPLE DRESSING
SERVES 6

I met Patrick Clark in 1990 when he was an up-and-coming chef at Los Angeles's Bice restaurant and I was the nutrition writer for the *Times*. One of the country's brightest culinary stars, let alone one of black America's culinary lights, he passed away suddenly while we were working on a cookbook proposal, translating his restaurant specialties for home kitchens. To honor his memory, Chicago's renowned chef Charlie Trotter assembled several of Clark's recipes and others from the industry's top chefs in a fundraising collection, *Cooking with Patrick Clark*. Grilled sweet potato salad with chile and ginger vinaigrette was among them.

The dish is a popular alternative to classic potato salad with a connection to the tropics. Several black authors have put their own spin on it, including Vertamae Smart-Grosvenor, and the Food Network's Pat and Gina Neely. But I offer this take on the dish from *B. Smith Cooks Southern-Style* as a tribute to the cookbook author, restaurateur, entrepreneur, and model Barbara Smith.

3 pounds sweet potatoes, peeled and cut into ¾-inch cubes
½ cup extra-virgin olive oil
2 tablespoons maple syrup
¼ cup orange juice
2 tablespoons balsamic vinegar
2 tablespoons minced fresh ginger
¼ teaspoon ground or freshly grated nutmeg
¼ teaspoon salt, plus more to taste
½ cup chopped green onions
½ cup chopped fresh parsley
¼ cup coarsely chopped toasted pecans
¼ cup golden raisins
¼ cup black raisins
Black pepper

1 In a large pot, combine the sweet potatoes and enough lightly salted water to cover. Bring to a boil, then reduce the heat and cook until just tender, about 15 minutes. Drain and allow the potatoes to cool to room temperature. (Alternatively, simmer the potatoes whole for 15 minutes, cool, peel, and slice ¾ inch thick, brush with vegetable oil, and grill over moderately hot coals until just cooked through, 3 to 5 minutes per side.) Cut the potatoes into ¾-inch cubes and transfer to a large bowl.

2 In a small bowl, whisk together the oil, maple syrup, orange juice, vinegar, ginger, nutmeg, and salt.

3 Add the onions, parsley, pecans, and raisins to the bowl of sweet potatoes and toss together. Gently stir in the dressing, tossing just until combined. Season to taste with salt and pepper. Refrigerate until ready to serve.

SOUTHERN FOOD HAS ELEMENTS OF AFRICAN
AMERICAN FOOD, BUT ALL AFRICAN AMERICAN
FOOD ISN'T SOUTHERN. LIKEWISE, SOUL FOOD
IS AFRICAN AMERICAN FOOD, BUT NOT ALL
AFRICAN AMERICAN FOOD IS SOUL FOOD.
—JENNIFER JENSEN WALLACH,
DETHRONING THE DECEITFUL PORK CHOP, **2015**

A Little Bit of This, a Little Bit of That

In 2004, a packet of National Park Service newsletters arrived in the mail for me from my uncle Thomas. The publications detailed the preservation activities of the descendants of Nicodemus, Kansas, one of the nation's last black towns. Established in 1877 by emancipated families as part of the "colored exodus" from Kentucky and Tennessee, Nicodemus reminded Thomas of the rural life his mother, my paternal grandmother, carved out on the eastern edge of Los Angeles.

My grandmother's husband descended from the "Exodusters" who were lured to Nicodemus by visions of a spacious frontier with rich land, game, and timber, a place to escape Southern oppression, a "Promised Land." They found desolation at first—about three hundred settlers living primitively, in dugouts "like prairie dogs among the grasses of the plains." In this barren, treeless dust bowl, the strong-willed settlers who stayed built homes, schools, churches, stores, postal services, hotels, and an ice cream parlor. They planted crops such as corn, millet, and sorghum; raised cattle and hogs; and established social services including a newspaper, a baseball team, and even literary and benefit societies. They named their new home after a New Testament character who personified freedom, tradition, and the chance to be "born again." (Some have argued that the town could have been named in response to "Wake Nicodemus!," a popular composition by abolitionist Henry Clay Work about a slave longing for freedom who wants to be reborn for the "great Jubilee.")

How hard was it for a few families to transform the rugged frontier into a prosperous town? Very. And only with great determination did a handful of residents survive the town's decline after it failed to attract a railroad line, and after the Great Depression and the Dust Bowl years. By the mid-1950s, Nicodemus's population was down to just sixteen. Hoping to revive its wheat-producing heritage, five black farmers founded the Nicodemus Flour Co-Op in 2001, milling a whole white wheat product, Promised Land Flour. The same year, Angela Bates-Tompkins published *Ernestine's Bar-b-que Cook Book and Autobiography*, an homage to her aunt and local restaurant owner, Ernestine Williams. Agriculture and cooking are traditions that help keep hope alive in Nicodemus.

Dad's mother, "Mommie" as we called her, was also born in a black town, Boley, Oklahoma, initially occupied by freedmen. Uncle Thomas calculated that the memories and lessons my grandmother taught us while raising animals and growing produce among the thorns, cactus, and coyotes of Southern California; the preservation efforts in Nicodemus; and the family connection to this historic place would motivate me to want to get involved. They did.

For years, I have imagined restoring an old historic house as a nurturing space where young women would exchange cultural ideas, learn to cook from one another, and break down the barriers that divide us. Until Ernestine's cookbook and that package from Uncle Thomas arrived, it never occurred to me that my dream wasn't just about preserving food history and reconciliation; it was part of a multicultural inheritance rooted in perseverance.

With memories of the African marketplace, where vendors trade spices, nuts, and homemade foods, Colonial market women tried to keep ancestral customs alive. In market towns and, later, in free black settlements like Nicodemus, away from oppression, black folks exchanged ideas and mixed a little bit of this and a little bit of that from other ethnicities. A nuanced cuisine grew beyond the slave village and the borders of the Old South based upon regional ingredients and a melting-pot philosophy.

As Juliet E. K. Walker explained in *The History of Black Business in America*, "Market towns throughout the colonies, even the northern colonies, provided places where slaves could sell their goods—provision ground commodities, poultry and farm animals, processed food, herb-based medicinal products and goods produced from both household handicraft activities and by skilled artisans."

Alethia Tanner demonstrated enterprising gardening and entrepreneurial skills when she purchased freedom for herself and nearly two dozen family members by selling fresh produce at a city market near "President's square" (now Lafayette Park) in Washington, DC; Thomas Jefferson was one of her customers. And at New York City's Catherine Fish Market, black men with "loads of cracked eggs, roots, berries, herbs, fish, clams, and oysters to sell for pocket change" danced in exchange for fresh fish or eels.

By the turn of the twentieth century, "Negro business districts" were popping up around the country to serve the needs of neighboring residents. Harlem markets were "culinary melting pots" where vendors peddled the fruits and vegetables of the African diaspora along with homemade foods. This observation appeared in a 1928 *New York Times* article: "Harlem is the cosmopolis of colored culture, of gaiety, of art, and the capital of Negro cookery. Harlem's visitors come from the Southern United States, the West Indies, from South America and even from Africa. In what it eats, Harlem shows itself less a locality than an international rallying point . . . a haven where food had the odd psychology, where viands solace the mind as well as the body."

The portraits of life out West, such as in Central California's San Joaquin Valley, paint an even broader picture, not just of cultures coming together, but of new lives and communities being made through hard work and land ownership. In the place known today as "food basket for the world," former servants proudly rebuilt their lives around agriculture. The land was cheap; ignorance, prejudice, poverty, and injustice were less severe. Some growers migrated from the South with a few seeds and "money enough to buy a pair of shoes," and others were "native sons"; all were "pioneers in spirit and deeds, willing to toil and hustle" for their independence, Delilah Beasley wrote with conviction in *The Negro Trail Blazers of California*, a pioneering register of the black elite she compiled and published in 1915.

A colony of ranchers in Bowles, California, overcame labor restrictions and poverty by raising and marketing sugar beets, chickens, turkeys, ducks, and hogs; managing livery stables; planting barley; and raising racehorses and Belgian hares. They invested their earnings and developed irrigation systems; established churches, schools, and libraries; accumulated land; purchased beautiful modern homes and automobiles; and sent their kids to college.

Mr. and Mrs. W. W. Eason owned 18 acres, which they planted with peach orchards and vineyards for producing raisins; on 160 acres Mr. and Mrs. J. E. Abernathy planted peaches, grapes, and alfalfa, devoting 80 of those acres to pasture for a dairy farm; and Mr. and Mrs. Lee Crane operated a truck garden. Farther south, Little Liberia, a short-lived settlement located in Baja California, encouraged the "economic uplift, racial self-sufficiency and land accruement" promoted by Booker T. Washington and Marcus Garvey through citrus orchards, fruit groves, and livestock.

Such agricultural prosperity "spurred a variety of different recipes, visible in cookbooks, and gave more complex flavors to regional dishes," Anne Yentsch explained in *African American Foodways: Explorations of History & Culture.* "No matter where one went, landowners had an abundance of bacon, fat, lard, butter, eggs, and cream." Access to convenience foods, kitchen tools and appliances, and local produce, which varied by region, spurred a cook's inventiveness: apples and wheat flour in the upland South; red and yellow plums, figs, dates, sweet oranges, sour oranges, grapes, pecans, and wild bananas near New Orleans; and along the Gulf Coast and in the Deep South, cabbage, rutabaga, turnips, onions, shallots, garlic, endive, mustard, radish, cauliflower, beets, cress, lettuce, parsley, leeks, English peas, and celery filled winter gardens.

Back in Nicodemus, agricultural adaptation and resilience mitigated the heartbreak of the 1930s and temporarily restored souls. Farmers replaced corn with more drought-resistant crops, such as wheat, sorghum, barley, and rye; seeds brought from Kentucky bloomed in gardens—lady peas, spring peas, black-eyed peas, crowder peas; foraging uncovered edible wild berries, currants, plums, wild lettuce (poke sallet), tomatoes, dandelions and other greens; the County Extension Service planted apple, peach, and pear trees; and teens participated in 4-H clubs. Ora Wellington Switzer, my step-great aunt, remembered foraging for wild foods: "We would have to go to the creek to find poke salad. . . . We use to have chokecherries down here on the river. We'd have to hunt for them."

The smell of chicken frying wafted through the open windows of Julia's Cafe, drawing hungry Nicodemus farmers and a few families across a dusty road, intoxicating nine-year-old Ernestine Williams during the 1940s. "Chub," as Ernestine was lovingly known, nurtured her passion for the art of cooking while working at the home-style restaurant. She polished by hand the silver that was brought from Kentucky; pressed and folded the pristine damask tablecloths; and set the tables where home-cured ham, hot fried chicken, homemade bread, boiled potatoes, pickled beets, mashed potatoes and gravy, collard greens, potato salad, black-eyed peas, and green beans filled polished white enameled tin plates. One dish, Ernestine's "Famous Bar-B-Q Baked Beans," is still served today, prepared by Angela for kin of Nicodemus's pioneer families attending homecoming on the last weekend in July.

Participation at the annual event, like the town's population, has dwindled over the years, but Uncle Thomas and Angela are optimistic. More than three hundred descendants observed Nicodemus's 140th anniversary in 2017. Buffalo Soldiers paraded. Travelers passed through. And a new generation found hope for a brighter future in the American West, and Ernestine's good cooking.

Field Peas and Beans

"Most ethnic groups had a variation of beans stewed or baked with meat; the dish is directly descended from the bean and pea potages of England and Europe, in which soaked beans were cooked slowly at a low temperature, usually with a piece of salt meat." The combination was generally associated with poverty, and the early bean dishes were savory and did not become sweet until the nineteenth century, when molasses entered the American diet, Sandra Oliver explained in *Food in Colonial and Federal America.*

Blending beans and peas with meat has a multiethnic lineage, as well. Several New World iterations of the West African mix of smoked fish or meat with vegetables (beans or peas), spices, and rice became a signature dish in the Caribbean diaspora: Barbados's peas and rice and Jamaica's rice and peas, Puerto Rico's *arroz con gandules* and Cuba's *moros y cristianos*, and *congris*, made with red beans and served in both Cuba and New Orleans, are just a few. The combination not only tastes good, it is good for you, too. When eaten with rice, beans form a complete protein, good for the body and the budget.

BAKED (BARBECUED) BEANS

SERVES 6 TO 8

Baked beans, a dish of navy beans stewed until richly glazed in a tomato sauce sweetened with molasses (and commonly salt pork or bacon), is generally associated with New England, as in Boston baked beans. It's been said the dish comes from Native Americans, but scholars have argued that "New England sea captains brought the idea home with them from Africa," where baked beans, called "skanah," had long been a Sabbath tradition among North African and Spanish Jews, according to John F. Mariani's *Encyclopedia of American Food & Drink*.

The dish has certainly found a home throughout the United States, using various bean types. Along the way, African American cooks made it their own—dried beans, soaked overnight and cooked, or canned, made savory with salt pork or bacon, sweetened with molasses and brown sugar, and spiced with prepared or dry mustard, ground spices—baked long and slow, up to four hours. Ernestine Williams's "Famous Bar-B-Q Baked Beans," published in the cookbook of recipes from her restaurant in Nicodemus, Kansas, is a just-right combination of canned pork 'n' beans, brown and/or white sugar, ground cinnamon, flour, and . . . Ernestine's Bar-B-Q Sauce.

I didn't have any of Ernestine's secret sauce, so instead I scaled back the sauce from Chicken Thighs and BBQ Beans from chef Todd Richards's *Soul: A Chef's Culinary Evolution in 150 Recipes,* replacing his browned chicken thighs with the customary pork. To turn the dish into a meal unto itself, as Richards does, caramelize the thighs in the same pan you're going to cook the beans in for a full-flavored dish.

6 slices bacon
1 cup minced onion
½ cup minced green bell pepper
2 garlic cloves, minced
1 cup packed dark brown sugar
½ cup molasses
½ cup ketchup or tomato sauce
2 tablespoons yellow mustard
2 tablespoons cider vinegar
1 tablespoon liquid hickory smoke (optional)
½ teaspoon crushed red pepper flakes
¼ teaspoon black pepper
2 teaspoons salt, or to taste
1 pound cooked navy beans, plus 3 cups cooking liquid, or 3 (15.5-ounce) cans, undrained

1 Preheat the oven to 350°F.

2 Cut 3 slices of the bacon into 1-inch strips. In a skillet, cook the cut bacon until browned and crisp. Use a slotted spoon to remove to paper towels to drain.

3 In the same pan, sauté the onion, bell pepper, and garlic over medium heat until tender and the onion is translucent, about 5 minutes. Stir in the brown sugar, molasses, ketchup, mustard, vinegar, liquid smoke (if using), pepper flakes, black pepper, and salt. Mix well. Cook over medium-low heat until the sugar is dissolved, about 1½ minutes.

4 In a large bowl, combine the beans, their liquid, the sauce, and the cooked bacon. Pour into a 13 × 9-inch baking dish or a 3-quart casserole. Place the remaining 3 slices of bacon on top of the beans. Cover and bake for 45 minutes. Uncover, increase the oven temperature to 425°F, and bake for 15 minutes more to brown the bacon slices.

BLACK-EYED PEAS AND RICE

SERVES 8

Watch Night Service is a gathering of the faithful to bring the New Year in with spirituals, prayers, and testimony. The celebration began on "Freedom's Eve," December 31, 1862, when the enslaved gathered in churches to await the news that the Emancipation Proclamation had set them free. With the news came shouts of jubilation and gratitude; today the service includes reflection, praise, and worship to God for His provision and protection.

Folklore in the *Penn School & Sea Islands Heritage Cookbook* described the Carolina Lowcountry tradition this way: "Early on New Year's Eve, the pots begin to cook, as the meal for New Year's day must be done by Midnight. The menu for New Year's day is a simple one: Hoppin' John, collard greens with hog jowls, and ribs for a side dish. Hoppin' John, or brown field peas cooked with rice, is eaten for good luck throughout the year. The collard greens represent dollar bills. It is said the more one eats, the more luck and money one will have."

This adaptation of Hoppin' John appeared in *Aunt Julia's Cook Book*, a collection of Atlantic Coast recipes published in the 1930s by the Standard Oil Company.

¾ pound salt pork or bacon, cut into ¼-inch dice

1 cup chopped onion

2 large garlic cloves, minced

8 cups Chicken Stock (page 133)

1 pound dried black-eyed peas, picked over for stones, rinsed, soaked in water overnight, and drained

½ cup diced (¼ inch) ham

1 teaspoon salt

¼ teaspoon black pepper

½ teaspoon crushed red pepper flakes

1 cup long-grain rice

1 In a large saucepan, sauté the salt pork over medium-high heat until crisp and the fat is rendered. Add the onion and garlic and cook until just translucent, about 3 minutes. Stir in the chicken stock, soaked peas, ham, salt, black pepper, and pepper flakes. Bring to a boil, then reduce the heat, cover, and simmer over medium-low heat until tender, about 1 hour.

2 Taste and season with more salt as desired. Stir in the rice. Cover and return the pot to a simmer over high heat. Reduce the heat to a gentle simmer, cover, and cook until the rice is tender, about 20 minutes longer. Remove from the heat and let stand, covered, 5 minutes, then fluff with a fork before serving.

PLANTATION BEAN POT

Mammy Pleasant's Cookbook: A Treasury of Gourmet Recipes from Victorian America, Helen Holdredge, 1970

Use 2 quarts of fresh, black-eyed peas. Soak them overnight in salted water to overcome any dryness. In the morning place the peas in a large roaster, preferably iron. Add ¾ of a pound of salt pork, cut into several pieces. Cover the peas with a liquid mixture which is ½ water and ½ claret. Tie into a [cheesecloth] sack containing leaves of marjoram, thyme, laurel, and flowers of papayas, 3 cloves and 4 black peppers. Start in a hot oven until heated, then cook over slow heat. The liquid will boil away. As it does, add dry white wine. Before removing from the heat add 1 water glass of strong coffee. Remove from heat and add 2 tablespoonsful of brown sugar and ¼ cup of brandy. The dish will take about 6 hours to cook.

LOUISIANA RED BEANS AND RICE

SERVES 8

In a story that inspired the title of her book, *A Date with a Dish*, Freda DeKnight recalled that Louis Armstrong, the "modern Gabriel," loved spicy foods and was known for a signature salutation: "Red beans and ricely yours." She captured his sentiments in a short story, "The Man, the Horn and Red Beans": "My favorite of all dishes (when I'm not on my diet and watching my calories) is just plain ham hocks and red beans," Armstrong said. "Old man, season them well! Add the right spices at the right time, and man, you have a 'Date with a Dish' that's just about the greatest."

There was a time when a leftover ham bone from Sunday dinner made Monday red beans and rice day, but Louis Armstrong was a man on the move who cooked and ate in different cities all the time. Ham hocks helped him keep the tradition alive.

The size and type of chile pepper you use will determine how much spice is in the dish. If you like it hot, select a larger pepper, or choose Scotch bonnet, a high scorer on the Scoville scale, which measures a pepper's burn.

2 tablespoons bacon drippings or vegetable or olive oil
1 small fresh red chile pepper, minced
1 cup diced onion
½ cup diced red bell pepper
½ cup diced celery
1½ tablespoons minced garlic (5 to 6 cloves)
1 pound dried small red or kidney beans, picked over for stones, rinsed, soaked in water overnight, and drained
1 bay leaf
1 pound smoked ham hocks or 1 baked ham bone
1 teaspoon salt, or to taste
½ teaspoon black pepper
½ cup minced parsley
½ cup minced green onions
Freshly cooked rice, for serving

1 In a skillet, heat the bacon fat over medium-high heat. Add the chile pepper, onion, bell pepper, celery, and garlic and sauté, stirring occasionally, until tender, about 6 minutes.

2 In a medium pot, combine 8 cups water, the sautéed vegetables, drained beans, bay leaf, and ham hocks. Stir to mix well. Bring to a boil over high heat, then reduce the heat to low, cover, and simmer for 2 hours. Season with the salt and pepper and continue to cook until the beans are tender, about 1 hour longer. Remove and discard the bay leaf.

3 Remove the ham hocks or ham bone from the beans to a cutting board. When cool enough to handle, use a sharp knife to remove the meat from the bone and coarsely chop the meat (discard any skin, fat, and bones). Stir the meat, parsley, and green onions into the beans, taste and adjust seasonings with salt and pepper. Serve the beans and ham over hot cooked rice.

VARIATION

To make soulful red beans and rice as chef Austin Leslie does in the *Chez Helene: House of Good Food Cookbook*, substitute picked pork rib tips for the ham hocks, and stir in ½ cup butter before serving.

Rice and Pilau

Rice pilau is a signature dish of the Carolina Lowcountry, influenced by Arab rice pilaf, accented with fresh herbs, spices, citrus juice, nuts, parsley, yogurt, or fruit. Often spelled purlow, perlu, or perloo, the dish was one of several rice plantation creations bondservants devised to deal with a standard ration of cracked rice, which they boiled with salt pork, fish, or game and vegetables, according to historian Charles Joyner.

White women writing cookbooks in the early twentieth century praised the region's black men and women for their knowledge and skill with pilau and other rice dishes. Blacks were so deeply entrenched in the rice culture of the Lowcountry that historical organizations in 1930s Charleston hired locals to demonstrate traditional African American folkways, including methods of flailing and husking rice, and a businessman marketed sweetgrass baskets as "handmade artifacts of slavery," Marcie Cohen Ferris explained in *The Edible South: The Power of Food and the Making of an American Region.*

As part of the West African technique of rice harvest and preparation, rice grains were pounded with a wooden mortar and pestle and tossed into the air or dropped from one wide coiled sweetgrass "fanner" basket to another to separate rice grains from their husks. "The resulting rice, scrubbed golden white through abrasion, contained whole and broken grains, with germ and flecks of bran intact. Its flavor and texture were exquisite," said Glenn Roberts, who markets Carolina Gold Rice and other heirloom grains through Anson Mills. This tradition is preserved by generations of Gullah-Geechee artisans; they are a people who descend from enslaved Africans who were isolated on the Sea Islands of Georgia and the Carolinas, and who retained much of their native culture in a unique language and way of cooking.

RED RICE

SERVES 4

Over time, a dish of long-grain rice simmered in a tomato broth has been known as Savannah Red Rice, Gullah Rice, or Mulatto Rice—"supposedly because its color resembles the skin tone of persons of mixed African, white, and Native American blood," John T. Edge explained in the *New Encyclopedia of Southern Culture: Foodways.*

The Savannah Cookbook, a 1930s collection of Lowcountry recipes that includes ones from the region's black cooks, characterized mulatto rice disparagingly as "the very chic name given to rice with a touch of the tarbrush." By contrast, African Americans believed a well-made bowl of mulatto rice displayed dignity and a connection to the Motherland and the Welcome table.

Pheoby Watson beamed with pride when she presented a heaping bowl of mulatto rice as a homecoming meal for Janie upon her return to Eatonville in Zora Neale Hurston's *Their Eyes Were Watching God.* (Eatonville is the historic black town featured in this and Hurston's other stories.) And Helen Mendes, in her 1971 collection of African and African-imbued soul foods, *The African Heritage Cookbook*, portrayed Gullah Rice as a modern version of an old African dish "consisting of rice, nuts, herbs, and oil." Pistachio nuts add a buttery crunch in her version. As red rice migrated West, it also adopted a few Spanish influences, including green bell pepper and a hint of cumin.

This recipe is one I reworked by seasoning the rice with minced fresh garlic and a dash of sugar. As you make yours, though, feel free to adapt it in any of the ways cooks have adapted it over the centuries—with aromatic vegetables and fresh herbs such as red bell pepper, celery, basil, or thyme.

3 slices bacon, diced, or 3 tablespoons butter
½ cup finely diced onion
1 teaspoon minced garlic (1 clove)
1 cup long-grain rice
1 (6-ounce) can tomato paste
1 teaspoon sugar (optional)
1 teaspoon salt
½ teaspoon black pepper
1 bay leaf
2 cups Chicken Stock (page 133) or water

1 If using bacon, sauté in a heavy saucepan over medium heat until crisp and the fat is rendered, 5 to 7 minutes. Remove the bacon to paper towels to drain. If using butter, simply heat in the pan over medium heat until melted.

2 Add the onion to the pan and sauté until translucent, about 2 minutes. Stir in the garlic and cook 1 minute longer. Stir in the rice and cook until the rice is no longer translucent, 2 to 3 minutes. Stir in the tomato paste, sugar (if using), salt, pepper, bay leaf, and chicken stock. Bring to a boil over high heat, then reduce the heat to low, cover, and simmer until the rice is tender, 20 to 25 minutes, stirring halfway through. Let stand at least 5 minutes when done. Remove and discard the bay leaf. Fluff with a fork before serving.

3 If you used bacon, sprinkle the rice with the bacon pieces. Taste and adjust the seasoning with salt and pepper.

VARIATION

SPANISH RICE
Stir in ⅓ cup minced green bell pepper with the onion and garlic, a pinch of cumin with the seasonings, and reduce the tomato paste to 3 tablespoons.

OKRA PILAU

SERVES 2 TO 4

Sally Washington was an old-fashioned "Negro" cook, whose cooking, according to the authors of *Two Hundred Years of Charleston Cooking*, "was of a kind to make one speculate as to whether she was a genius in her own right or whether Charleston was gifted by the gods." Okra Pilau was one of her specialties. Washington's was a four-ingredient dish of ingenuity—bacon, rice, okra, and water. To dazzle guests, cooks may also add tomatoes, onions, and garlic. Vertamae Smart-Grosvenor stirred in shrimp just to mix things up a bit.

You can call this nimble dish Limpin' Susan, if you like; Verta says it's a "relative" of Hoppin' John. And just to show you how recipes change as they migrate, celebrity caterer, soul cook, and author Bob Jeffries used neither okra nor bacon, swapping in red beans and salt pork.

The touch of garlic turns up the flavor a bit. The addition of chicken stock is also mine. Double the recipe to feed a crowd.

3 thick-cut slices bacon, cut into ¼-inch dice
2 cups sliced (½-inch) fresh okra
½ cup chopped onion
1 teaspoon minced garlic (1 clove)
1 cup long-grain rice (preferably Carolina Gold)
2 cups Chicken Stock (page 133)
1 teaspoon salt
½ teaspoon black pepper

1 In a skillet with a tight-fitting lid, cook the bacon over medium heat until crisp, 5 to 7 minutes. Use a slotted spoon to remove the bacon from the pan and drain on paper towels.

2 Add the okra to the pan and cook for 5 minutes. Stir in the onion and garlic. Cook and stir over medium heat until softened, about 3 minutes. Stir in the rice and sauté until the onion is lightly browned, about 3 minutes more. Stir in the chicken stock, salt, and pepper and bring to a boil over high heat, stirring to loosen any browned bits in the bottom of the pan.

3 Reduce the heat to the lowest temperature possible, cover the pan, and cook until the rice is tender and cooked through, about 20 minutes. During the last 5 minutes of cooking time, use a fork to stir the bacon into the rice. Fluff lightly with a fork to serve.

BOILED RICE

New Orleans Cookbook, Lena Richard, 1939

1 cup rice
4 cups water
1 tablespoon salt

Wash rice and rub well between hands. Drop into salted boiling water and boil rapidly, uncovered, for fifteen to twenty minutes until kernels are cooked through. Put rice in a colander and pour boiling water over it to remove loose starch and separate grains. Drain well and place in a slow oven with the door open until grains are thoroughly separated and dry, or about twenty minutes.

JAMBALAYA

SERVES 12

"The name jambalaya is pure Louisiana Creole: *jamb* comes from the French word for ham, *ala* is French or Acadian and means 'of' or 'with,' and *ya* is an African word for rice. According to folklorist Rebecca Henry, it has also been called 'long gravy' because of its versatility in stretching any combination of ham, sausage, chicken, seafood, and vegetables into a rice-filling meal," Heidi Haughy Cusick explained in *Soul and Spice: African Cooking in the Americas.*

Some chefs never put rice *in* their jambalaya sauce, they serve it *over* rice, while others make a quick sauce and add leftover rice for a casserole that can be heated in the oven.

When Creole chef and cookbook author Austin Leslie introduced New Orleans haute cuisine and his special fried chicken recipe to diners at the restaurant Chez Helene, he created a hybrid Creole-soul food restaurant that was world class. In his 1984 recipe collection, *Chez Helene: House of Good Food Cookbook,* his jambalaya featured subtle celery, shrimp stock, and a prodigious amount of sausage and ham. For my version, I double the characteristic Louisiana punch of green peppers and call for more chicken stock. I also use a parched-rice technique to keep the grains separate (which I learned from a Creole chef in Los Angeles) for a dish that is both hearty in satisfaction and light in texture.

2 cups long-grain rice
½ cup finely diced salt pork
1½ cups chopped onions
1 cup chopped green bell pepper
3 garlic cloves, minced
½ cup chopped green onions, white part only
1 pound smoked sausage (andouille), cut into
    ½-inch-thick coins
½ cup diced (½ inch) ham
2 cups diced tomatoes

4 cups Chicken Stock (page 133)
1½ cups diced (½ inch) cooked chicken
1 tablespoon dried thyme
2 bay leaves
½ teaspoon paprika
¼ teaspoon black pepper
1 teaspoon salt, plus more to taste
½ pound small shrimp, peeled and deveined
Cayenne pepper
2 tablespoons minced fresh parsley

1 Preheat the oven to 400°F. Line a 15 × 9-inch rimmed baking sheet with parchment paper.

2 Pour the rice onto the baking sheet in a single layer. Parch in the oven, stirring occasionally, until lightly browned, about 10 minutes. Set aside.

3 In a large, heavy ovenproof pot or Dutch oven, sauté the salt pork over medium heat until the fat is rendered and the pork is lightly browned. Use a slotted spoon to remove the pork to paper towels to drain.

4 Add the onions and bell pepper to the fat in the pot and cook over medium-low heat until starting to soften, about 5 minutes. Stir in the garlic, green onions, sausage, and ham and cook, stirring occasionally, until the vegetables are tender and the meat is lightly browned, about 5 minutes. Stir in the tomatoes and chicken stock and bring to a boil over high heat. Reduce the heat to a simmer and cook for 10 minutes. Stir in the parched rice, chicken, thyme, bay leaves, paprika, pepper, and salt.

5 Transfer to the oven and bake, uncovered, for 20 minutes. Stir in the shrimp and bake until the rice is tender and the shrimp are pink. Remove and discard the bay leaves. Season to taste with salt and cayenne, sprinkle with parsley, and serve.

RICE AND PEAS WITH COCONUT

SERVES 6 TO 8

Rice and peas is Jamaica's "coat of arms" in cooking, and it usually means small red beans (peas) and rice simmered with coconut, often also seasoned with a hint of thyme, bay, and cinnamon. Rather than red beans, you can also try a mix of red peas and *gungo* (pigeon peas or *gandules*), or use frozen green peas or limas for a change of pace. If you are concerned that the coconut milk will overpower the beans, don't be. The milk adds a creamy quality to the dish, and the taste is subtle and mild. It's my new favorite.

1 cup dried small red beans, picked over for stones, rinsed, soaked in water overnight, and drained

1 large onion, chopped

2 garlic cloves, minced

1 small dried red chile pepper, left whole

½ teaspoon dried thyme

1 bay leaf

1 cinnamon stick

1 tablespoon butter or oil

1 (13.5-ounce) can coconut milk

1 quart Chicken Stock (page 133)

2 cups long-grain rice

Salt and black pepper

1 In a large saucepan, combine the beans, onion, garlic, chile pepper, thyme, bay leaf, cinnamon, butter, coconut milk, and chicken stock. Bring to a boil over high heat, then reduce the heat to medium-low, cover, and simmer until the beans are just tender, about 1¼ hours.

2 Place the rice in a bowl and rinse under cool running water until the water is clear. Drain the rice well. Stir the rice into the beans and cook over low heat, covered, until the rice is tender and most of the liquid is absorbed, 20 to 30 minutes longer.

3 Discard the chile pepper, bay leaf, and cinnamon stick, and season to taste with salt and pepper.

RIZ ISLE BREVELLE [RED RICE CROQUETTES]

Melrose Plantation Cookbook,
Francois Mignon and Clementine Hunter, 1956

Wash one-half cup of raw rice and drain well.
Place three pints of salted water in a stewpan.
Set over fire and bring to a fast boil.
Dash in the rice. Boil for ten minutes and then drain.
Prepare a cup of tomato juice seasoned with one-fourth teaspoon salt, pinch of pepper, and dessert spoon of sugar.
Heat this and pour over the rice.
Cook about ten minutes more or until rice is tender.
Take from the fire and add one tablespoon of the butter, one teaspoon of onion juice.
Whip in the beaten yolks of three eggs.
Then stir in two tablespoons of grated Parmesan cheese.
Set the mixture, in the stewpan, in a pan of boiling water and stir over the fire for several minutes.
Then remove from heat and allow to cool.
Make into croquettes.
Beat the yolk of an egg and add one tablespoon of milk.
Spread cracker crumbs on a platter.
Dip the croquettes in the egg yolk, then roll in cracker crumbs. Chill the croquettes for an hour. Then fry in hot, deep vegetable oil. Drain and serve.

MACARONI CROQUETTES, CHEESE SAUCE

The Kentucky Cook Book: Easy and Simple for Any Cook, by a Colored Woman, Mrs. W. T. Hayes, 1912

For the croquettes take enough cold boiled macaroni to make 2 cups when cut into small pieces. Add to this 1 teaspoon lemon juice, ½ teaspoon of onion juice, a little celery salt and seasoning to taste. Mix with 1 cup of white sauce made of 2 tablespoons of butter, 2 tablespoons of flour, seasoning, and one cup of boiling milk. Let the mixture cool. Form in cone shaped croquettes, roll in egg and bread crumbs and fry in deep fat till a very light brown. Stick a small spray of parsley in the top of each croquette. Cheese Sauce: To 1 cup of white sauce add ½ cup grated cheese and 1 tablespoon of chopped walnut meats.

BAKED MACARONI AND CHEESE

SERVES 8 TO 10

In *Soul Food: The Surprising Story of an American Cuisine, One Plate at a Time*, James Beard Award winner Adrian Miller asked, "How did macaroni and cheese get so black?" The answer: James Hemings.

Hemings was an enslaved chef in Thomas Jefferson's home who mastered the sophisticated techniques of French classical cooking in Paris, including the operation of a "maccaroni" press. As Monticello's *chef de cuisine*, Hemings handwrote his recipes; the ones whose records have survived include fried potatoes (French fries), burnt cream (crème brûlée), and *"Nouilles a maccaroni"* (macaroni noodles). It's known that he prepared a "macaroni pie" for a White House dinner in 1802. The macaroni recipe turns up topped with grated cheese following its publication in *The Virginia Housewife* published in 1845 by Mary Randolph, a Jefferson relative.

But that was just the beginning. Black chefs continued to adapt macaroni and cheese for their menus. In 1911, chef Rufus Estes of the Pullman railroad layered cooked macaroni, cheese, melted butter, salt, and black pepper in a baking pan, then poured milk over it all before baking. In her 1912 cookbook, the *Kentucky Cook Book: Easy and Simple for Any Cook, by a Colored Woman*, Mrs. W. T. Hayes spotlighted two African American culinary practices—croquette making and frying—in her macaroni croquettes, a special-occasion dish. And of course, today, mac and cheese is still a staple on soul food and holiday menus.

This mac and cheese resembles the one Texas caterer Bess Gant rolled up in ham jackets, made of thin slices of ham, like crêpes, in 1947. If you're so inclined, feel free to add chunks of ham, cooked shrimp, or lobster.

Softened butter, for the baking dish
1 pound elbow macaroni
2 cups shredded Cheddar cheese
2 cups shredded Jack cheese
1 stick (4 ounces) butter, melted
½ cup sour cream
3 large eggs, well beaten
1 (12-ounce) can evaporated milk
½ teaspoon salt, plus more to taste
¼ teaspoon white pepper
⅛ teaspoon cayenne pepper
Paprika

1 Preheat the oven to 350°F. Generously butter a 13 × 9-inch baking dish.

2 Bring a large pasta pot or saucepan of generously salted water to a boil. Add the macaroni and cook until al dente. Drain.

3 In a large bowl, combine the Cheddar and Jack cheeses. Measure out 1 cup of the cheese mixture and set aside for the top of the dish. Layer the remaining combined cheeses and macaroni in the buttered baking dish, beginning and ending with the macaroni.

4 In a medium bowl, whisk together the melted butter, sour cream, eggs, evaporated milk, ½ teaspoon salt (or to taste), white pepper, and cayenne. Pour the cream sauce over the macaroni and cheese. Top with the reserved 1 cup cheese and sprinkle generously with paprika. Place the dish on a rimmed baking pan to catch any juices that spill over.

5 Bake until the cheese is bubbling and the top is browned and crusty, 30 to 45 minutes. Remove from oven and let stand 10 minutes before serving.

Cornbread Dressing

Cornbread dressing is Southern; it is also African. Just ask culinary historian Michael Twitty. It descends from a memory dish some of the enslaved called kush (also spelled cush), made from cooked cornmeal mush or crumbled cornbread. The one-pot meal reminded West African captives of *kusha*, a couscous-like dish of steamed or boiled grains of millet or sorghum, Twitty explained in his James Beard Award–winning memoir, *The Cooking Gene*.

Kush became a darling of Louisiana Cajuns, who Twitty said "adopted many of the Senegambian people's foodways, including okra, rice, the liberal use of hot pepper, and a breakfast cornmeal preparation they came to know as 'couche couche,' eaten with milk and cane syrup."

Twitty unearthed memories of both dishes in the Slave Narratives, a Federal Writers' Project, that between 1936 and 1938 collected interviews with the formerly enslaved. Anna Wright of North Carolina remembered: "Kush was cornbread, cooked on de big griddle mashed up with raw onions an' ham gravy poured over hit . . . de old southern way of makin' baked chicken dressin' . . . wuz made from soft cornbread wid some bacon grease, onions, black pepper an' boiled eggs."

Julius Nelson, also of North Carolina, described kush as a "good supper dish . . . made outin' meal, onions, salt, pepper, grease an' water."

While the WPA was conducting interviews, Arturo Schomburg suggested that cakes, cookies, and puddings concocted from leftover bread, biscuit, wafer, and cornbread crumbs exemplified efficiency cooking, and that many of these dishes should be credited to creative black cooks. Regional cookbooks being written by white women at the time did occasionally do that.

CORNBREAD DRESSING

SERVES 12 TO 16

The authors of *Two Hundred Years of Charleston Cooking* offered high praise for the cornbread dressing created by Sally Washington and gubernatorial butler William Deas. This recipe reminds me of the cornbread dressing I grew up on and still serve at Thanksgiving. I've offered a few more details than the dish recorded on behalf of Deas, whom the authors call "one of the great cooks of the world."

During the busy holiday season, you can prepare it ahead, which allows the flavors to mingle. I bake the Extra-Light Buttermilk Cornbread (page 99) several days before putting the dressing together, crumble it, and store it tightly covered. Stale or dried leftover cornbread is sometimes suggested, but I'm not a fan. Once assembled, I cover the casserole dish tightly with plastic wrap and store it in the refrigerator for up to 24 hours. Simply bring the dressing to room temperature and remove the plastic to bake it. I pour stock into the dish just before it goes into the oven for moist, rich flavor. For smaller gatherings, cut this recipe in half; it makes enough dressing for second helpings.

Softened butter, for the baking pan
Double recipe Extra-Light Buttermilk Cornbread (page 99), crumbled
1½ cups dried bread crumbs, toasted
2½ teaspoons dried sage
2 teaspoons dried thyme
1 teaspoon poultry seasoning
½ teaspoon dried marjoram
2 teaspoons salt
1 teaspoon black pepper
¼ teaspoon cayenne pepper
1 stick (4 ounces) butter
1 cup finely diced onion

⅓ cup finely diced green bell pepper
⅓ cup finely diced celery
2 teaspoons minced garlic
3 large eggs, beaten
2 cups turkey or chicken stock
Giblet Gravy (page 251) or Chile-Pecan Sauce (page 250), for serving

1 Preheat the oven to 325°F. Generously butter a deep 13 × 9-inch baking pan.

2 In a large bowl, stir together the cornbread crumbles, bread crumbs, sage, thyme, poultry seasoning, marjoram, salt, black pepper, and cayenne.

3 In a large skillet, heat the butter over medium-high heat. Add the onion, bell pepper, and celery and sauté until softened, 7 to 10 minutes. Stir in the garlic and cook 30 seconds longer. Cool slightly. Gently stir the vegetables into the cornbread mixture, then stir in the eggs. (At this point, the dish may be refrigerated for later baking; just let it come to room temperature before baking.)

4 Drizzle the turkey stock over the cornbread mixture, tossing with a fork until the mixture is just moistened. Spoon the dressing into the baking pan and cover with foil. Bake for 30 minutes. Remove the foil, rotate the pan, and bake until hot, set, and crusty, about 30 minutes longer.

5 Serve with either giblet gravy or chile-pecan sauce.

Summer Garden Vegetables

I love the handed-down garden tradition that ties self-sufficiency and self-determination together with fresh vegetables—from the so-called yam gardens some captive women hid behind plantation flower beds to protect them from the overseer; to George Washington Carver's "moveable school," a horse-drawn vehicle called a Jesup Agricultural Wagon, designed so Tuskegee's faculty could take their healthy-eating teaching into the community; to truck gardens, 4-H clubs, and the urban farm my mother nurtured in our city backyard so that fresh organic produce was always at hand.

I thought of all of this while ferreting out recipes for mid-twentieth-century garden vegetable recipes in black cookbooks as suggested by the long, long list of dishes in Arturo Schomburg's African American cookbook proposal.

The recipes I encountered sounded wonderful, but there were just too many to include here: scalloped, as in anything one could braise in a cream sauce and perch on toast; pickled into relish; pannéd, meaning to dust with bread crumbs and fry; French-fried everything—from eggplant to beets; vegetables filled with stuffings made of other vegetables, meat, and rice; plus creatively titled specialties like cabbage pudding, potato puffs (which resembled the frozen food phenomenon Tater Tots), and turnips buttered à la "Kingston."

Fast-forward to the soul food era of the 1960s, and the vegetable recipe choices surged even more. I could easily have written an entire book based around summer crops alone—corn, beans, tomatoes, okra, veggies for the salad bowl, herbs, and such. Instead, I grouped together and updated the time-honored preparations, exalting my favorites.

MAQUE CHOUX (FRIED CORN WITH GREEN PEPPERS)

SERVES 2 TO 4

The 2000 publication of *Food for the Soul: A Texas Expatriate Nurtures Her Culinary Roots in Paris* accomplished two goals for its author Monique Wells. Collecting the recipes resolved her—and other Parisian African Americans'—hankering for a taste of home, and sharing lovely, seasonal dishes like maque choux (adapted here) opened the eyes of elite French cooks to the flavors of the American South and Southwest. This led noted French chef Alain Ducasse to write Wells's preface, lauding generations of black cooks who, like Monique, dedicated themselves to uplifting the image of soul food.

3 to 4 ears corn, shucked
2 tablespoons butter
½ cup finely diced onion
½ cup finely diced green bell pepper
½ teaspoon minced garlic
¼ teaspoon dried thyme
½ teaspoon crushed red pepper flakes
⅛ teaspoon black pepper, or to taste
½ teaspoon salt, or to taste
½ teaspoon sugar (optional)
¾ cup heavy whipping cream or half-and-half
1 tablespoon minced fresh parsley
2 tablespoons minced green onions

1 Use a sharp knife to cut the kernels off the corn cobs, then turn the knife and use the dull side to scrape the cob down to release any remaining bits of corn and corn milk.

2 In a heavy skillet, heat the butter over medium-high heat until melted and sizzling. Add the onion, bell pepper, and garlic and sauté until softened, about 3 minutes. Stir in the thyme, red pepper flakes, black pepper, salt, sugar (if using), and corn. Cook, stirring, until the corn is cooked through, about 5 minutes. Add the cream and cook 5 minutes more to thicken. Stir in the parsley and green onions. Taste and adjust seasoning with more salt and pepper.

STEWED FRESH CORN

Soul Food Cookery, Inez Yeargan Kaiser, 1968

corn on cob
milk
butter
salt
pepper
flour

CUT . . . . . . *corn from cob, cutting twice.*

ADD . . . . . . *milk, butter, salt and pepper.*

SLOWLY . . . . . . *stir in flour.*

COOK . . . . . . *over low heat until gravy thickens and corn is cooked.*

CORN PUDDING

SERVES 6

Corn pudding is a way for families to enjoy corn in a lush custard. Served as a savory side dish for roast beef, or slightly sweeter with pork or ham, it is customary at Thanksgiving. In Rebecca West's recipe collection, it's referred to as Corn Soufflé, which gives you a sense of how refined and light it can be.

Carla Hall is a celebrity chef—she was a finalist on *Top Chef* and hosted *The Chew* on daytime television for many years—who has dedicated her career to spinning the beloved flavors of home into stunning new dishes with global appeal. Of all the techniques I discovered in recipe books to ensure this pudding is light and fluffy—from folding stiffly beaten egg whites into the mix, baking the corn pudding in a water bath, and underbaking the mixture so that it has a jiggly center when removed from the oven—I like the ideas in *Carla's Comfort Foods* best. Hers gets a flavor boost from a little cornmeal, a quick browning in a hot oven, and a midbake stir. (Carolyn Quick Tillery's *A Taste of Freedom: A Cookbook with Recipes and Remembrances from the Hampton Institute* bound the pudding with cornmeal alone.)

To serve the dish during winter, do what farm cooks who canned their own stewed corn did: Replace flavorless out-of-season fresh corn with canned cream-style corn for a super soft custard.

Softened butter, for the baking dish
3 large eggs, separated
2 tablespoons sugar
1 teaspoon salt
½ cup all-purpose flour
¼ cup stone-ground cornmeal
3 cups whole milk
1 cup heavy whipping cream
4 tablespoons (½ stick) butter, melted
1 tablespoon minced onion
3 cups fresh corn kernels

1 Preheat the oven to 450°F. Generously butter a 3-quart shallow baking dish.

2 In a large bowl, whisk the egg yolks until they are light and form a ribbon. Gradually whisk in the sugar 1 tablespoon at a time, then add the salt. Whisk in the flour, cornmeal, milk, cream, and melted butter. Stir in the onion until well blended.

3 In a very clean bowl, with a whisk or hand mixer (or in a stand mixer), whisk the egg whites until stiff peaks form. Gently fold the beaten whites into the yolk mixture. Pour this into the buttered dish. Scatter the corn evenly over the top.

4 Bake for 20 minutes, or until the top of the pudding is lightly browned. Remove from the oven, stir with a fork to mix in the browned crust, then return to the oven. Reduce the oven temperature to 350°F and continue baking until the pudding is just set, about 20 minutes more.

GREEN BEANS AMANDINE

SERVES 4 TO 6

In 2009, First Lady Michelle Obama did something unthinkable to the White House's South Lawn: She turned it into a kitchen garden. A year later, I was blessed to be among seven hundred chefs from around the country invited to tour the garden, as part of her healthy kids initiative, Chefs Move! to Schools. She shared inspirational stories about her struggles, joys, and worries as a novice gardener in a cookbook, *American Grown: The Story of the White House Kitchen Garden and Gardens Across America.*

The recipes in the book appear as healthier alternatives to some heritage dishes, such as the Old South's string beans braised in a smoky pork stock until they were so tender you could mash them with a fork. These days, when I serve green beans, they go to the table with a slight crunch, from blanching in boiling water, and garnished with something fresh—garlic sautéed in browned butter, cooked minced red bell peppers, or nuts, as with this interpretation of an almond-studded classic, green beans amandine.

Green beans are versatile: You can cook them to your own desired doneness. And, if you like crunchy beans or less garlic, no problem. Cooking teacher Mrs. T. P. (Sarah Helen) Mahammitt gave no amounts for the ingredients in her version of the dish in her 1939 cookbook, *Recipes and Domestic Service: The Mahammitt School of Cookery*, encouraging students to engage their senses when cooking: "It's completely up to your tastes."

Salt
1½ pounds French green beans (haricots verts), trimmed
1 tablespoon extra-virgin olive oil
1 tablespoon butter
1 teaspoon minced garlic or shallots
½ teaspoon paprika
Black pepper
½ cup slivered almonds, toasted
1 tablespoon minced fresh parsley

1 Set up a large bowl of ice and water. In a large skillet, bring a couple cups of well-salted water to a boil over high heat. Add the beans and cook until they turn bright green and tender-crisp, 3 to 4 minutes (or longer, to your desired tenderness, adding water if necessary), shaking the pan occasionally to cook evenly. Drain the beans and plunge them into the bowl of ice water to stop them from cooking further. Drain again and set aside or refrigerate until ready to cook, if making ahead.

2 In the same skillet, heat the oil and butter over medium-high heat. Add the garlic and sauté until tender, about 30 seconds. Return the beans to the pan. Season with the paprika and salt and pepper to taste. Cook for 2 to 3 minutes, stirring the pan occasionally, to heat through. Serve garnished with the almonds and parsley.

STRING BEANS À LA CREOLE

SERVES 6

Green beans steeped in Southwestern flavors are an unusual but appropriate use of the term *à la Creole,* meaning "of mixed heritage." This dish is a quick adaptation of Bertha Turner's 1910 book, *The Federation Cook Book: A Collection of Tested Recipes, Contributed by the Colored Women of the State of California.* She poached her beans in a broth laced with mild green chiles, then simmered them with tomatoes and more chiles.

Salt

1½ pounds green beans, trimmed and cut into 1-inch pieces

2 tablespoons bacon drippings or vegetable or olive oil

1 cup diced onion

1 teaspoon minced garlic

1 (10-ounce) can diced tomatoes and green chiles (such as Ro-Tel)

¼ teaspoon smoked paprika

Black pepper

1 Set up a large bowl of ice and water. In a large skillet, bring a couple cups of well-salted water to a boil over high heat. Add the beans and cook until they turn bright green and tender-crisp, 3 to 4 minutes, shaking the pan occasionally. Plunge the beans in the ice water to stop them from cooking further. Drain and set aside.

2 In the same skillet, heat the bacon fat over medium-high heat. When hot, sauté the onion and garlic until translucent, 2 to 3 minutes. Add the tomatoes and chiles, paprika, and beans. Season with salt and pepper and continue to cook 5 to 10 minutes, or to desired tenderness.

SPICY SAUTÉED OKRA AND TOMATOES

SERVES 4

Some cooks avoid okra because of its natural sliminess. Others have found workarounds, recommending that okra be prepared whole or dredged in flour or cornmeal, or blanched briefly before use. The mucilage seems to be minimized when cooked hot and fast and combined with tomatoes.

2 tablespoons olive oil

2 slices bacon, diced

1 cup chopped onion

1 tablespoon minced garlic (3 to 4 cloves)

1 pound fresh okra, trimmed and cut into ¼-inch slices

1 cup chopped fresh tomatoes

½ cup Chicken Stock (page 133)

½ teaspoon salt, or to taste

¼ to ½ teaspoon crushed red pepper flakes, to taste

Black pepper

Freshly cooked rice, for serving

1 In a large skillet, heat the oil over medium heat. Add the bacon and, once it has rendered its fat and is just starting to crisp, stir in the onion and cook until translucent, 2 to 4 minutes. Stir in the garlic and cook 30 seconds longer. Add the okra and sauté for 2 minutes, until the okra begins to soften.

2 Stir in the tomatoes, chicken stock, salt, and red pepper flakes. Bring to a simmer, partially cover, and cook, stirring occasionally, about 15 minutes, until the okra is tender. Do not overcook the okra or it will be too soft. Season one more time with salt and pepper, if desired. Serve with hot rice.

BRAISED CELERY

SERVES 4 TO 8

I created this dish one Easter Sunday, with memories of a dish served at Mary Mac's Tea Room in Atlanta still on my lips and recipes published in 1912 by S. Thomas Bivins on my mind. Bivins wrote a massive work of more than six hundred recipes, including his take on the stewed celery dish known in fine-dining restaurants as Celery Victor.

I sautéed the celery in drippings left over from roasting our holiday leg of lamb and garnished the dish with sliced almonds, Monticello-style (one of the fancy upgrades under James Hemings's watch). I also followed Edna Lewis's lead: She steeped celery in beef broth and butter and served it sprinkled with chopped fresh parsley.

Give the dish body, just as chef S. Thomas Bivins did, with beurre manié (butter and flour rubbed together)—a French technique you can use at the last minute to thicken most any dish. It's a delicate alternative to the custom of smothering vegetables in a roux-based gravy.

1 tablespoon reserved meat drippings
    or olive oil

2 small bunches celery (about 2 pounds),
    trimmed and cut into 3-inch pieces

½ cup coarsely chopped onion

2 cups Chicken Stock (page 133)

Pinch of crushed red pepper flakes

1 teaspoon salt, plus more to taste

Pinch of ground or freshly grated nutmeg
    (optional)

1 tablespoon butter, cut into small dice

1 tablespoon all-purpose flour

¼ cup heavy whipping cream

Black pepper

1 In a Dutch oven, heat the meat drippings or olive oil over medium heat. When hot, add the celery and onion and sauté 10 to 12 minutes, until softened. Add the chicken stock, red pepper flakes, salt, and nutmeg (if using). Simmer until the celery is tender, about 30 minutes.

2 Meanwhile, on a work surface, use the side of a knife or your fingertips to rub together the butter and flour until well mixed, resembling a smooth, thick paste.

3 Whisk the butter-flour mixture into the celery, whisking until completely dissolved. Stir in the cream. Simmer, uncovered, until thickened, 2 to 3 minutes more. Taste and adjust seasoning with salt and pepper, and serve.

BRAISED SUMMER SQUASH WITH ONIONS

SERVES 4

Creative cooks have myriad ideas for dealing with the squash that can overrun the summer garden. Two of the most common are squash baked in a cheesy casserole topped with bread crumbs and squash pan-fried with onions.

The butter/oil/rosemary mix in Maya Angelou's 2004 cookbook, *Hallelujah! The Welcome Table: A Lifetime of Memories with Recipes,* is a refreshing alternative to classic smothered squash seasoned with bacon drippings. Other black cookbooks have offered their own variations, stirring in diced green pepper, chopped shrimp, or curry powder, but Angelou's suggestion of rosemary adds a deep herbal flavor that is unforgettable.

2 pounds yellow summer squash

2 tablespoons butter

2 tablespoons vegetable or olive oil

1 cup thinly sliced onion

1 teaspoon minced garlic

¾ teaspoon salt, or to taste

¼ teaspoon black pepper

¼ teaspoon dried rosemary or ½ teaspoon chopped fresh

2 tablespoons minced chives

1 Use a mandoline or a sharp knife to cut the squash into ¼-inch-thick slices. In a large skillet, heat the butter and oil over medium-high heat until hot. Add the onion and garlic and sauté until the onion is translucent, about 2 minutes. Add the squash, salt, black pepper, and rosemary and sauté over medium heat, 2 to 3 minutes until fragrant, stirring occasionally, adding up to 2 tablespoons water as needed to prevent sticking.

2 Reduce the heat to medium-low, cover, and cook, turning frequently, until the squash is very tender, about 30 minutes. Garnish with the chives and serve.

Roots and Tubers

While researching potato recipes in African American cookbooks I encountered root vegetables of every kind—boiled and fried; scooped with a melon baller, poached in water, and then browned all over in butter; boiled and mashed to a puree; shaped into croquettes and fried.

It didn't take long to realize that black chefs have been adept at turning ordinary boiled vegetables into something decadent and silky with little more than stock, butter, and milk or cream, but vegetable mashes are pure African, too—the Kenyan dish *irio* (a corn, potato, and bean mash) comes to mind.

Root vegetables are delicious when they are cut into a small dice and tossed with olive oil before roasting in a hot oven until the edges are slightly browned and crisp. This method concentrates the vegetables' naturally sweet juices, preserving their nutritious goodness.

MASHED TURNIPS AND CARROTS WITH RUM

SERVES 4 TO 6

Old-school caterer Jessie Payne cut root vegetables decoratively using a melon baller, then sautéed them in butter and served them attractively in cups cut from sweet green bell peppers in her 1955 cookbook, *Paynie's Parties*.

You, too, can broaden the appeal of turnips or rutabagas, which are underappreciated and sweet, by whipping them with carrots, onions, and a splash of rum. This dish was inspired by a recipe in Norma Jean and Carole Darden's *Spoonbread and Strawberry Wine*. If you choose to add the rum, do so gradually, to your own tastes.

½ pound turnips (or rutabaga), peeled, trimmed, and quartered

1 pound carrots, trimmed and halved lengthwise

2 tablespoons sugar

1 tablespoon honey

1 teaspoon salt, or to taste

4 tablespoons (½ stick) butter

¼ cup chopped onion

1 to 2 tablespoons heavy cream, to taste

1 tablespoon rum (optional)

Black pepper (optional)

1 In a medium saucepan, combine 2 cups water, the turnips, carrots, sugar, honey, and salt. The water will not cover the vegetables. Bring to a boil over medium-high heat, then reduce the heat to a simmer and cook the vegetables, covered, for 15 minutes. Pierce with a fork to test doneness, then continue to cook to your preferred degree of doneness, up to 15 minutes more, adding water as needed to prevent sticking and to keep the vegetables steaming. (The more tender the vegetables, the smoother the mash will be, but don't overcook them totally or the mash will be watery.)

2 Drain the vegetables in a colander, reserving the cooking water. Mash the vegetables with a spoon, ricer, or food mill, or in a food processor, until smooth.

3 In the same saucepan, heat the butter over medium-high heat. Add the onion and sauté until translucent, 1 to 2 minutes. Add the onions to the turnips and carrots and blend well, adding cream as desired and enough reserved cooking water or rum (if using) to adjust the consistency and flavor to your liking. Taste to adjust the seasoning with salt and pepper.

PUREED PARSNIPS

SERVES 4 TO 6

In *B. Smith Cooks Southern-Style*, former model, restaurateur, and chef Barbara (B.) Smith showed her fondness for parsnips, a humble, sweet, carrot-like root: "With a hint of sweetness and a pinch of spice, parsnips can be boiled, steamed, roasted, braised, or mashed." But it was Pullman Railroad chef Rufus Estes's Parsnip Puree, published in *Good Things to Eat, as Suggested by Rufus* in 1911, that is behind this recipe. Chef Estes mashed the cooked parsnips and fried them as fritters, or he served them simply, flavored by stock instead of water, milk, or cream. The butter is nonnegotiable.

2 pounds parsnips, peeled and cut into ½-inch-thick slices
2 to 3 cups Chicken Stock (page 133)
4 tablespoons (½ stick) butter
1 teaspoon salt
¼ teaspoon black pepper
1 tablespoon heavy whipping cream
Minced fresh chives (optional)

1 In a large saucepan, combine the parsnips and enough chicken stock to cover. Bring to a boil over medium-high heat, then reduce the heat, cover, and simmer until very tender, 15 to 20 minutes. Drain in a colander, reserving the stock.

2 Return the parsnips to the pan. Add the butter, salt, pepper, and cream and mash them with the back of a wooden spoon or a vegetable masher, adding enough reserved stock to make a smooth puree. (Or puree in a blender or food processor.) Cook over low heat to warm through. Taste to adjust seasonings. Garnish with chives, if desired.

PARSNIP BALLS

Recipes and Domestic Service: The Mahammit School of Cookery, Mrs. T. P. [Sarah Helen] Mahammit, 1939

6 parsnips
1 tbsp. butter
½ tsp. salt
white pepper
1 egg

Cook parsnips and mash. Season with butter, salt, pepper, and 1 egg yolk. When cold, roll in balls. Dip in egg white and crumbs. Fry in deep fat.

BAKED PARSNIP

¾ cup bread crumbs
2 cups parsnip puree
1 tbsp. grated onion
½ cup very rich milk
2 tbsp. butter
salt and pepper

Boil parsnips, peel and put through a coarse sieve. Season this puree with salt and pepper to taste and put in the bottom of a baking dish. Add the grated onion. Sift crumbs. Put the fine crumbs over the parsnips onion, and pour over all the milk to which has been added one tablespoon of the butter melted. Melt the remaining tablespoon of butter in a small pan and with this blend the coarse crumbs which were left after the sifting. Dress the top of the dish with these and bake in oven at 400 degrees F., for about half an hour.

BEETS ÉTOUFFÉE

SERVES 4

This recipe is a mash-up of inspiration taken from recipes for sweet-and-sour beets, "Harvard" beets, and beets with onions and cream. It is cleverly disguised by the name of the revered rural Louisiana dish, étouffée, which generally means meats smothered in a dark, red-brown gravy, and it was originally created by Ida Guillory in *Cookin' with Queen Ida: "Bon Temps" Creole Recipes (and Stories) from the Queen of Zydeco Music*.

I updated the savory dish by layering on pungent garlic and ginger and tossing tart green apples into the mix for variety.

1 tablespoon butter

1 cup thinly sliced red onion

1 garlic clove, minced

1 teaspoon minced fresh ginger

3 cups beets, peeled and cut in ¼-inch matchsticks

1 small tart green apple, peeled and cut in ¼-inch matchsticks

¼ teaspoon salt

2 teaspoons sugar

½ cup seasoned rice or cider vinegar

¼ teaspoon freshly grated lemon zest

½ teaspoon fresh lemon juice

1 In a large skillet, heat the butter over medium heat until sizzling. Add the onion and sauté until it begins to get translucent, about 2 minutes. Stir in the garlic and ginger and cook 30 seconds more. Stir in the beets and apple and toss gently to coat with the aromatics. Add ½ cup water, the salt, sugar, and vinegar. Bring to a boil, then reduce the heat to medium-low, cover, and cook until the beets are fork-tender, about 20 minutes. (For very tender beets, cook 10 minutes longer, adding up to ¼ cup additional water to prevent sticking.)

2 Stir in the lemon zest and juice and let cool slightly. Serve warm.

Going to the Sweet Potato Bank

Sweet potatoes were a dietary staple for South Carolina's bondservants, its field workers and hunters. Sallie Ann Robinson, the Gullah-Geechee griot, wrote of this in her poignant record of life in the Carolina Sea Islands, *Gullah Home Cooking the Daufuskie Way*: "Grandmomma always grew a big field of sweet potato vines. When we dug the sweet potatoes right after the first frost in the late fall, we separated out the small tubers for seed to be planted in the spring and 'banked' both them and the eating sweet potatoes in the special, tin-roofed, A-frame shed. Sweet potatoes don't keep well in a refrigerator or at room temperature, and when any part of one rots, the flavor of the whole tuber is spoiled. The banking kept them cool, but not cold, moist but not wet, and away from varmints."

Formerly enslaved black people interviewed in the 1930s described intense love for sweet potatoes roasted in ashes, which brings out the natural sweetness of the tuber. Field workers carried "baked sweet 'tadas'—with their skins serving as a natural wrapper—in their pockets or aprons for a midday meal."

So why do we add sugar, molasses, maple syrup, or fruit juice to a luscious vegetable already sweet as the first kiss? William Ed Grimé might have discovered the answer in a cooking method described by a French observer: "The negros' who make sugar do not fail to throw their potatoes in the sirup pot, where they let them cook for a half hour."

From this ancestry, sweet potatoes are enjoyed in many forms, of course, and America's spiced yam balls, sweet potato pones, puffs, and croquettes are descendants of African *fufu* and Caribbean *batata*—pounded yuca, yams, or sweet potatoes. Dr. George Washington Carver was a champion of sweet potatoes for their consistent yields in the fields and their nutritive value at home. In his bulletins, he suggested several options for stuffing fried sweet potato puffs with minced meat or nuts. He also created a highly spiced, doughnut-shaped treat he called "puffers." Some domestic cooks and caterers tucked a marshmallow inside of sweet potato fritters.

Sweet potato casserole and candied yams became soul food classics, upgrades from the old days when cooks roasted possum or shoats with plain sweet potatoes or pounded them into pones and baked. Later, sliced potatoes and apples poached in a glaze of sugar and spices were beautiful and delicious. In some kitchens, corn syrup and marshmallows or a crown of praline topping nudged mashed sweet potatoes, sometimes called "compote," toward dessert.

SWEET POTATO CASSEROLE

SERVES 6 TO 8

In most of the recipes I encountered for sweet potato casserole, the praline topping was like candy, sweet enough to set your teeth on edge, a throwback to the days when crushed pineapple or marshmallows uplifted basic grated sweet potato pone and molasses. But not quite so with Bob Jeffries, who tweaked his grandmother's recipes to suit more modern tastes, making this dish slightly less sweet.

Butter, for greasing the dish
½ cup light brown sugar, packed
¼ cup all-purpose flour
2 cups chopped toasted pecans
1 cup melted butter
3 cups cooked mashed sweet potatoes
1 cup granulated sugar
2 eggs, beaten
⅓ cup evaporated or whole milk
1 teaspoon vanilla extract
Pinch of salt
1 teaspoon ground cinnamon
½ teaspoon ground nutmeg

1 Preheat the oven to 350°F. Grease a 2-quart baking dish with butter.

2 In a small bowl, combine the brown sugar, flour, pecans, and ½ cup of the melted butter. Set aside.

3 In the bowl of a stand mixer, beat the sweet potatoes on medium speed until light. Beat in the remaining ½ cup butter, the granulated sugar, eggs, milk, vanilla, salt, cinnamon, and nutmeg. Pour the mixture into the baking dish. Sprinkle with praline topping. Bake until the top is browned and firm, 30 to 35 minutes.

CROQUETTES

How the Farmer Can Save His Sweet Potatoes: And Ways of Preparing Them for the Table, Bulletin No. 38, George Washington Carver, 1936

Take two cupfuls of mashed, boiled, steamed or baked sweet potatoes; add the beaten yolks of two eggs and season to taste; stir over the fire until the mass pulls from the sides of the pan. When cold, form into small croquettes, roll in egg and bread crumbs, and fry in hot lard to amber color. Serve on napkins.

SWEET POTATO BALLS

Prepare the same as for croquettes, make into balls and enclose within the center of minced meat.

GLACE, NO. 1

Boil and cut in halves medium-sized sweet potatoes, lay evenly in braising pan, baste with syrup and butter warmed together, sprinkle lightly with brown sugar, put in hot oven until brown, and serve in the syrup.

GLACE, NO. 2

Cut in slices 1–2 inch thick, wash and place in deep sauce pan; spread with butter; season with a little grated nutmeg and salt; moisten with broth or water, cover and let simmer over a slow fire for three-fourths of an hour, turning the slices so that they will glace on both sides. Serve with drawn butter or other sauce.

A Mess o' Greens

Whole Foods Market caused quite a stir in 2014 when the health food superstore declared "collard greens the new kale" and tweeted a recipe for sautéed collards garnished with peanuts. I admit I had to laugh. It reminded me of the author's words in *A Good Heart and a Light Hand: Ruth L. Gaskins' Collection of Traditional Negro Recipes:* "It's amazing to us to think that anyone could grow up without greens, but every time we shop in the supermarket, White women ask in surprise, 'What in the world do you do with those things?'"

For many on Twitter, this recipe was a bridge too far. "For other people collards are a trend—for us they are a tradition," food writer and historian Michael Twitty said at the time. But it's also fair to ask: What is that tradition? In this case it may have been the peanuts that shocked people. But there is also an impression that old-fashioned, Southern, or country-style greens must be boiled to death to be authentic soul food. Any other way, and you might as well just designate the dish #fakesoul. That notion, though, hasn't always been set in stone.

Descendants of the African diaspora have always prepared cultivated and wild greens by myriad methods. Here is what Frankie Field had to say in *The Chef,* published by the City Federation of Colored Women's Clubs of Tulsa in 1944: "Select the best vegetables. Pick carefully, wash thoroughly and cook over a low flame, only water that clings to the leaves. Cook until tender as wanted. Never over-cook. When using meat to season greens, cook the meat until well-done, leaving only a small amount of water with meat, then add greens and cook for a short time, or until done."

With those words in mind, I tweaked the recipe for sautéed greens so they cook quickly and their bright color and firm texture are preserved. The unexpected addition to our holiday dinner table thrilled my niece Aliya the year she turned vegetarian.

COLLARD GREENS
WITH CORNMEAL DUMPLINGS
SERVES 6

Cornmeal dumplings dropped into a bubbling pot of turnip greens, collards, or cabbage will remind some of African *fufu*, the pones made from pounded yam, cassava, or potato flour—or their contemporary adaptations featuring cream of wheat, farina, or even instant potato flakes. This is a totemic soul food dish—greens simmered long and slow until quite tender, though young greens cook in half the time. Choose a state of doneness that best suits your tastes and your collards.

I like the way this poem by Aneb Kgositsile, which I first saw in *The African American Heritage Cookbook: Traditional Recipes and Fond Remembrances from Alabama's Renowned Tuskegee Institute* (2001), honors the memory of the dish:

> *Collards and cornbread,*
> *communion meal of*
> *daily resurrection.*
> *I ate the survival leaf as I stood at*
> *the field's edge,*
> *soaking its cure through pores*
> *and spirit.*

1½ quarts Smoky Soul Stock (recipe follows)

½ cup chopped onion

1 garlic clove, minced

1 pound collard greens

2 small dried red chile peppers or 1 teaspoon crushed red pepper flakes

¾ teaspoon salt, plus more to taste

Black pepper

½ cup all-purpose flour

1½ cups coarsely ground cornmeal

1 teaspoon baking powder

1 teaspoon sugar

2 tablespoons butter

1 In a saucepan, bring the stock, onion, and garlic to a boil over high heat. Reduce the heat, cover, and simmer while preparing the greens.

2 Thoroughly wash the greens and trim away the stems, if desired. Discard the stems or coarsely chop. Stack 2 or 3 leaves on a cutting board and roll tightly into a log. Slice the greens crosswise into ¼-inch-wide ribbons. Place the greens and the chiles in the broth and return to a simmer. Cook, covered, about 1½ hours for very tender greens; you may cook them for less if you have young greens or prefer greens with more chew. Season to taste with salt and black pepper. Spoon out ½ cup of the potlikker and set aside.

3 Meanwhile, in a small bowl, whisk together the flour, cornmeal, baking powder, sugar, and ¾ teaspoon salt. In a small saucepan, melt the butter. Add the reserved potlikker, and heat to just below boiling. Remove the potlikker mixture from the heat and whisk it into the dry ingredients. Let stand 5 minutes. When cool enough to handle, use wet fingertips to shape the dough into 6 dumplings.

4 During the last 15 minutes of the collards' cooking time, carefully drop the cornmeal dumplings into the pot with the greens, making sure the dumplings rest in the potlikker. Cover the pot and simmer until the dumplings are cooked through, 10 to 15 minutes.

5 Serve greens and dumplings in bowls with plenty of potlikker.

SMOKY SOUL STOCK

MAKES ABOUT 2 QUARTS

2 smoked ham hocks or 2 smoked turkey
   wings
2 medium onions, quartered
4 celery stalks, including leaves, halved
2 carrots, trimmed and quartered
2 garlic cloves, peeled and smashed
½ teaspoon black peppercorns
2 bay leaves

1 In a large heavy stockpot, bring 3 quarts
water, the smoked meat, onions, celery,
carrots, garlic, peppercorns, and bay leaves
to a boil. Reduce the heat, and simmer,
partially covered, until the flavors are
well blended, about 2 hours. The broth
develops stronger flavor the longer you let
it simmer.

2 Remove the meat from the broth. When
cool enough to handle, pull the meat off
the bones (discard the skin, fat, and bones).
Chop the meat and reserve for another use.
Use a fine-mesh sieve to strain the stock.
Refrigerate the stock until the fat floats
to the top. Use a slotted spoon to skim off
the fat and discard. Store the stock tightly
covered in the freezer.

SAUTÉED GREENS

SERVES 4

Inspired by the Brazilian style in which *couve*
(greens) are sautéed raw, this brightly colored
dish comes in handy when chard, beet greens,
spinach, and tender sweet potato greens turn
up at the farmers' market. My addition of vinegar and maple syrup comes by way of Ruth
Gaskins and the singer Isaac Hayes.

2 pounds mixed greens (mustard or turnip
   greens, spinach, chard, arugula, baby kale,
   or young collards)
2 tablespoons olive oil
1 cup chopped onion
2 garlic cloves, minced
½ teaspoon crushed red pepper flakes
1 tablespoon cider vinegar
1 tablespoon maple syrup (optional)
Salt and black pepper

1 Wash the greens, removing the stems
and thick midribs. (Or keep them and
slice them thinly.) Stack 2 or 3 leaves, roll
tightly into a log and slice it into ¼-inch-
wide ribbons. Repeat with the rest of
the greens.

2 In a large heavy skillet, heat the oil over
medium heat. Add the onion and garlic
and sauté until translucent, 2 to 4 minutes.
Reduce the heat to medium-low. Add
half the greens and sauté until limp, 3 to
5 minutes. Add the remaining greens and
cook until tender, 7 to 8 minutes more (or
less, if using tender greens). Stir in the red
pepper flakes, vinegar, and maple syrup (if
using). Season to taste with salt and black
pepper. Increase the heat to medium-high
and cook, stirring, until the flavors come
together and the greens are cooked to your
desired doneness.

NEVER LET THE PEOPLE BE
KEPT WAITING . . .
—TUNIS G. CAMPBELL, 1848

Comfort in Dining

The vacation destinations that affluent blacks began to establish during the 1890s, in tiny enclaves on the fringes of picturesque resort areas for white people, were idyllic settings. They affirmed my ancestors' ambitions for getaway communities of their own, much like the hospitality offered by black women during the Colored Conventions Movement or the "vacation without aggravation" aid offered to Jim Crow–era tourists by *The Negro Motorist Green-Book*, a guide to safe places to eat and sleep—or get gas, car repairs, or a haircut—published by Victor H. Green from 1936 to 1967.

It's not a stretch to say that these communities and service providers helped their children believe they could achieve anything.

By the 1920s, Highland Beach, Maryland; Bruce's Beach in Manhattan Beach, California; and Oak Bluffs on Martha's Vineyard had earned reputations for nurturing black excellence that galvanized well-heeled blacks all around the country. Near my hometown, a group of prominent black Angelenos picnicked, swam, and rode horses free from the restrictive covenants and oppressive laws that characterized urban living in the rolling hills west of the Santa Clarita Valley—a Promised Land.

Well-to-do professionals and celebrities, including Sidney P. Dones, Norman O. Houston, Joe and Charlotta Bass, and James Earl Jones, drove nearly forty miles north of Los Angeles to Eureka/Val Verde (Spanish for green valley). They invested in half-acre lots and built vacation homes where they celebrated special occasions, threw holiday parties, and splashed in the crystal blue waters of a magnificent swimming pool. Eventually, a clubhouse, tennis courts, baseball fields, a golf course, restaurants, and inns turned Val Verde into a retreat community, nicknamed the "Black Palm Springs."

"Oh, that swimming pool," my uncle Melvin chortled exuberantly when I asked him about Val Verde. "That pool was the gathering place. You had to have a car, or you went with the church. We went horseback riding and brought our own food. Your aunt was even crowned Miss Val Verde."

With Val Verde, investors realized a hospitality tradition begun by gracious hosts and hostesses of color who operated boardinghouses, inns, hotels, and resorts frequented by hungry, weary travelers in the pre–Civil War era. Modeled on the refined lodging services that black innkeepers offered to white people, such as Wormley's Hotel in the District of Columbia, African American inns offered clean sheets and a good hot meal to enslaved workers traveling with planters and free people of color attending social justice meetings.

In antebellum Detroit, Benjamin "Pap" Singleton's boardinghouse welcomed fugitive slaves; the Dumas Hotel in Cincinnati was a place where African American servants socialized with other black people while traveling with their owners. Gracy Jones advertised board and lodging in New York for all "genteel persons of color." A month later, her competitor Eliza Johnson stepped up her game, advertising that she not only provided lodging and boarding but also oysters and "a quantity of the best Refreshments."

Fine foods served on white linen with polished silver helped business grow.

An 1848 advertisement revealed the kind of food service George Downing offered in Rhode Island at his Sea Girt Hotel: "a suite of Game and Oyster Supper Rooms on Cottage Street, where he will have on hand New York Oysters, Woodcock, Soft Crabs, Lobster Salid [sic], Green Turtle soup, Ice Cream, Confectionary, &c." Malinda Russell kept a boardinghouse where she pleased visitors with delectable breads, cakes, pies, and pastries in Tennessee. Later she opened her own bakery and published recipes from her enterprises—the first cookbook published by a black woman. And successful businesswomen Mary Ellen Pleasant of San Francisco, Rebecca Howard in Olympia, Washington, and Lucretia "Aunt Lou" Marchbanks in the Black Hills of South Dakota earned formidable reputations out West, providing excellent service, good food, and fine hospitality in boardinghouses, hotels, and dining halls that they purchased themselves.

But it was the health resort-getaway that Annie Box and Curly Neal operated in Oracle, Arizona, that got me thinking about the ambitious aspirations behind the founding of Val Verde and all that black lodging had accomplished. "The most luxurious hotel in the west"—that's how observers described the Mountain View Hotel, a 160-acre ranch, health sanatorium, and recreational playground where fine music, entertainment, rodeos, and exquisite dining for the very wealthy were the "epitome of Western opulence."

I never visited Val Verde. By the time my vacation memories started forming, segregation was in its waning years, and black families had stopped driving long distances to create social, cultural, and recreational activities for themselves. Instead, my parents and their friends formed a boat club, named themselves the Sea Searchers, and intentionally launched their speed boats in Southern California's friendlier lakes and beaches—many of them located in that same region of Eureka. I learned to water ski just west of Val Verde on Lake Cachuma; we fished for bluegill and large-mouth bass at nearby Castaic Lake.

We ate simply but well. As if to sustain the ancestors' hospitable spirit, families often fried the day's catch in a communal pot near the campfire. Mom channeled Western cooks on the ranch and on wagon trains, simmering a big pot of chili, beef stew, or beans during the day. The men carried on cowboy barbecue traditions with slow-smoked ribs and sausage, or grilled steaks marinated in cracked black pepper, soy sauce, and Worcestershire sauce.

Today, I savor my connection to generations who extended food and fellowship in public spaces, as well as the homemakers and hosts listed in *The Negro Motorist Green-Book*. They provided safe places to eat and sleep during segregation, healed bodies and spirits with comforting and lavish meals, treated weary travelers like distinguished guests, and made it all seem commonplace, as it should be.

Beef Stew with a French Attitude

Braising tough meat harkens back to a time when cooks of every station made ends meet by tenderizing lesser cuts with long simmering. Remember the oxtails, short ribs, and pot roasts that bubbled for hours in velvety gravy before being served by Grandmother with mashed potatoes, noodles, or rice?

In elite circles, African American caterers and cooks to the wealthy, Jesse Lewis among them, became "adept at making other cuisines besides southern food, and most often it was French food, the 'official cuisine' of high society in America," Adrian Miller wrote in *The President's Kitchen Cabinet*. First as a teenager waiting tables in a boardinghouse, then as a cook on a Mobile–New Orleans tug, Lewis refined his dexterity with regional dishes in the resort town of Bay St. Louis, Mississippi. Whether it was the "ragout of oxtail supreme" Lewis spiced with cloves and allspice in his 1954 recipe collection, *Jesse's Book of Creole and Deep South Recipes*, or any one of the dishes created for American presidents, black professionals have intoxicated politicians, socialites, their wealthy friends, and guests with Frenchified cooking that is still evident in African American cookbooks to this day.

Recipe titles hinted at French techniques. *Roti de boeuf*, beef with *lardons*, or beef *à la mode* levitated ordinary beef stew on status-seeking menus, but know that while the results in these recipes impress, the method for making them isn't too far from the all-too-familiar beef stew. You'll want to pass around plenty of crusty bread or hot buttered Rice Muffins (page 106) to soak up the exquisite pan juices—whatever you decide to call the dishes.

BEEF WITH ONIONS AND WINE

SERVES 6

This is a version of the French stew beef bourguignon. If the thought of making what legendary singer Mahalia Jackson called "oven beef Burgundy" seems fussy, though, think of it as she did—just as beef pot roast with a bunch of onions, dressed up with red wine.

In the classic French preparation, layered flavors from sautéed meat, vegetables, and long-simmered pearl onions give the dish a robust character. Edna Lewis grated onions and added an additional onion stuck with cloves to the braising liquid for a refined sweetness and depth. Mahalia Jackson stirred everything together for an effortless dish. Mine is a mash-up of those (with a bit of Julia Child's version mixed in) that tastes even better the next day.

1 pound pearl onions

½ pound sliced bacon

2½ pounds beef stew meat or chuck, cut into 1½-inch pieces

2 teaspoons salt, plus more to taste

1½ teaspoons black pepper

½ teaspoon dried thyme

2 tablespoons all-purpose flour

2 cups sliced onions

2 large carrots, cut into ½-inch-thick slices

4 garlic cloves, minced

1 pound mushrooms, cut into ¼-inch-thick slices

4 cups red wine

1 tablespoon tomato paste

1 bay leaf

Minced parsley, for garnish

Freshly cooked mashed potatoes, noodles, or rice, for serving

1 Preheat the oven to 350°F.

2 Place the pearl onions in a bowl. Pour in enough water to cover the onions and set aside to soak for 10 to 15 minutes to loosen the skins. Use your fingers to rub the skins loose and peel the onions. Use a sharp knife to make a small X on the stem end.

3 In a large Dutch oven, cook the bacon in batches over medium heat until crisp, about 7 minutes per batch. Remove the bacon, leaving the drippings in the pan, and crumble the bacon when cool enough to handle.

4 Pat the meat dry with paper towels. In a shallow dish or paper bag, combine salt, pepper, thyme, and flour. Place the beef in the dish and dust or shake the meat with the seasoned flour to entirely coat.

5 In the Dutch oven, heat the bacon fat over medium-high heat. Add the meat to the pan in batches, being careful not to crowd the pan, and sear until deeply browned, then turn and sear on all sides. This can take some time. Use a slotted spoon to remove the seared meat to a platter and set the meat aside.

6 Add the sliced onions and carrots to the pan and cook, stirring, over medium-high heat until tender-crisp. As you stir, scrape the bottom of the pan to pick up any browned bits and dissolve them into the vegetables. Add the garlic and cook 30 seconds. Remove the vegetables to the platter with the meat. Add the mushrooms to the pan and sauté until tender. Return the meat, vegetables, and any juices that collect on the plate to the pot. Stir in the wine, tomato paste, and bay leaf.

7 Bring to a simmer, cover the pot tightly, and transfer to the oven. Bake for 2 hours. Stir the pearl onions and bacon into the pan and add salt to taste, remembering that it will concentrate somewhat as it continues to cook. Bake until the meat is very tender, about 1 hour more. If necessary, add a little water or stock if the liquid seems thick.

8 Before serving, remove and discard the bay leaf. Sprinkle the stew with parsley and serve with mashed potatoes, noodles, or rice.

POT ROAST WITH RUM

Recipes and Domestic Service: The Mahammitt School of Cookery, Mrs. T. P. [Sarah Helen] Mahammitt, 1939

3 pounds rump roast
1 small bottle of stuffed olives
1 garlic clove
¼ cup water
¼ pound salt pork
2 tablespoons rum
2 teaspoons salt
⅛ teaspoon cayenne pepper
¼ cup butter
¼ cup shortening
2 cups tomatoes

Lard the roast with salt pork. Wipe roast and cut small slits in roast with sharp knife, alternate with the pork. Stuff olives in the slits. Brown the roast in butter and place in cooker kettle. Cook 1½ hours. During the last hour add the tomatoes and rum and continue to cook one hour. Serve sliced, with gravy made from liquid in the cooker kettle.

COFFEE-SCENTED SHORT RIBS BRAISED IN RED WINE

SERVES 4

This dish is an innovation on classic braised short ribs. I massage the ribs with a seductive mixture of coffee, cocoa, and spices before simmering in red wine and beef stock until the meat practically falls from the bone—a trick I discovered in contemporary writer Nicole Taylor's *The Up South Cookbook*. I retained the molasses traditionally called for because I love its somewhat tannic character, and I gave the dish a boost of sweetness with brown sugar. Extra beef stock ensures there is plenty of it to soak into the hot, creamy grits.

1 tablespoon brown sugar
1 tablespoon unsweetened cocoa powder
1 tablespoon ground coffee
½ teaspoon chili powder
½ teaspoon ground allspice
½ teaspoon ground cinnamon
2 teaspoons salt, plus more to taste
1 teaspoon black pepper
4 pounds bone-in short ribs, cut into 2-inch pieces by the butcher
⅓ cup bacon drippings or vegetable oil
1½ cups coarsely chopped onions
1½ tablespoons minced garlic (5 to 6 cloves)
1 cup coarsely chopped carrots
1 cup coarsely chopped celery
2 teaspoons dried thyme
2 teaspoons dried rosemary
3 cups red wine
3 cups Beef Stock (recipe follows)
2 bay leaves
1½ cups molasses
Freshly cooked grits or mashed potatoes

RECIPE CONTINUES

1 In a small bowl, stir together the brown sugar, cocoa powder, ground coffee, chili powder, allspice, cinnamon, salt, and pepper. Pat the short ribs dry with paper towels, and rub and press the seasoning mixture into the meat with your fingers. Let sit for 1 hour, or up to 1 day, covered and refrigerated.

2 In a Dutch oven, heat the bacon fat over medium-high heat until shimmering. Add the ribs, working in batches if necessary to prevent crowding, and sear until well browned, about 5 minutes per side. Transfer the ribs to a plate and set aside.

3 Add the onions, garlic, carrots, and celery to the pot and cook, stirring to loosen any browned bits and dissolve them into the vegetables, until the onions are translucent, about 8 minutes. Add the thyme and rosemary and cook for 30 seconds. Add the wine and bring to a boil over high heat. Reduce the heat to medium-low and simmer for 5 minutes. Stir in the beef stock, bay leaves, and 1 cup of molasses. Return the short ribs and any juices that have accumulated on the plate to the pan. Taste and season with more salt if necessary to balance the sweetness, but keep in mind that the sauce will cook and concentrate. Bring to a boil, then reduce the heat to a gentle simmer, partially cover, and cook for 1 hour.

4 Use a slotted spoon to remove the ribs to a clean plate. Strain the braising juices in a colander and discard the solids. Refrigerate the juices until the fat rises to the top. Skim off and discard the fat. Return the juices to the pan, stir in the remaining ½ cup molasses and more salt, as needed, and return the ribs to the pan. Bring back up to a simmer and cook until the meat is tender, about 30 minutes.

5 Spoon the grits or mashed potatoes onto serving plates. Top with the ribs and spoon the sauce around the edge of the plate, or pass the sauce separately.

BEEF STOCK
MAKES ABOUT 1 QUART

2½ pounds beef soup bones
1 carrot, peeled and cut in half
1 celery stalk, cut in half, with leaves
1 garlic clove, smashed
½ onion, quartered
1 bay leaf
2 thyme sprigs
1 teaspoon black peppercorns

1 Preheat the oven to 425°F.

2 Place the bones in a roasting pan and roast for 45 minutes, until well browned. Transfer the bones to a large, heavy soup pot. Add the carrot, celery, garlic, onion, bay leaf, thyme, peppercorns, and 4 quarts water. Bring to a boil over high heat, then reduce the heat to medium-low and simmer, partially covered, for at least 8 hours, adding water as needed to keep the bones submerged.

3 Use a fine-mesh sieve to strain the broth. Discard the solids and refrigerate the stock overnight. The next day, remove and discard the layer of fat that has formed on the top of the stock. Reduce the stock, or add water, if need be, to maintain 1 quart. Pour the stock into jars and refrigerate for up to 1 week, or freeze for up to 6 months.

Lamb

Caroline Randall Williams's grandmother Joan didn't hand down china or jewelry when she passed away. But she left her collection of more than one thousand cookbooks, a source of pride and empowerment that was "a central aspect of her identity," Caroline and her mother, Alice Randall, passionately explained in *Soul Food Love: Healthy Recipes Inspired by One Hundred Years of Cooking in a Black Family*.

"While remaining rooted to black Southern country cooking, hard-times-in-Harlem cuisine, and the fare of intellectual black expatriates abroad," the recipes in the cookbook collection reveal one woman's connection to kitchens around the world. From these, the mother-daughter duo crafted a healthier approach to soul cooking.

Their roast leg of lamb is accented with garlic and fresh herbs—a simplified reworking of an Easter classic that African Americans adapted from barbecued mutton. Reading that recipe, and recalling the diverse, global perspectives in Caroline's cookbook collection, had me thinking about the appropriateness of lamb on the African American table. Lamb spans so many traditions on the African continent: from a chunky stew imbued with Moroccan spices, or cooked with okra and tomatoes in Egypt, to lamb chops simmered with garlic-pepper-laced tomato gravy in Ghana, to the many lamb curries from South Africa and throughout the Caribbean. American adaptations in this canon are right where they belong.

ROAST LEG OF LAMB WITH ROSEMARY

SERVES 8 TO 10

Edna Lewis's third cookbook, *In Pursuit of Flavor*, is not as popular as her other titles, but I love it. She describes her secret for coaxing the natural goodness from the flavorful cut of roasted lamb leg she portrayed as "exotic": "I rub the outside of the tied-up leg with butter to help it brown, to add flavor, and to keep it from drying out. Deglaze the pan with less than 1 tablespoon of water and scrape up all the browned bits and juices. Turn into a warm bowl and pass with the slices of lamb after it is carved," with small white roasted potatoes and fresh asparagus. Heavenly.

Oil, for the roasting pan

1 (4- to 5-pound) trimmed boneless leg of
    lamb, butterflied

4 tablespoons olive oil

¼ cup minced fresh flat-leaf parsley,
    plus 4 sprigs

2 tablespoons minced fresh rosemary,
    plus 4 sprigs

6 garlic cloves, minced

1 tablespoon salt, or to taste

1 teaspoon black pepper

20 small red potatoes, peeled and quartered

1 Preheat the oven to 375°F. Lightly grease a large roasting pan with oil.

2 Place the leg of lamb on a board. Open the lamb and place it fat side down. Pat dry with paper towels, if needed. Drizzle the lamb with 2 tablespoons of the olive oil. In a small bowl, combine the minced parsley, minced rosemary, and garlic. Rub over the entire surface of the lamb. Season with 1½ teaspoons of the salt and ½ teaspoon of the pepper. Roll up the lamb into as tight a cylinder as you can, and tie it with kitchen twine at 1-inch intervals so the meat holds its shape. Rub the lamb with the remaining 2 tablespoons oil, and season with the remaining 1½ teaspoons salt and ½ teaspoon pepper.

3 Place the herb sprigs in the bottom of the roasting pan. Arrange the potatoes on top of the herbs. Add the lamb, resting it on the potatoes so they will be flavored with its juices, and roast until a meat thermometer inserted into the center of the meat registers 130°F for medium-rare or 140°F for medium, 1 to 1½ hours.

4 Transfer the roast to a carving board, tent with foil, and let rest for 10 minutes. Strain the pan juices into a cup. Let sit or refrigerate until the fat rises to the top, then skim off fat. Remove and discard the twine, and thinly slice the roast. Surround the lamb with roasted potatoes, drizzle with the juices, and serve.

ROAST SHOULDER OR LEG OF MUTTON STUFFED

Hotel Keepers, Head Waiters, and Housekeepers' Guide,
Tunis G. Campbell, 1848

Stuff a leg of mutton with mutton-suet, salt, pepper, nutmeg, grated bread, and yolks of eggs; then stick it all over with cloves, and roast it; when it is about half done cut off some of the under side of the fleshy end in little bits; put those into a pipkin with a pint of oysters, liquor and all, a little salt and mace, and half a pint of hot water; stew them till half the liquor is wasted, then put in a piece of butter rolled in flour, shake all together, and when the mutton is done enough take it up; pour the sauce over it, and send it to table.

BRAISED LAMB SHANKS WITH PEANUT SAUCE
(MAFÉ)

SERVES 4 TO 6

Chef Pierre Thiam's spectacular cookbook *Senegal: Modern Senegalese Recipes from the Source to the Bowl* is breathtakingly beautiful, with modern interpretations for old-world standards like this lamb shank mafé. Traditionally a braise given depth with tomato paste and peanut butter, it bears resemblance to the West African Groundnut Stew (page 140), but is richer.

For a fresh finish, this recipe concludes with a punch from a condiment that combines Senegalese *rof,* a parsley stuffing for fish, with Italian gremolata, a topping made traditionally with herbs, lemon zest, and garlic.

Serve this with rice pilaf, cooked couscous, or fonio, a West African "superfood" grain.

2 tablespoons tomato paste

4 cups Beef Stock (page 210)

1 cup creamy peanut butter

4 lamb shanks, about 2 pounds total

1½ teaspoons salt

¾ teaspoon black pepper

2 tablespoons vegetable or olive oil

2 cups thinly sliced onions

3 garlic cloves, minced

½ to 1 teaspoon minced Scotch bonnet pepper, to taste

1 teaspoon dried thyme

2 large bay leaves

2 carrots, peeled and cut in quarters

Rof Gremolata (recipe follows), for serving

Hot cooked rice, couscous, or fonio, for serving

1 In a small bowl, combine the tomato paste with ¼ cup of the stock. Stir the peanut butter into the remaining stock. Set both mixtures aside.

2 Place the shanks on a board and pat dry with paper towels. Season with ½ teaspoon salt and ¼ teaspoon black pepper. In a Dutch oven, heat the oil over medium-high heat until shimmering, then add the shanks and cook until evenly browned on all sides, about 15 minutes total. Work in batches if necessary. Do not crowd the pan.

3 Remove the shanks to a platter and set aside. Add the onions to the pan and brown, stirring occasionally, about 10 minutes. Add the garlic, chile pepper, and thyme and cook for 30 seconds. Reduce the heat to low, add the tomato paste mixture to the onions, and cook 7 to 10 minutes, until the broth is completely evaporated.

4 Stir in the peanut butter-stock mixture, bay leaves, and carrots. Season with the remaining 1 teaspoon salt and ½ teaspoon black pepper. Return the lamb and any juices that have collected on the platter to the pan. Bring the pot to a boil, then reduce heat to low and simmer, covered, 1 hour.

5 Uncover, increase the heat to medium, and simmer 30 minutes more to allow the gravy to thicken and the meat to become fork-tender. If necessary, let it cook longer, until the shanks are very tender. Add a little more stock or water if doing so, to prevent the sauce from getting too thick. Taste and adjust seasonings.

6 Garnish with a spoonful of rof gremolata, and serve with rice, couscous, or fonio.

ROF GREMOLATA

MAKES ABOUT 1 CUP

½ cup minced fresh parsley

3 green onions, minced

2 garlic cloves, minced

½ Scotch bonnet pepper, seeded and minced,
   or to taste

Grated zest of 1 lemon

Salt and pepper

In a small bowl, combine the parsley,
onions, garlic, chile pepper, and lemon
zest. Season to taste with salt and pepper.
Refrigerate up to 1 week, tightly covered.

LAMB CURRY

SERVES 4

South African curries are a blend of Malay and Indian influences. To make a good curry, *The Africa News Cookbook* insists, the cook must quickly sauté onions in ghee (clarified butter) until golden, then simmer together lamb cubes, a fragrant spice blend, and tomatoes until the flavors are well married. Curry traveled to the Caribbean, where gamey mutton or goat became a Jamaican favorite; in the French islands, lamb is the meat of choice. Stateside, home cooks have stewed lamb chunks with allspice, cloves, and vegetables.

I weaved together aspects of three dishes for this lamb curry to make it my own: toasting the spices and creating a layer of sweetness from green apples. My inspiration for this recipe comes from Alexander Smalls and J. J. Johnson's *Between Harlem and Heaven: Afro-Asian-American Cooking for Big Nights, Weeknights, and Every Day;* elements of African technique are courtesy of Marcus Samuelsson's *The Soul of a New Cuisine*; and the splash of rum and lime juice added just before serving, to complement the mild spice, was something I discovered in Dunston Harris's *Island Cooking: Recipes from the Caribbean.*

2 pounds lamb shoulder or leg, cut into 1-inch cubes
Salt and black pepper
2 tablespoons olive or vegetable oil
2 tablespoons butter
1 cup coarsely chopped onions
2 tablespoons minced green bell pepper
2 tablespoons minced celery
2 teaspoons minced garlic
2 tablespoons curry powder, to taste
1 tablespoon tomato paste

1½ cups diced tomatoes
2 cups Chicken Stock (page 133) or water
1 bay leaf
2 medium green apples, peeled and cubed
2 tablespoons rum (optional)
1 tablespoon fresh lime juice (optional)
Freshly cooked rice

1 Place the lamb on a platter and pat dry with paper towels. Season all over with 1½ teaspoons salt and ½ teaspoon pepper. Let stand for 2 hours.

2 In a large Dutch oven or deep skillet, heat the oil over medium-high heat until sizzling. Working in batches to avoid crowding the pan, add the lamb and sear until browned and crusty, turning to cook on all sides, 5 to 8 minutes. Use a slotted spoon to remove the lamb to a plate.

3 Add the butter to the pan and sauté the onions, bell pepper, celery, and garlic until the onion is translucent, about 5 minutes. Sprinkle the curry powder over the vegetables and cook, stirring constantly, until fragrant, about 30 seconds. Return the lamb to the pan with the tomato paste, tomatoes, chicken stock, and bay leaf.

4 Reduce the heat to medium-low, cover, and simmer until the meat is tender and the sauce is thick, about 1½ hours. Add the apples to the pan during the last 30 minutes of cooking time. Remove and discard the bay leaf. Stir in the rum and lime juice, if using, and heat for 1 minute. Serve with rice.

Barbecue and Roast Pork

"The thirty-thousand year old practice of cooking over an open fire continues to be an integral part of Africa's culinary heritage," Heidi Haughy Cusick explained in *Soul and Spice: African Cooking in the Americas*. "In Togo today, street vendors cook *michui*, spicy skewered fish and meat, over charcoal. In Mali, whole goats are still ceremoniously roasted for weddings and other special occasions. Sidewalk vendors from West Africa to the Caribbean grill plantains to eat as a snack or with spicy grilled meats or stews; and in Bahia they carry small lighted charcoal-filled drums with grates on top for cooking fresh cheese."

But when we think of American barbecue, images of well-seasoned ribs, brisket, whole hog, and poultry slow-roasted and smoked over hardwood charcoal replace Old World techniques that grilled quickly over an open flame. The practice is attributed to the Taino, an Arawak tribe in the West Indies, who preserved food by smoke-drying it over a pit fire on a wooden grate called a barbacoa. Spanish explorers brought the device and the word to the American Southeast during the early sixteenth century. By 1709, the word "barbecue" was in use in America; it had taken on the implications of a social gathering by 1733; and George Washington mentioned attending a barbecue in his journal in 1769, according to *The Encyclopedia of American Food & Drink*.

The enslaved barbecued whole suckling pigs, called shoats, during hog killing time. Mutton and rabbits went into the pit to celebrate special occasions. And when the meat on the grill was of poor quality, they fashioned a barbecue sauce from spicy red peppers mixed with vinegar to mask the taste. After the Civil War, barbecuing became an integral part of Juneteenth celebrations.

I love the story of Bluebill Yancey, one of those "pit artists" whose legendary barbecue was a fixture of Mississippi politics during the mid-1930s. Candidates hired him often because his barbecue brought "dead enemies" together to chat "as if food and drink have eradicated all differences," a WPA interviewer recalled. Yancey was eccentric, too. He cooked according to the stages of the moon, believed that the presence of women stopped the meat from breathing freely, used chicken fat in his mop sauce, and paced "ceaselessly—up one side to turn the meat, down the other to baste it"—all night long. Yancey's secret sauce of vinegar, bay leaves, lemon, pickling spices, onion, and generous amounts of garlic and paprika is a throwback to the plantation legacy that miraculously transformed simple meats into an American tradition.

This legacy was remembered by pitmaster Wesley Jones. In the Slave Narratives, Jones described a similar barbecue ritual on a South Carolina farm: "Night befo' dem barbecues. I used to stay up all night a-cooking and basting de meats wid barbecue sass. It made of vinegar, black and red pepper, salt, butter, a little sage, coriander, basil, onion, and garlic. Some folks drop a little sugar in it. On a long pronged stick I wraps a soft rag or cotton fer a swab, and all de night long I swabs dat meat 'till it drip into de fire. Dem drippings change de smoke into seasoned fumes dat smoke de meat. We turn de meat over and swab it dat way all night long 'till it ooze seasoning and bake all through."

Barbecue—and its cousin, roast pork—is one of those everlasting dishes: a mainstay on our menus, whether it's a dish of pulled or chopped pork roast, spareribs, or baby backs nursed in a ten-foot pit with wire mesh stretched over smoldering hot coals. From Puerto Rican–seasoned back bones to shoulder roasts rubbed with Creole spices or marinated in Jamaican jerk seasonings and citrus juice, our barbecue is kissed with a touch of the African diaspora.

CARIBBEAN ROAST PORK

SERVES 6 TO 8

The power behind the dish Arturo Schomburg called "West Indies pork" is the spice-blending prowess of cooks in the Dominican Republic, Puerto Rico, and Jamaica. This roast calls on beloved island flavors like ginger, allspice, and rum and was influenced by recipes from both photographer/cookbook author John Pinderhughes and superstar singer/cookbook author Kelis.

1 (4- to 5-pound) bone-in pork shoulder
4 garlic cloves, thinly sliced, plus 2 teaspoons minced garlic
1 tablespoon salt
1 teaspoon garlic powder
1 teaspoon onion powder
1 teaspoon ground coriander
1 teaspoon paprika
1 teaspoon black pepper
1½ teaspoons ground allspice
1½ teaspoons ground ginger
½ cup packed light brown sugar
¼ cup dark rum
1 teaspoon fresh lime juice

1 Place the pork on a board and pat dry with paper towels, if needed. Place the pork on a rack in a heavy roasting pan. Using the tip of a sharp knife, make 1-inch-deep incisions all over the surface of the roast. Insert the garlic slices into the slits.

2 In a small bowl, combine the salt, garlic powder, onion powder, coriander, paprika, pepper, and 1 teaspoon each of the allspice and ginger. Use your fingers to press the rub into the roast to completely coat it on all sides. Let rest for 30 minutes or refrigerate, covered, up to 24 hours. (If refrigerated, let stand at room temperature 1 hour before roasting.)

3 Preheat the oven to 350°F.

4 Carefully pour about 1 cup water into the bottom of the roasting pan. Set a rack in the roasting pan and the pork on the rack. Cover with foil. Roast for 3 hours, basting every 45 minutes.

5 Meanwhile, in a small bowl, combine the brown sugar, rum, lime juice, minced garlic, and remaining ½ teaspoon each of the allspice and ginger. Uncover the roast. Spread the paste over the meat and return it to the oven. Continue to roast until the outside is nicely browned, about 1½ hours, until the internal temperature reaches 185°F and the paste is sealed onto the roast. Let rest 10 minutes before slicing.

PICKLED ROAST PIG

A Domestic Cook Book, Malinda Russell, 1866

Dress and stuff your pig, put it into a dripping pan and put it baking; take one pint of strong vinegar, Madeira wine, or currant wine, put into a basin with half lb butter; boil together; stir in a little batter made of flour and water; baste the meat with this quite often until done.

BARBECUED PORK SHOULDER

SERVES 8 TO 10

Heidi Haughy Cusick celebrated the tastes and textures of the American South, plus Brazilian, Creole, and Caribbean cuisines, in *Soul and Spice: African Cooking in the Americas*. She discovered a smoky sandwich meat with a recipe much like this one in Memphis, Tennessee, that recalls the mop sauces pitmasters have used for generations to deeply infuse meat with flavor during the long, slow cooking process. It is boldly spiced, moist, and absolutely delicious with its pairing of dark, sweet, mysterious molasses barbecue sauce.

1 (4- to 5-pound) pork shoulder, bone-in or
   boneless
1 tablespoon garlic powder
1 tablespoon salt, or to taste
1 teaspoon black pepper
1 teaspoon cayenne pepper
1 teaspoon smoked paprika
¼ cup vegetable oil
Molasses Barbecue Sauce (recipe follows),
   for serving

1 Place the pork on a board and pat it dry with paper towels. In a large zip-top plastic bag, combine the garlic powder, salt, black pepper, cayenne, smoked paprika, and oil. Add the pork to the bag, close the bag, and turn it over several times to thoroughly coat the pork with the spice paste. Refrigerate for at least 8 hours, or overnight.

2 Prepare a charcoal fire on one side of a barbecue grill or heat one side of a gas grill. When the temperature inside the grill is 250°F, place the pork on the cooler side of the grill, away from the heat. Cover the grill and grill the pork, turning occasionally,

until a meat thermometer inserted in the center of the meat reaches 185°F, 3 to 4 hours. Add additional wood or coals as needed to maintain the temperature at 250°F. (Use smoke chips, if desired, according to manufacturer's directions, if using a gas grill.) Remove the pork to a board and let stand for 10 minutes. Use a sharp knife to slice the pork across the grain and chop. Or, when cool enough to handle, use a fork to pull the pork into shreds. Serve with Molasses Barbecue Sauce.

MOLASSES BARBECUE SAUCE

MAKES ABOUT 2½ CUPS

2 tablespoons butter
1 garlic clove, minced
2 tablespoons minced onion
1⅓ cups ketchup
¼ cup cider vinegar
¼ cup molasses
1 tablespoon Worcestershire sauce
1 tablespoon fresh lemon juice
2 tablespoons brown sugar
2 teaspoons yellow mustard
½ teaspoon smoked paprika
½ teaspoon cayenne pepper
½ teaspoon salt
¼ teaspoon black pepper
¼ teaspoon chili powder

In a saucepan, heat the butter until sizzling. Add the garlic and onion and cook over medium-low heat until tender, about 2 minutes. Stir in ½ cup water, the ketchup, vinegar, molasses, Worcestershire sauce, lemon juice, brown sugar, mustard, smoked paprika, cayenne, salt, black pepper, and chili powder. Bring to a boil over medium-high heat, then reduce the heat to a gentle simmer, cover, and cook for 20 minutes to allow the flavors to mingle.

Ribs

When the intoxicating perfume of hardwood is as thick as coastal fog, you will have arrived at Rodney Scott's Whole Hog BBQ in Charleston. The James Beard Award–winning pitmaster, originally from Hemingway, South Carolina, started slow-smoking pork when he was just eleven years old, on hog pits his family built themselves behind a convenience store located on an old highway that ran through town. Scott descends from a tradition perfected by black men who have been cooking whole hogs over glowing coals to celebrate hog butcherings, summer holidays, and family reunions since slavery days.

For many, that image is the essence of the barbecue tradition, and these same people may not appreciate the baked ribs with sauce I'm suggesting here as an alternative to pit barbecue—for when the pit is just too far away, or it's too cold outside, or you just can't get your hands on a whole pig. For the fully committed, or if you are just plain curious about the long, slow process, the Scott family's recipe is presented on page 226. And for the rest of us, I recommend the two rib recipes that follow; they are divine.

JAMAICAN JERK RIBS
WITH PINEAPPLE-MANGO SALSA

SERVES 4

Kelis once sang, "My milkshake brings all the boys to the yard"; now she's pumping out culinary jams as a classically trained chef, author, and restaurant owner. In one of her many new-fashioned approaches, she massages pork ribs with classic jerk seasonings, then bastes them with a sweet-hot sauce while they bake. Found all along the highway between Montego Bay and Ocho Rios, jerk pork was created by escaped slaves, called maroons, who survived in the Jamaican mountains on a highly spiced delicacy of wild boar slow-cooked over a fire of green allspice branches. The list of savory jerk spices and fragrant herbs is long, traced to the West and Central African custom of smoking and drying highly-seasoned bush (wild game) meats, but that is what makes the dish so appealing.

Serve these ribs as I do, with a cooling side of Pineapple-Mango Salsa, and you'll be singing, "Damn right, it's better than yours," too. The explosive contrast between the tropical fruit and the high spice on the meat is superb.

6 pounds pork spareribs, St. Louis-style, or
    baby back ribs
Jerk Rub (recipe follows)
¼ cup packed brown sugar
½ cup cider vinegar
½ cup fresh orange juice
2 tablespoons fresh lime juice
2 tablespoons olive oil
1 to 2 minced Scotch bonnet peppers, to taste
1 cup minced onion
½ cup minced green bell pepper
4 garlic cloves, peeled but whole
¼ cup molasses
¼ cup soy sauce
Pineapple-Mango Salsa (recipe follows),
    for serving

1 Place the ribs on a board and pat dry with paper towels, if needed. Use your fingers to press the jerk rub into the ribs to completely coat. Place the ribs, bone side down, in 2 large roasting pans. Refrigerate for at least 1 hour or overnight.

2 Preheat the oven to 400°F.

3 Cover the pans tightly with foil and roast 1½ hours, switching the pans from the top to the bottom rack halfway through the cooking time.

4 Meanwhile, in a blender or a food processor, combine the brown sugar, vinegar, orange juice, lime juice, olive oil, chile pepper, onion, bell pepper, garlic, molasses, and soy sauce. Process until smooth. Transfer the mixture to a medium saucepan and bring to a boil over high heat. Reduce the heat to medium and simmer until the jerk sauce is darkened in color, 10 to 15 minutes.

5 Remove the ribs from the oven. Uncover, and use a basting brush or the back of a spoon to coat the ribs evenly with the jerk sauce. Cook, uncovered, basting with the sauce every 5 minutes, until the ribs are well glazed and sticky, about 15 minutes more. Serve with pineapple-mango salsa and the remaining jerk sauce on the side.

RECIPE CONTINUES

JERK RUB

Try this exceptional seasoning mix on chicken as well as ribs and grill over hardwood coals.

1 tablespoon ground allspice
½ teaspoon ground cinnamon
½ teaspoon ground or freshly grated nutmeg
1 teaspoon ground sage
2 tablespoons garlic powder
4 teaspoons salt, or to taste
1 teaspoon black pepper
1 teaspoon cayenne pepper
1 teaspoon smoked paprika

In a small bowl, combine the allspice, cinnamon, nutmeg, sage, garlic powder, salt, black pepper, cayenne, and paprika.

PINEAPPLE-MANGO SALSA

MAKES ABOUT 3½ CUPS

2 cups finely diced pineapple
1 cup chopped fresh mango
¼ cup minced red bell pepper
¼ cup minced red onion
1 tablespoon chopped fresh cilantro
½ hot chile pepper, minced, to taste
1 small garlic clove, minced
¼ cup fresh lime juice
¼ cup vegetable oil
¼ teaspoon salt

In a small bowl, combine the pineapple, mango, bell pepper, onion, cilantro, chile pepper, and garlic. Stir in the lime juice, oil, and salt. Let stand at room temperature at least 1 hour to allow the flavors to mingle. May be refrigerated, but bring to room temperature to serve.

THE SCOTT FAMILY'S
SOUTH CAROLINA WHOLE HOG

Smokestack Lightning: Adventures in the Heart of Barbecue Country,
Lolis Eric Elie, 1996

1 hog, 80 to 130 pounds, dressed and butterflied
Vinegar and water
Salt, black pepper, and red pepper

Burn oak or another hard wood down to coals. Shovel the coals into the pit in such a way as to form a square roughly the size of the butterflied hog. Put the hog on the grill. Cook it skin side up [basting with a sop sauce of vinegar, water, salt and pepper], adding coals to the pit approximately every 25 to 30 minutes and adding wood to the coal fire as needed. Cook skin side up for approximately 4 to 6 hours. When the skin has begun to curl, it's time to turn the hog over. Once the hog is on the pit skin side down, spread coals under the entire body, rather than in a square. Pour sauce into the body of the hog as the skin is crisping. Once the skin is crisp, remove the hog from the fire and serve.

OVEN-BAKED RIBS
WITH COLA BARBECUE SAUCE

SERVES 8

Activist. Comedian. Drummer. Carpenter. A man of many talents and skills, Bobby Seale cofounded the Black Panther Party, initiating community-based food service programs such as free breakfast for schoolchildren.

He had a love of hickory-smoked meat. His Uncle Tom taught him the nuanced skills of a Texas barbecue pitmaster: how to place the wood in the pit and burn it down and spread the coals, the importance of having a pit fire without any flames, and a secret tenderizing method—meat dunked into a washtub of watery drippings that he calls "base" or "baste-marinade." The base is also mopped onto the meat throughout the pit-smoking process as it browns.

With a helping hand from Seale and Uncle Tom's smoky baste-marinade, in this dish I re-created the "fascinating aroma and taste" of the pit, but in the oven.

2 (4-pound) slabs pork spareribs,
   St. Louis-style
1½ teaspoons salt
1 teaspoon black pepper
1 teaspoon garlic powder
1 teaspoon onion powder
1 teaspoon smoked or sweet paprika
½ teaspoon celery salt
Baste-Marinade (recipe follows)
2 cups Cola Barbecue Sauce (recipe follows)

1 Place the spareribs on a board and pat dry with paper towels. In a small bowl, combine the salt, pepper, garlic powder, onion powder, paprika, and celery salt. Use your fingers to press the seasoning mixture into the ribs to completely coat on all sides. Let stand for 1 hour.

2 Preheat the oven broiler. Line 2 large roasting pans with foil.

3 Place the ribs in the roasting pans and broil one pan at a time, 4 to 6 inches below the heat, until browned, 3 to 5 minutes. Turn the ribs over and sear on the other side. Drain any fat that accumulates in the pan, if needed. Turn off the broiler and set the oven temperature to 375°F. Pour ¾ cup of the baste-marinade over each slab of the ribs and cover carefully but tightly with foil. Bake for 1 hour, switching the pans from the top to the bottom rack and basting with some additional marinade after 30 minutes.

4 Uncover the ribs, brush with the cola barbecue sauce, and bake, basting with the sauce every 5 minutes, until the ribs are well browned and the sauce is sticky, about 30 minutes more. When the ribs are cool enough to handle, use a sharp knife to cut the slabs between the bones. Serve the bones with any remaining barbecue sauce on the side.

RECIPE CONTINUES

BASTE-MARINADE

MAKES ABOUT 2 CUPS

1 lemon

5 sprigs parsley

⅓ cup chopped onion

¼ cup chopped red or green bell pepper

2 tablespoons chopped green onions

⅓ cup chopped celery

1 teaspoon minced Scotch bonnet or other chile pepper, or to taste

1 small garlic clove, minced

⅛ teaspoon black pepper

½ teaspoon salt

¼ teaspoon onion salt

¼ teaspoon garlic salt

1 small bay leaf

¼ cup apple juice

3 tablespoons cider vinegar

2 tablespoons liquid hickory smoke

2 tablespoons Worcestershire sauce

1 With a sharp knife or vegetable peeler, carefully strip off the yellow zest from the lemon, then juice the lemon and set aside. Trim the stems from the parsley and reserve the leaves for another use.

2 In a large saucepan, combine 2 cups water, the parsley stems, lemon zest, onion, bell pepper, green onions, celery, chile pepper, garlic, black pepper, salt, onion salt, garlic salt, and bay leaf. Bring to a boil, then reduce the heat to a gentle simmer, and cook for 30 minutes, until broth is well-seasoned and vegetables are very tender. Remove from the heat and let cool.

3 Strain the marinade through a fine-mesh sieve and return to the saucepan. Stir in the reserved lemon juice, the apple juice, vinegar, liquid smoke, and Worcestershire sauce. Bring to a boil, then reduce the heat, cover, and simmer over medium-low heat to blend the flavors, 7 to 10 minutes. Remove from the heat. Cool to room temperature. Use immediately or refrigerate, covered, up to a week.

COLA BARBECUE SAUCE

MAKES ABOUT 1½ CUPS

2 tablespoons butter

1¼ cups ketchup

3 tablespoons brown sugar

6 tablespoons cider vinegar

¼ cup Worcestershire sauce

¼ teaspoon cayenne pepper

¼ teaspoon salt

¾ teaspoon paprika

2 teaspoons liquid hickory smoke

1 cup cola

In a small saucepan, combine the butter, ketchup, brown sugar, vinegar, Worcestershire sauce, cayenne, salt, paprika, and liquid smoke. Bring to a boil, then reduce the heat to simmer. Add the cola, cover, leaving a little vent for steam, and simmer very gently, stirring occasionally, until thick enough to cling to a spoon, about 1 hour.

BAKED HAM GLAZED WITH CHAMPAGNE

SERVES 15

To many descendants of America's servant class, who at hog killing time helped smoke the very best parts of the pig or prepared those cuts for the planter's table, a succulent, golden-brown ham is more than sustenance; it is the centerpiece whenever special occasions are celebrated.

We see this over and over throughout the history of black foodways. A succulent ham, studded with cloves and roasted with a brown sugar-mustard glaze, is part of the food tradition at The Big Quarterly, a religious celebration of the Africa Union Church, begun in 1814 in Wilmington, Delaware. Cooking school teacher Sarah Helen Mahammitt taught students to boil ham the old-fashioned way and offered a modern approach—baking ham with wine—in her 1939 cookbook. A decade later, *Ebony* food editor Freda DeKnight invited readers to bake ham with sherry or port, and to place tiny pieces of garlic in the fat covering the ham for a zesty, pungent taste. Leonard Roberts learned the craft of French cooking from his father, a railway and hotel chef, and wrote of his Frenchified soul cooking in *The Negro Chef Cookbook* in 1969; he glazed his ham with Champagne to make it elegant, and I adapt his recipe here.

1 (9- to 10-pound) bone-in smoked ham
2½ cups packed brown sugar
2 (750 ml) bottles extra-dry Champagne or
    other sparkling wine
3 tablespoons honey or maple syrup
2 tablespoons Dijon mustard
1½ teaspoons ground ginger
Pineapple slices, for serving (optional)

1 Preheat the oven to 325°F. Line a roasting pan with foil and place a rack on top of the foil.

2 Place the ham on the rack, fat side up. Using a sharp knife, score the fat across the top in a crisscross pattern, cutting just through the fat to the meat. Spoon 1 cup of the brown sugar over the top of the ham, pressing with your fingers or the back of a spoon. Carefully pour 1 bottle of Champagne over the ham and the brown sugar. Cover the ham with foil and bake for 2 hours.

3 Meanwhile, in a saucepan, combine the remaining bottle of Champagne, 1½ cups brown sugar, the honey, mustard, and ginger. Bring to a boil, then reduce the heat and simmer, uncovered, until the glaze thickens, about 15 minutes.

4 Remove the ham from the oven and spoon half of the glaze on top. Keep the remaining glaze warm over low heat. Return the ham to the oven and bake, basting with the remaining glaze every 15 minutes, until a meat thermometer inserted in the ham registers 145°F, 1 hour longer or more. Tent with foil and let stand for 15 minutes before serving. Garnish with pineapple slices, if you'd like.

SMOTHERED PORK CHOPS

A Good Heart and a Light Hand: Ruth L. Gaskins'
Collection of Traditional Negro Recipes,
Ruth L. Gaskins, 1968

Dip the chops in a mixture of flour, salt and pepper.
Have ¼ inch of shortening very hot, but not smoking,
in an iron skillet. Fry, uncovered, on both sides until
they are brown and crispy. Chops should be fried
quickly but thoroughly by keeping the shortening
hot and the heat around medium.

PORK CHOPS
WITH RICH CAPER-LEMON SAUCE
SERVES 4

Chef Nathaniel Burton learned about the masters of Creole and French culinary classics—including Escoffier—while clearing tables as a busboy at the Hotel New Orleans. He went on to refine his skills at the Hotel Pontchartrain and Broussard's before teaching the Culinary Institute of America's apprentice cooks. He told the fascinating life stories and shared imaginative recipes from some of Louisiana's best chefs in *Creole Feast: Fifteen Master Chefs of New Orleans Reveal Their Secrets.*

To update the many homestyle dishes black cooks recorded in their books, I turned to Burton's collection of recipes. Caper sauce caught my eye. Burton's is a classic, roux-based gravy with capers and vinegar added for punch. I exchanged his lamb with bone-in pork loin chops because the bits of fat near the bone make the meat flavorful and juicy. I replaced the vinegar with lemon juice and zest, as suggested in *B. Smith Cooks Southern-Style,* and simmered stock and butter together for a velvety-smooth emulsion. I love this sauce so much that I also serve it on pan-roasted veal chops.

4 bone-in pork loin chops (about 8 ounces each)
1 teaspoon salt, plus more to taste
¼ teaspoon black pepper, plus more to taste
½ teaspoon dried thyme
2 tablespoons olive oil
4 tablespoons (½ stick) butter, at room temperature
1 teaspoon minced garlic
1 tablespoon minced shallot
1½ teaspoons all-purpose flour
1 cup white wine
1½ cups Chicken Stock (page 133)
2 tablespoons capers, drained
1 teaspoon freshly grated lemon zest
2 tablespoons fresh lemon juice
¼ teaspoon hot pepper sauce (optional)
2 tablespoons minced fresh parsley

1 Preheat the oven to 400°F.

2 Place the chops on a board and pat dry with paper towels. Season with the salt, pepper, and thyme, rubbing with your fingers to press the seasonings into the meat. In a large ovenproof skillet, heat the oil over medium-high heat until shimmering. Add the chops and cook until well browned, 3 to 4 minutes per side. Transfer the skillet to the oven and roast until a meat thermometer inserted in the chops registers 145°F, 5 to 7 minutes, depending upon the thickness. Remove the chops from the oven, transfer to a plate, and cover to keep warm. Drain off and discard the fat.

3 In the same skillet, heat 2 tablespoons of the butter until sizzling. Add the garlic and shallot and sauté until tender, about 1 minute. Sprinkle in the flour and cook for 2 minutes more. Whisk in the wine and chicken stock and bring to a boil over high heat, scraping up the browned bits in the bottom of the pan. Reduce the heat to medium-high and cook, uncovered, until the liquid is reduced by half, about 5 minutes. Stir in the capers, lemon zest, lemon juice, hot pepper sauce (if using), and parsley and simmer 1 to 2 minutes more. Add the remaining 2 tablespoons butter to the pan ½ tablespoon at a time, shaking the pan between additions until the butter melts and the sauce looks smooth. Season to taste with salt and pepper. Pour the sauce over the pan-roasted chops and serve.

Stewed Chicken

Known as classic French fricassee, simmering meat in a rich cream gravy is a centuries-old French blueprint elaborated on by black cooks over time to create delicacies from tough or less desirable meats, fish, or poultry. Malinda Russell simmered catfish; Rufus Estes liked it with rabbit; Mrs. W. T. Hayes enriched squirrels; Jesse Lewis, who catered in Bay St. Louis, Mississippi, during the 1950s, preferred a meaty stewing hen.

From this foundation, stewed chicken, also known as chicken and gravy, is the basis of a wide range of entrées—from one-pot meals like pot pie to composed specialties, such as chicken with rice—and there are just about as many varieties for chicken and dumplings as there are cooks who prepare it. Just don't be confused by the name. These dishes are based on the same method as the comforting smothered chicken with onion gravy that Grandmother served on Sundays with cornbread dressing or macaroni and cheese.

CHICKEN AND DUMPLINGS

SERVES 4 TO 6

In her soul-era *Black American Cook Book*, Willa Mitchell recalled catching a wild hen, dressing and boiling it, then making "slick downs," a type of noodle to help a little bit of chicken go a long way. "This is called chicken and dumplings nowadays," she explained.

Now that chickens are easy to catch at the nearby supermarket, I brown chicken parts in butter, add a splash of white wine to the gravy for grandeur, and cut the dumplings into squares so each serving is as pretty as it is savory. For extra richness, stir warm cream into the gravy just before serving—a tip I learned from Jennifer Hill Booker's *Field Peas to Foie Gras: Southern Recipes with a French Accent*. She also saves time stirring leftover roasted chicken into this dish instead of cooking a whole bird.

1 (3½- to 4-pound) frying chicken, cut into pieces

2 teaspoons salt, plus more to taste

1 teaspoon black pepper

½ teaspoon paprika

⅓ cup all-purpose flour

¼ cup bacon drippings, vegetable or olive oil, or butter

1 cup chopped onions

½ cup (¼-inch) diced celery

½ cup (¼-inch) diced carrots

2 garlic cloves, minced

½ teaspoon dried thyme

4 to 6 cups Chicken Stock (page 133; see Note)

½ cup white wine (optional)

1 small bay leaf

Dumplings or Drop Dumplings (recipes follow)

1 cup heavy whipping cream or half-and-half

1 tablespoon minced fresh parsley

1 Place the chicken parts on a board and pat dry with paper towels. Season the chicken with the salt, pepper, and paprika. In a paper bag or shallow dish, coat the chicken parts with the flour. In a large heavy pot or Dutch oven, heat the bacon fat over medium-high until sizzling, and then reduce the heat to medium. Working in batches, add the chicken a few pieces at a time (do not crowd the pan) and cook until well browned, about 8 minutes per side, depending upon the size of the bird. Transfer the chicken to a plate. Add the onions, celery, carrots, garlic, and thyme to the pot and sauté until tender and fragrant, 6 to 8 minutes. Stir in the chicken stock (see Note) and wine (if using), scraping up any browned bits that are stuck to the bottom of the pan. Add salt to taste. Add the bay leaf and return the chicken to the pot. Bring to a boil, then reduce the heat to medium, cover, and simmer until the chicken is cooked through, about 40 minutes. Remove and discard the bay leaf.

2 Increase the heat to medium-high and heat until bubbles begin to appear around the sides of the pot. Drop the dumplings into the chicken and gravy. Reduce the heat to medium-low and simmer, covered, without opening the lid so the dumplings steam and become tender, about 15 minutes. They will resemble thick egg noodles.

3 Meanwhile, in a small saucepan, heat the cream. When the dumplings are cooked through, stir the warmed cream into the pot. Sprinkle with parsley before serving.

NOTE: Drop dumplings absorb more liquid than rolled. Start with 4 cups stock, then add ½ cup at a time during cooking, as needed, depending on how thick you want the gravy to be.

DUMPLINGS

MAKES 4 TO 6 SERVINGS

2 cups all-purpose flour
½ teaspoon baking powder
½ teaspoon salt
½ teaspoon dried thyme
2 tablespoons rendered chicken fat or shortening, chilled and cut into pieces
2 large eggs
½ cup whole milk

In a medium bowl, whisk together the flour, baking powder, salt, and thyme. Sprinkle the chicken fat over the flour mixture. Use your fingertips, a pastry blender, or two knives to cut the fat into the dry ingredients. In a small bowl or measuring cup, combine the eggs and milk. Use a fork to stir the egg mixture into the flour mixture, stirring just until a sticky dough forms. Turn the dough out onto a lightly floured work surface and knead for 5 minutes, until the dough is smooth and resembles pie dough. Chill the dough for 30 minutes. Lightly flour the work surface again. Roll the chilled dough out to a ¼-inch thickness, then cut into 1½-inch squares.

VARIATION

DROP DUMPLINGS

In the dough for the dumplings, stir together the flour, salt, and thyme and increase the baking powder to 2 teaspoons. Omit the chilled chicken fat. Make a well in the center of the dry ingredients. Stir in the eggs, milk, and 2 tablespoons melted shortening or oil until well mixed. When the chicken and gravy are bubbling in step 2 of the recipe, drop this batter onto the surface by the tablespoon. Proceed with recipe as directed.

HAND ROLLED DUMPLINGS

Black American Cook Book, Volume 2,
Willa Mitchell, 1977

To cook the slick downs, take one good dipper of water and a pinch of salt, add one good handful of flour to make your dough soft. Pat out until very thin. Pinch in strips, not so wide. Stretch them before laying them in the liquid broth. Cook until tender. This makes the broth thick as they cook. Add your cut up hen and serve hot.

BISCUIT-TOPPED CHICKEN POT PIE

SERVES 4 TO 6

Before chickens were plentiful, African American cooks stewed small game birds they hunted themselves, such as doves or pigeons, and served the creamy mixture on toast, with a simple biscuit, or with a pastry crust topping. Chicken pie was reserved for and especially beloved on Christmas Day.

In the 1950s, Clementine Hunter, a master of fine and culinary arts, included creamed chicken on toast, which she named *salmi a la yucca* in a small selection of extraordinary recipes, *Melrose Plantation Cookbook,* which she penned with Francois Mignon. Hunter layered Creole flavors in a roux-based gravy—smoky ham, aromatic vegetables of the Holy Trinity (onion, green pepper, and celery), consommé, cloves, and a blade of mace. She simmered it for an hour to develop a deep richness, then stirred in cooked chicken and served it with fried bread on the side.

Alternatively, my adaptation follows the time-honored preparation for pot pie, topping the silky chicken gravy with a crust of flaky biscuits. If Hunter's Creole style intrigues you, swap in chopped green bell peppers for half of the carrots and add a pinch of cloves and mace. Notice that the vegetables are diced, not coarsely chopped; they are prettier that way.

1 stick (4 ounces) butter, plus softened butter
    for the pan
1 cup diced onion
1 cup (¼-inch) diced carrots
½ cup (¼-inch) diced celery
1 tablespoon minced garlic (about 3 cloves)
½ cup all-purpose flour
2 cups Chicken Stock (page 133), warmed
2 cups whole milk, plus 1 tablespoon for
    the egg wash
1 teaspoon salt, or to taste

½ teaspoon black pepper
2 cups (¼-inch) diced potatoes, cooked
½ cup baby peas (optional)
2 cups diced cooked chicken
Pot Pie Biscuit Dough (recipe follows)
1 egg

1 Preheat the oven to 450°F. Generously butter a shallow 6-cup baking dish.

2 In a heavy saucepan, melt the stick of butter over medium heat until sizzling. Stir in the onion and cook for 2 minutes. Stir in the carrots, celery, and garlic and cook until the onions are translucent and starting to soften, about 2 minutes longer. Whisk in the flour. Cook and stir 3 to 5 minutes to make a blonde roux. Gradually whisk in the chicken stock, a few tablespoons at a time, stirring after each addition, until the mixture is smooth. Whisk in 2 cups of the milk and the salt and pepper. Cook until the mixture comes to a boil, then reduce heat to a simmer, stirring, until the mixture is thickened, 2 to 3 minutes.

3 Place the potatoes, peas (if using), and chicken in the baking dish. Pour in the sauce.

4 On a floured board, roll out the biscuit dough to a ¼-inch thickness. Cut with decorative or 2-inch round biscuit cutters. Place the biscuits on top of the filling, leaving ¼ inch between biscuits. (You can also roll the dough into one sheet and fit it over the baking dish; just be sure to cut 2 or 3 slits in the crust to let the steam escape.) In a small bowl, stir together the egg and 1 tablespoon milk. Lightly brush this egg wash all over the crust. Bake until the filling is bubbling and the crust is golden brown, 15 to 20 minutes. Serve immediately.

POT PIE
BISCUIT DOUGH

**MAKES ENOUGH FOR A
DOUBLE-CRUST PIE**

2 cups all-purpose flour
1 tablespoon baking powder
1 teaspoon salt
¼ cup shortening, cut into ½-inch
   pieces and chilled
⅔ cup cold whole milk

In a large bowl, combine the flour, baking
powder, and salt. Sprinkle the shortening
over the flour mixture. Using your
fingertips, a pastry blender, or two knives,
cut in the shortening until the mixture
resembles coarse crumbs. Use a fork to
stir in the milk. Turn the dough out onto a
floured board. Knead 5 to 10 seconds, just
until dough is smooth.

Fried Chicken

In the rural Virginia community of Gordonsville, Bella Winston was one of the "waiter carriers"—vendors who sold homemade dishes near the railroad platform to weary travelers during the post–Civil War years. Their menus were described by Psyche Williams-Forson in *Building Houses Out of Chicken Legs*: fried chicken, biscuits and breads, hard-boiled eggs, fruit pies, and "their famous hot coffee, which was sold in old-fashioned pots." These were enterprising, pioneering women, who had families, owned land, and used chicken to break down economic barriers and build lives for themselves, and who would influence future generations.

We have seen many iconic figures thrive in the waiter carriers' tradition. Possibly the most famous is André Prince Jeffries of Nashville, whose success relies upon a family recipe for chicken, made hot as hell with a hefty dose of ground red pepper. And, if you grew up in Los Angeles in the 1970s, Zelma Stennis's Golden Bird was the only place to get fried chicken outside of your own kitchen, unless you wanted your bird served alongside Roscoe's hot and crisp waffles. While testing recipes based on various Creole techniques, I was delighted to recognize the taste of my beloved Golden Bird in those employing a rich egg/cream batter and cracker or bread crumbs for crunch.

Then, of course, there is "regular" fried chicken, the kind I ate at home—basic floured chicken, shallow-fried in fat. Across the country, cooks added a little of their own soul to the old-school method of cooking with lard. Early on, my mom fried her chicken in hot shortening, then switched to vegetable oil for better health, whereas Edna Lewis dropped a quarter-pound of country ham—and butter—into the fat for chicken fried in her Virginia country style. Helen Dickerson, also from Virginia and who cooked at the historic Chalfonte Hotel in Cape May, New Jersey, divulged her special touch in *I Just Quit Stirrin' When the Tastin's Good: The Chalfonte Hotel Recipe Collection*. She added a thick slice of onion to the cooking oil for "soul food with its Sunday clothes on." Soul era cooks Pearl Bowser and Joan Eckstein fried their "gospel bird" in a mix of salt pork and butter. One of their contemporaries was a cookbook author named Jimmy Lee, who prided himself on his recipe, calling it "Jimmy's Best Fried Chicken." And it came with this declaration: "Ever hear that old white-haired chicken-cooking man who brags so much about that 'secret blend of 11 herbs and spices' he uses to fry chicken? I don't care much for making a mystery out of cooking."

So here, I present the recipes for my finest fried chickens.

HOMESTYLE FRIED CHICKEN

SERVES 6

There was a time when cooks considered a three-step pan-fry in shallow oil the best method for achieving mouthwatering chicken. They started the chicken with a short fry in a cast-iron skillet in hot oil to give the chicken a light browning. Next, the pieces were crowded into the pan, covered (sometimes with a glass lid), and steamed over medium-high heat to create moistness. At the end of cooking time, the cook turned the heat back to high to crisp the skin. It was a good process that author Kathy Starr said was the key to success in the art of "Southern" fried chicken in *The Soul of Southern Cooking*. Today we count on a deep-fry thermometer to help maintain the temperature for perfectly crisp, juicy chicken.

1 (3- to 4-pound) frying chicken, cut up into 8 or 10 pieces
2 teaspoons to 1 tablespoon salt, or to taste
½ teaspoon black pepper, or to taste
½ teaspoon cayenne pepper
1½ teaspoons paprika
1½ teaspoons garlic powder
¼ teaspoon celery salt (optional)
1 cup all-purpose flour, or as needed
Peanut or vegetable oil, for shallow-frying

1 Place the chicken on a board and pat dry with paper towels, if needed. Place the chicken in a large bowl and sprinkle with the salt, black pepper, cayenne, paprika, garlic powder, and celery salt. Use your hands to rub the seasonings well into the chicken, turning to coat evenly on all sides. Place the flour in a small paper bag. Add the chicken to the bag, a few pieces at a time, shaking to coat well. Use tongs to transfer the chicken pieces from the flour to a wire rack to rest while you flour the remaining pieces.

2 Pour about ¾ inch of oil into a heavy, deep cast-iron skillet and heat to 375°F over medium-high heat. (Use a thermometer, or if a small cube of bread sizzles immediately but does not burn when dropped into the pan, the oil is ready.) Adjust the heat to maintain this temperature. Working in batches of a few pieces at a time (do not crowd the skillet), add the chicken and cook until golden brown, about 12 minutes, turning once. Drain the chicken on paper towels and serve hot.

PRESSURE COOKER FRIED CHICKEN WITH 11 HERBS AND SPICES

Soul Food Cook Book, Jimmy Lee, 1970

1 [3- to 4-pound] frying chicken, cut up
Water
1 egg, beaten
A good pinch each: dried parsley, sage, rosemary, thyme, oregano, paprika, chili powder, celery salt, onion salt, garlic salt and black pepper
2 cups crushed cracker or dry bread crumbs
½ pound butter or bacon drippings

Place chicken in a pressure cooker with sufficient water to cook 20 minutes. Remove chicken pieces, drain, and allow to cool slightly. In a shallow bowl, mix egg and 1 tablespoon water. In a separate shallow bowl, blend together cracker crumbs, herbs and spices. Dip chicken pieces in egg, then roll in seasoned crumbs. In a large skillet, heat butter until sizzling. Fry chicken in hot butter until browned and crisp, turning once. Serve hot.

BUTTERMILK FRIED CHICKEN

SERVES 6

I once wrote that an informal review of the most influential Southern cookbooks in my collection revealed as many ways to fix fried chicken as there are cooks making the iconic dish, with innovations appearing in all time periods.

A lemonade bath before frying moistens the chicken legs served by chef Chris Scott, a finalist on Bravo's *Top Chef. Mojo criollo* infuses Cuban chicken with garlic, orange, and lemon juice. Evaporated milk gives Creole chicken a New Orleans flair. I learned from a far-reaching 1987 culinary opus, *The Black Gourmet Cookbook: A Unique Collection of Easy-to-Prepare, Appetizing, Black American, Creole, Caribbean, and African Cuisine,* that birds soaked overnight in a marinade of soy sauce, lime juice, and rum will transport you to the islands. There are salt water brines, pickle brines, vodka brines—chef Todd Richards's buttermilk brine leans into the hot chicken style, adding a dose of hot pepper sauce and red pepper flakes to the mix in *Soul: A Chef's Culinary Evolution in 150 Recipes.*

While all of these methods can produce wonderful chicken, through it all, marinating in buttermilk remains a classic go-to technique for succulent chicken; the acidic cultured milk tenderizes the meat. For the blazing taste of Prince's Hot Chicken, add a couple of tablespoons of hot pepper sauce to the buttermilk marinade and increase the cayenne pepper exponentially, depending upon your heat tolerance.

1 tablespoon salt, or to taste
¼ teaspoon celery salt
1 teaspoon black pepper, or to taste
½ teaspoon cayenne pepper
1 teaspoon paprika
½ teaspoon garlic powder
½ teaspoon onion powder
1 (3- to 4- pound) frying chicken, cut up
2 cups buttermilk
1 cup self-rising flour
Peanut or vegetable oil, for shallow-frying

1 In a small bowl, combine the salt, celery salt, black pepper, cayenne, paprika, garlic powder, and onion powder. Pat the chicken dry so the spices will stick, then place the chicken in a long, shallow glass baking dish. Rub half of the seasoning mixture onto the chicken pieces, turning to coat all sides. Carefully pour the buttermilk over the chicken and refrigerate, covered, at least 4 hours and overnight if possible, turning once or twice.

2 In a plastic or lunch-size brown paper bag, combine the flour and the remaining seasoning mixture. Remove the chicken from the buttermilk, shake off each piece to remove any excess, and place 1 piece at a time in the bag. Close the bag and shake well to coat evenly on all sides. Let the coated chicken rest on a wire rack while you repeat until all the chicken has been coated with the seasoned flour. (Discard the buttermilk.)

3 Pour about ¾ inch oil into a heavy, deep cast-iron skillet and heat to 375°F over medium-high heat. (Use a thermometer, or if a small cube of bread sizzles immediately but does not burn when dropped into the pan, the oil is ready.) Adjust the heat to maintain this temperature as needed. Working in batches of a few pieces at a time (do not crowd the skillet), add the chicken and cook until golden brown, about 12 minutes, turning once. Drain the chicken on paper towels and serve hot.

CREOLE FRIED CHICKEN

SERVES 4 TO 6

What is it that gives Creole fried chicken that NOLA swagger? Some would argue that it's the sliced pickle and a garnish of minced garlic and parsley served with the fried chicken in chef Austin Leslie's French Quarter restaurant, Chez Helene. But Leslie omitted that popular embellishment in the printed recipe published in the 1978 edition of *Creole Feast: Fifteen Master Chefs of New Orleans Reveal Their Secrets* and in his own recipe catalogue, *Chez Helene: House of Good Food Cookbook.*

So I queried other Creole authors to see what they had to say. Leah Chase soaked chicken parts in evaporated milk and added a sprinkle of dried thyme to the marinade. Queen Ida Guillory stirred a bit of baking powder into the flour before dusting the chicken to give it an extra-crispy, light crust. Between Leslie's cream-based batter and Lena Richard's 1939 recipe for chicken parts rolled in a mixture of flour batter and cracker meal, Richard's is the one I like best.

It doesn't get much better than this.

1 tablespoon salt, or to taste

1 teaspoon black pepper, or to taste

1½ teaspoons paprika

1½ teaspoons garlic powder

1 (3- to 4-pound) frying chicken, cut into pieces

2 large eggs, beaten

½ cup evaporated milk or half-and-half

1 cup all-purpose flour

1 cup finely crushed cracker meal or fine dried bread crumbs

Peanut or vegetable oil, for shallow-frying

1 In a small bowl, combine the salt, pepper, paprika, and garlic powder. Place the chicken on a board and pat dry with paper towels. Place the chicken in a large bowl. Sprinkle with half the seasoning mixture. Use your hands to rub the chicken with the seasonings, turning to coat evenly on all sides.

2 In a small bowl, combine the eggs, evaporated milk, and 1 cup water. Pour the mixture over the chicken and mix well to thoroughly coat. Refrigerate for 1 to 2 hours to allow the flavors to soak into the chicken.

3 In a small paper bag, combine the flour, cracker crumbs, and the remaining seasoning mixture. Add the chicken to the bag, a few pieces at a time. Close the bag and shake to coat the pieces well. Remove the chicken to a wire rack to rest for 20 minutes.

4 Pour about ¾ inch oil into a heavy deep cast-iron skillet and heat to 375°F over medium-high heat. (Use a thermometer, or if a small cube of bread sizzles immediately but does not burn when dropped into the pan, the oil is ready.) Adjust the heat to maintain this temperature as needed. Working in batches of a few pieces at a time (do not crowd the skillet), add the chicken and cook until golden brown, about 12 minutes, turning once. Drain the chicken on paper towels and serve hot.

Roast Turkey

A big turkey has been a special-occasion focal point since bondsmen hunted wild turkeys and other game in the woods and fried them, a practice remembered in *What the Slaves Ate: Recollections of African American Foods and Foodways from the Slave Narratives*. Cookbook author, novelist, and peach farmer Dori Sanders's memories of wild turkeys involved marinating the birds in buttermilk and using a sherry stuffing to draw out some of the gamey taste. Domesticated turkey was the purview of professionals. Charleston's Nat Fuller, the "renowned prince of caterers," for instance, achieved fame during the early 1860s for stellar meat cookery that included boned turkey, excellence cited again and again in David Shields's *Southern Provisions: The Creation and Revival of a Cuisine.*

Purists may find it heretical to celebrate winter holidays without classic roast turkey and giblet gravy as the center of attention, but I am not one of them. I learned from Freda DeKnight, *Ebony* magazine's midcentury food editor, that diners can be comforted with traditional dishes and also excited by innovative recipes that surprise tastebuds. She favored roasting turkey in one's own sweet way—rubbed in a peanut butter paste made with butter and cream; baked in port in a heavy brown paper bag; cut into quarters and basted with milk so that it creates its own rich gravy; or in a Spanish or Creole sauce, redolent with flavorful vegetables and ambrosial spices.

My advice to the purists: Just go with it.

ROAST TURKEY
WITH CHILE-PECAN SAUCE
SERVES 10 TO 12

One of the rarest black cookbooks known to librarians, historians, and collectors is also one of the last remaining first editions I wanted to add to my collection when *The Jemima Code* was published. I finally obtained an autographed copy of the *Lone Star Cook Book and Meat Special (From the Slaughter Pen to the Dining Room Table)* at auction, and what a treasure it turned out to be! Published in 1929 by Artaway Fillmore, it offered a glimpse into the mindset and recipe files of a chef making a name for himself in the business of hotel hospitality.

Fillmore was chef at the Hilton in Dallas when the *Lone Star Cook Book* was published, but the recipes and menus were from the Lubbock Hotel, which was advertised as modern and luxurious with one of the finest dining rooms in the region. As testimony to the important legacy he left behind and the talent he took with him, the Lubbock Women's Club celebrated Fillmore's accomplishments in 2018.

What draws me to Fillmore's fine-dining style? Flavors that are culturally and regionally familiar: Creole and Southwestern dishes dominated by tomatoes, green bell peppers, chile peppers, chili powder, and hefty amounts of paprika. His Tamala Loaf was a layered dish of leftover meat mixed with chili powder, browned "cominos [cumin] seed," and a cornmeal paste that reminds me of the tamale pie my mother made when I was growing up in Southern California. And his Spanish Sauce, a mix of fragrant vegetables, tomatoes, and paprika, sparked the chile-pecan sauce that I serve with this Southwestern-seasoned roast turkey. Start the stock for the sauce first, as soon as you retrieve the giblets and neck.

1 (10- to 12-pound) turkey
1 small apple, cored and quartered
1 small onion, quartered
4 large garlic cloves, smashed
2 celery stalks with leaves
2 carrots, halved lengthwise
¼ cup vegetable oil or melted butter
Chile Rub (recipe follows)
Chile-Pecan Sauce (recipe follows)
Cornbread Dressing (page 180), for serving

1 Preheat the oven to 325°F.

2 Remove the giblets and neck from the turkey and begin making the stock for the chile-pecan sauce. Tuck the wings under the bird, then use string to tie the wings and legs close to the body. Place the turkey, breast side up, in a deep, heavy roasting pan. Insert a meat thermometer into the lower part of the thigh, without touching the bone.

3 Fill the turkey neck cavity and body cavity with the apple, onion, garlic, celery, and carrots. Use skewers to close the body cavity. Rub the turkey all over with the oil, then use your hands to rub the turkey with the chile rub. Tent the turkey with foil.

4 Roast the turkey, basting with pan juices every 30 minutes, until the temperature on the thermometer reaches 180°F, 3 to 3½ hours. Remove the foil during the last 30 minutes and do not baste, so the turkey will brown.

5 Reserving the pan drippings for the chile-pecan sauce, transfer the turkey to a platter and remove the skewers and strings. Let stand for 20 minutes. Meanwhile, finish making the chile-pecan sauce. Serve the turkey with the sauce and cornbread dressing.

RECIPE CONTINUES

CHILE-PECAN SAUCE

MAKES ABOUT 2 CUPS

Giblets and neck (reserved from a whole
    turkey)

1 small onion, quartered, plus 2 tablespoons
    minced onion

1 celery stalk with leaves, quartered

1 garlic clove, crushed, plus 2 teaspoons
    minced garlic

½ teaspoon salt, plus more to taste

¼ teaspoon black pepper, plus more to taste

2 tablespoons pan drippings from a roast
    turkey

1 small Scotch bonnet pepper, minced,
    or to taste

1 tablespoon chili powder

1 teaspoon ground cumin

½ cup chopped toasted pecans

1 In a large saucepan, combine 3 cups
water, the turkey giblets and neck, onion
quarters, celery, crushed garlic clove,
½ teaspoon salt, and ¼ teaspoon black
pepper. Bring to a boil, then reduce the heat
to low, cover, and simmer while the turkey
roasts, adding water as necessary to keep
the water level. Remove the stock from
the heat when the turkey is done. Strain
the stock through a colander and reserve.
Discard the solids.

2 Pour off and discard all but 2 tablespoons
of the pan drippings from the turkey
roasting pan. Place the pan over medium-
high heat. Add the minced onion, minced
garlic, and chile pepper and sauté until
softened, about 1 minute. Sprinkle in the
chili powder and cumin and sauté for
2 minutes. Gradually whisk the reserved
stock into the pan in a slow, steady stream,
scraping up browned bits at the bottom of
the pan. Cook until the sauce is reduced
by one-third, about 20 minutes. Stir in the
pecans and season to taste with salt and
black pepper.

CHILE RUB

MAKES ABOUT ½ CUP

Try this rub on flank steak or pork ribs to
give them a Southwestern kick.

2 tablespoons paprika

1 tablespoon chili powder

1 tablespoon ground cumin

1 tablespoon brown sugar

1 tablespoon salt

1 tablespoon black pepper

1½ teaspoons chipotle chile powder

1½ teaspoons dried oregano

1½ teaspoons garlic powder

1½ teaspoons onion powder

In a small bowl, combine the paprika, chili
powder, cumin, brown sugar, salt, black
pepper, chipotle chile powder, oregano,
garlic powder, and onion powder.

GIBLET GRAVY

MAKES ABOUT 5 CUPS

Of course, some families insist their Thanksgiving traditions aren't to be messed with, and so here I also present a classic giblet gravy to go with a roast turkey.

Giblets and neck (reserved from a whole turkey)
1 large onion, quartered
2 celery stalks with leaves
1 garlic clove, crushed
½ teaspoon celery seeds
¼ teaspoon poultry seasoning
1 bay leaf
¼ teaspoon whole black peppercorns
1 teaspoon salt, plus more to taste
2 tablespoons pan drippings from a roast turkey
6 tablespoons butter
½ cup all-purpose flour
Black pepper

1 In a large saucepan, combine 2 quarts water, the turkey giblets and neck, onion, celery, garlic, celery seeds, poultry seasoning, bay leaf, peppercorns, and 1 teaspoon salt. Bring to a boil, then reduce the heat, partially cover, and simmer while the turkey roasts, at least 3 hours, adding water as necessary to keep the meat and vegetables covered.

2 Remove the stock from the heat when the turkey is done. Reserving the giblets, strain the stock and return to the saucepan to keep warm. When cool enough to handle, coarsely chop the giblets and set aside. Return the stock to medium heat and simmer, uncovered, until reduced to 5 cups.

3 Pour off and discard all but 2 tablespoons pan drippings from the turkey roasting pan. Place the pan over medium-high heat, add the butter, and heat until sizzling. Sprinkle with the flour and stir to mix. Cook the flour and fat until browned as desired, about 5 minutes for medium-colored gravy. Gradually stir the hot stock into the pan, scraping up browned bits at the bottom of the pan. Continue to cook, stirring until the gravy thickens. Add the giblets to gravy and season to taste with salt and pepper.

TURKEY TRUFFLES

Good Things to Eat, as Suggested by Rufus,
Rufus Estes, 1911
[In addition to being a creative way to flavor turkey, this recipe, over a century old, proves that black chefs were adept with the most prized luxury ingredients—in this case, what today would be thousands of dollars' worth of truffles.]

Take a fat turkey, clean and singe it. Take three or four pounds of truffles, chopping up a handful with some fat bacon and put into a saucepan, together with the whole truffles, salt, pepper, spices and a bay-leaf. Let these ingredients cook over a slow fire for three-quarters of an hour, take off, stir and let cool. When quite cold place in body of turkey, sew up the opening and let the turkey imbibe the flavor of the truffles by remaining in a day or two, if the season permits. Cover the bird with slices of bacon and roast.

Fish and Seafood

A barefoot, curly-haired black man, dressed in overalls, is seated on an over-turned bucket. He's next to a drop pole, close to the shore, and wiping sweat from his brow. Another man has rolled up the legs of his overalls; he is standing under a tall tree where a fat catfish hangs from a nail. A third man can be seen gripping the reins on a large wagon. His wife and four children, their poles, and several buckets fill up the wagon bed.

These are a few of the enigmatic sketches illustrating the fish and seafood recipes in Ethel Dixon's cookbook, *Big Mama's Old Black Pot*. Published in 1987, the folklore and stories recall her youth in a small rural community in Louisiana; the recipes for country-style cooking are simple and classic Southern, and this book remains a darling of cooks and collectors.

Her memory of "stumpin" for catfish took me to a time and place beyond Southern California, where I grew up with families ordering fish at "you buy, we fry" fish markets.

Frying fish has been at the center of black social events for generations, an essential activity at Emancipation Day and July Fourth celebrations, revivals, and camp meetings. Fried porgies tucked between two slices of bread and dressed with mustard were central to Saturday-night social and fund-raising affairs in the Sea Islands, and "hot fish," so named because it was quickly eaten after being freshly fried in hot oil, is still a staple on Southern and soul menus.

Outside of the South, early black cookbooks seldom included recipes for fried fish. And Arturo Schomburg's proposal for a black cookbook listed choice dishes in the African American seafood pantheon such as curry of catfish, Lowcountry crab boil, and shrimp Creole, plus exquisite-sounding fish and seafood baked in pie crust, creamed in béchamel sauce, cloaked in puff pastry, molded into timbales, simmered "West Indies style," and baked, stuffed, and sauced.

With that in mind, and with all due respect to Big Mama's reasoning that "Nothing is better than 'stumpin' for catfish—except eatin' um on the creek bank," this little group connects the past and the present, the humble with the elegant, the fried and the un-fried.

OYSTER LOAF
(PO' BOYS)

SERVES 2 OR 3

Creoles stuff po' boys with fried oysters, but for that hero-type sandwich, the long loaf of crusty French bread could be filled with any number of inexpensive ingredients that poor boys could afford, from potatoes to fish fillets, topped by a layer of sliced tomatoes, crisp shreds of lettuce, and a mayonnaise dressing.

The oyster loaf may be the antecedent of this combination. Fried oysters piled in a box made from a loaf of bread is referred to as the mediatrice—"the Peace Maker"—in early twentieth-century cookbooks. Back then, when a man came home late from a night of carousing in the French Quarter and told his anxiously waiting wife he had been detained on business downtown, he brought her a mediatrice to curb her anger and make peace. The success of the plan depended upon an exquisitely prepared sandwich filled with delicate oysters.

This twist on the overflowing sandwich, which comes by way of chef Marvin Woods's recipe for oysters stuffed in a garlic-bread loaf, is a stunner on the buffet. To make individual servings easier, you may also adapt the recipe by using small rolls instead of one long loaf. That way, guests can pile on their own mix of crisp oysters, sweet tomatoes, and pungent rémoulade sauce.

1 (14-inch) loaf of unsliced white bread, also known as a Pullman loaf or pan bread

4 tablespoons butter, melted

1 garlic clove, minced

Vegetable oil, for deep-frying

1½ cups cornmeal

2 teaspoons Old Bay seasoning

½ teaspoon cayenne pepper

¼ teaspoon salt, plus more as needed

1 large egg, beaten

¼ cup whole milk

3 dozen shucked oysters (about 2 cups)

Shredded lettuce, tomato slices, and pickles, for serving

Rémoulade Sauce (page 44), for serving

1 Preheat the oven to 350°F.

2 Use a sharp knife to trim the crust from the sides and ends of the bread loaf. Cut off the top one-third of the loaf and hollow out the inside of the loaf to create a box-like shell with 1-inch-thick sides. In a small bowl, combine the melted butter and garlic. Brush the bread loaf inside and out with the garlic-butter. Bake until crisp and lightly browned, about 10 minutes. Set aside.

3 Pour 3 to 4 inches of oil into a large Dutch oven or other wide, deep pot and heat to 375°F over medium-high heat. (Use a thermometer or flick in a small cube of bread; if it sizzles immediately but doesn't burn, the oil is ready.) Adjust the heat to maintain this temperature as needed.

4 In a medium bowl, combine the cornmeal, Old Bay, cayenne, and salt. In a small bowl, whisk together the egg, milk, and a pinch of salt. Drain the oysters and pat dry with paper towels. (Discard the oyster liquor or save it for another use.) Dip the oysters into the egg mixture, then into the cornmeal mixture, turning to coat all sides. Shake off any excess cornmeal. Working in small batches (do not crowd the pan), fry the oysters until golden-brown, about 3 minutes. Use a slotted spoon to remove the oysters and drain on paper towels. Pile them into the bread loaf with lettuce, tomatoes, and pickles. Spoon rémoulade sauce over the oysters and serve.

CATFISH ÉTOUFÉE

SERVES 4

Leonard Roberts's 1969 cookbook, *The Negro Chef Cookbook*, expressed his pride in the legacy of fusion cooking that occurs when black chefs reimagined humble ingredients, mixed sauces and spices from various cultures, and applied culinary technique in dishes such as catfish steaks with "green-lime maître d'hôtel butter," "Oriental" king mackerel steaks, tuna tetrazzini, and salmon curry.

Ethel Dixon's Catfish Étoufée demonstrates that country cooks also performed in the kitchen with that same kind of nimble ingenuity, minus the pageantry. Classic Louisiana country cooking, étoufée is a brick-red roux-based gravy ordinarily swimming with swamp crawdads (crawfish) or shrimp from the bayou and served over rice, but Dixon substitutes mild-tasting catfish.

This is a rendition of the catfish and gravy remembered by a former bondservant in Alabama. It combines Dixon's nostalgia for the ancestors' ways with the bottom-feeding fish that were so abundant in Southern streams, rivers, and lakes with Roberts's chefy sauce-making skills.

1 pound catfish fillets, or any other firm-fleshed white fish, cut into 4-inch pieces
1 teaspoon cayenne pepper
½ teaspoon salt, or to taste
½ teaspoon black pepper
¼ teaspoon dried thyme
½ cup vegetable oil
6 tablespoons all-purpose flour
¼ cup minced onion
2 tablespoons minced green bell pepper
2 tablespoons minced celery
1 teaspoon minced garlic
1 small bay leaf
1½ cups Fish Stock (page 136), warmed
1 tablespoon tomato paste
8 tablespoons (1 stick) butter
2 tablespoons minced green onions
1 tablespoon chopped fresh parsley
Freshly cooked rice

1 Place the catfish pieces on a plate and dry with a paper towel to help the seasonings adhere to the fish. In a small bowl, combine the cayenne, salt, black pepper, and thyme. Season the fillets with half of the seasoning mixture.

2 In a large skillet, heat the oil over high heat until sizzling and nearly smoking. Reduce the heat to medium-high. Gradually whisk in the flour until smooth, being careful not to splatter any of the hot roux on your skin. Cook, stirring constantly, until the roux is medium-brown, about 5 minutes. Remove from the heat and stir in the onion, bell pepper, celery, garlic, bay leaf, and the remaining seasoning mixture. Return to the heat and cook, stirring constantly, until the vegetables are softened, about 2 minutes. Gradually stir in ½ cup of the warm fish stock and the tomato paste and stir until the sauce begins to thicken, about 1 minute, then remove from the heat.

3 In a separate skillet, heat 4 tablespoons of the butter until sizzling. Add the catfish and green onions and cook until the catfish is opaque (it does not need to brown), 2 to 3 minutes per side.

4 Transfer the fish, the remaining 4 tablespoons butter, and the remaining 1 cup stock to the skillet with the vegetables and cook for 2 to 3 minutes, shaking or stirring the pan constantly to melt the butter and emulsify it into a rich sauce. Remove and discard the bay leaf. Sprinkle the étoufée with the parsley and serve over rice.

SHRIMP CREOLE

SERVES 4 OR 5

Not long ago, I wrote that Lena Richard may be the twentieth century's least celebrated celebrity chef, but today she is compared with Martha Stewart for expanding her brand through an empire built on restaurant ownership, cookbook publishing, and food manufacturing. She was a great cook and creator of joy who appeared on a television cooking show *twenty years* before Julia Child was a household name. To honor Richard, I selected the dish she called Shrimp Fricassee à la Creole, from the *New Orleans Cookbook*. I learned to refine it from chef Homer Luke of Homer and Edy's Bistro in Los Angeles.

Richard allowed the shrimp to linger in the sauce for a long braise so the flavors could mingle, while chef Luke poached shrimp in their shells so they retained their flavor and kept their snappy texture, then peeled them just before adding them to a sauce of fresh tomatoes seasoned with the Holy Trinity (celery, bell pepper, and onions). Here I do as Homer does. (The flavor of the broth intensifies as the shrimp cooks, so please reserve it to boil additional shrimp, or strain the stock and freeze it for another use.)

1 lemon, halved

1 small onion, quartered, plus 1½ cups chopped

1 celery stalk with leaves, halved, plus ½ cup chopped

Stems from 2 sprigs fresh parsley, plus 2 teaspoons minced parsley

1 large and 1 small bay leaf

1½ teaspoons Worcestershire sauce

1½ tablespoons plus ½ teaspoon salt

10 whole black peppercorns

5 whole cloves

½ teaspoon dried thyme

½ teaspoon cayenne pepper

1 pound shell-on shrimp

2 tablespoons bacon drippings, vegetable or olive oil, or melted butter

¾ cup chopped green bell pepper

2 teaspoons minced garlic

1 cup chopped tomatoes

Freshly cooked rice

1 In a large Dutch oven or saucepan, bring 1 quart water to a boil. Add the lemon halves, onion quarters, celery pieces, parsley stems, large bay leaf, Worcestershire sauce, 1½ tablespoons salt, the peppercorns, cloves, and ¼ teaspoon each of the thyme and cayenne. Bring to a boil, then reduce the heat and simmer for 10 to 15 minutes to allow the flavors to mingle.

2 Add the shrimp to the pot and return to a boil, then reduce the heat to medium and cook until the shrimp just turn pink, about 5 minutes. If necessary, remove faster-cooking shrimp from the pan as they are done. Drain and reserve 1 cup of the shrimp stock for the sauce. (Refrigerate or freeze the remaining stock for later use.) Once cool enough to handle, peel and devein the shrimp.

3 In a large skillet, heat the bacon fat over medium until sizzling. Add the bell pepper, chopped celery, and chopped onion and sauté until they start to soften, about 5 minutes. Stir in the garlic and cook for 30 seconds. Stir in the tomatoes, reserved shrimp stock, small bay leaf, and the remaining ½ teaspoon salt and ¼ teaspoon each thyme and cayenne. Cook until the vegetables are tender and the tomatoes are saucy, about 20 minutes. Remove and discard the bay leaves.

4 Stir in the shrimp and cook just a few minutes to heat them through. Sprinkle with minced parsley and serve spooned over rice.

LOWCOUNTRY SHRIMP AND GRITS

SERVES 4

Shrimp and grits are everywhere on restaurant menus, but harder to find in African American cookbooks unless you know what you're looking for: The historian Arturo Schomburg called it "breakfast shrimp with hominy." In Gullah-Geechee parlance, it's gone by names like shrimp gravy or smuttered shrimp. Casual Louisiana Creoles might call it breakfast shrimp with tomatoes.

Whatever you call it, this is a luscious version of the dish, inspired by chef Chris Williams of the Houston restaurant Lucille's, which he named after cookbook author Lucille Bishop Smith, his great-grandmother. The tips for preparing perfect grits here are from Dora Charles's *A Real Southern Cook in Her Savannah Kitchen*. It combines cheese grits, which are simmered low and slow so they are creamy, with plump, slightly briny Gulf Coast shrimp paired with a rich gravy infused with bacon and green onion. It is outstanding served at breakfast; I also like to serve it as an elegant first course for dinner with special friends. Try it my way, then the next time, if you'd like, dice a few mushrooms or a small tomato and toss them into the pan with the onions and garlic.

1¼ cups Chicken Stock (page 133)
1½ teaspoons salt, plus more to taste
1 cup old-fashioned or quick (not instant) grits
2 tablespoons butter
6 tablespoons half-and-half
½ cup shredded Cheddar cheese
¼ teaspoon white pepper
3 slices bacon, finely diced
¼ cup all-purpose flour
1 pound shrimp, peeled and deveined
½ cup chopped green onions
¼ teaspoon crushed red pepper flakes
1 garlic clove, minced
1 tablespoon fresh lemon juice
1 tablespoon minced fresh parsley

1 In a large saucepan, bring 3½ cups water, 1 cup of the chicken stock, and ½ teaspoon of the salt to a boil over high heat. Gradually whisk in the grits 1 tablespoon at a time, stirring until blended. Return to a boil, then reduce the heat to low, cover, and simmer, whisking occasionally to prevent lumps, until tender, about 30 minutes. Add water, if necessary, to keep it thick but not stiff. Remove the grits from the heat. Stir in the butter, half-and-half, Cheddar, and white pepper. Keep warm.

2 In a large skillet, cook the bacon over medium heat until crisp, about 7 minutes. Spoon out the bacon and drain on paper towels. Discard all but 2 tablespoons of the bacon drippings.

3 In a small bowl, combine the flour and the reamaining 1 teaspoon salt. Toss the shrimp in the flour mixture to coat lightly on all sides.

4 Heat the bacon fat in the pan over medium-high until sizzling. Add the shrimp and sauté for 2 minutes. Stir in the green onions, red pepper flakes, and garlic. Cook, turning once, until the shrimp turn fully pink, about 2 minutes more. Stir in the remaining ¼ cup stock and cook, stirring, until the shrimp gravy is smooth and thick, 2 to 3 minutes. Stir in the lemon juice and minced parsley. Taste and add salt if necessary.

5 Divide the grits evenly among serving bowls. Pour the shrimp and gravy over the grits. Sprinkle with the bacon.

LOUISIANA BARBECUED SHRIMP

SERVES 2 TO 4

You won't find any barbecue sauce in the model/chef/restaurateur B. Smith's dish of shrimp in spiced butter sauce: "Barbecue shrimp" is just the name Louisiana Creole cooks assigned to shrimp braised in wine, beer, or a garlic-butter sauce.

I like to make this dish spicy, in a cast-iron skillet, and served in shallow bowls with hunks of crisp French bread to soak up the sauce. It's classic NOLA. Shaking the pan back and forth during cooking time is a trick that helps give the sauce more body than stirring.

½ teaspoon cayenne pepper
¼ teaspoon black pepper
½ teaspoon salt
¼ teaspoon crushed red pepper flakes
½ teaspoon dried thyme
½ teaspoon dried oregano
¼ teaspoon paprika
2 bay leaves, crushed
4 tablespoons (½ stick) butter
2 garlic cloves, minced
¼ cup white wine
½ cup Fish Stock (page 136)
2 tablespoons fresh lemon juice
2 tablespoons Worcestershire sauce
1 pound shell-on shrimp
2 tablespoons minced fresh parsley
Hot crusty French bread, for serving

1 In a small bowl, combine the cayenne, black pepper, salt, red pepper flakes, thyme, oregano, paprika, and bay leaves.

2 In a large cast-iron skillet, heat the butter over medium-high until melted and sizzling. Add the garlic, seasoning mixture, wine, fish stock, lemon juice, and Worcestershire sauce. Bring to a boil, then reduce the heat and simmer until the sauce thickens enough to lightly coat a spoon, about 5 to 7 minutes; shake the pan as it cooks to help bring the sauce together.

3 Add the shrimp, reduce the heat to low, and cook, turning once, until the shrimp turn pink and firm, 3 to 5 minutes.

4 Sprinkle the shrimp with the parsley and serve immediately with hot French bread.

HOW THE WOMEN WHO LIVE ON REMOTE FARMS IN KENYA FIND THE TIME AND ENERGY TO DEVOTE TO THE FINER POINTS OF BAKING WHILE DEALING WITH INVADING LIONS, LEOPARDS AND LOCUST PLAGUES IS REMARKABLE. . . .
—LETTER FROM MRS. ERNEST HEMINGWAY, KIMANA SWAMP, KENYA, 1954

The Sweet Life

"All I want to know is who is bringing the chocolate cake," Aunt M. quietly demanded in a way that let everyone know she wasn't pleased.

Aunt M. (for Meredieth) was wonderful and warm most of the time. Just don't forget to write back, and don't mess with her family reunion. But on a blistering hot weekend in July 1994, we were guilty of at least one of those crimes—we just didn't know it yet.

Although my husband, Bruce, and I roared through several north-eastern Ohio counties on US 422 toward the Pennsylvania border, we were going to be late for the annual Martin homecoming. The family had gathered in Warren or Youngstown, Ohio, or Sharon, Pennsylvania, on the fourth Sunday of July every year for the past sixty-five or so—a way for the family to celebrate the birth of new babies, congratulate graduates, or welcome brides and grooms to the clan. The gathering is also about great food and eating. Especially dessert. No amount of hectic living or working overtime was going to destroy the tradition.

Aunt M. was frantically pacing about, mumbling, "Oh, this is just terrible," at every turn around the long cloth-covered table. Already well past 1 p.m. and aware of the delay, family members arrived steadily, hurriedly situating favorite dishes in place—some still warm from the oven. It was a wonderful spread: three versions of macaroni and cheese, scalloped potatoes, baked beans, green beans, fresh beets, crusty fried chicken, potato and macaroni salads, homemade cloverleaf rolls.

But there was no chocolate cake.

In the same way that Mrs. Hemingway seemed baffled in Africa, several busy generations of our family were stunned by Aunt M.'s exasperation. We forgot that homemade treats are like a birthright, essential to special-occasion traditions, an expression of appreciation, conviviality, love. Our African ancestors made puddings from fruits and nuts; sweet potato, rice, or coconut breads spiced with ginger; cassava pone; and fruit salads so heavenly they earned the name "ambrosia" in America. In plantation kitchens, pastry cooks earned formidable reputations for temperamental desserts like "omelette soufflé," and free black pastry cooks and confectioners fashioned business enterprises from their knowledge and experience in baking, forming a key segment of the black economy.

But to Aunt M., we had caved to the lure of store-bought goodies. The long table displayed plastic tubs filled with miniature brownies and sugar cookies studded with M&M's candies, pies with machine-formed crusts in see-through clamshell boxes, and bubble trays of cupcakes topped with brightly colored neon frosting and confetti sprinkles. No chocolate cake—none that was made from scratch in a home, anyway.

We copped to our misdeed, acknowledged our need to atone for indifference to homemade chocolate cake, and decided a family griot (a West African term for a storyteller who uses the arts to preserve oral tradition) could hand down revelations of the perseverance, resistance, self-reliance, and power of baking throughout African American history—and be someone to remind us that baking is just plain *fun*.

That someone turned out to be me. For help, I looked to the culinary historian David S. Shields, author of *The Culinarians: Lives and Careers from the First Age of American Fine Dining* and *Southern Provisions: The Creation and Revival of a Cuisine*. Shields's stunning research chronicles ignored and forgotten cooks and restaurateurs, primarily from the nineteenth-century Carolina Lowcountry, including some of the influential black confectioners and pastry shop owners I celebrate in this chapter. I encountered pastry cooks in historical probes exploring the lives of free people of color, African American women, and black entrepreneurs as well.

These portraits of accomplishment stand in stark contrast to African American stereotypes and literary characters dutifully baking cakes in wash tubs and tomato cans for the mistress, industriously creating sweets of scarcity—vinegar and mock fruit pies, cakes baked with leftover bread crumbs leavened with corncob soda, and molasses candies. The ancestors did make those things, and their ingenuity is to be honored; they *also* left a legacy of recipes for elaborate cakes baked at Christmastime and for secret special-occasion celebrations in the woods—evidence of access to precious ingredients and tremendous skill they used both in enslavement and servitude, and to empower themselves and their communities.

"Of slaves, among the most valuable, rating next to skilled carpenters, were pastry cooks," Shields affirmed in *Southern Provisions*. In advertisements announcing slave sales, pastry cooks were "always distinguished from mere 'cooks,'" Shields added, and "the usual descriptor for a kitchen artist of the highest accomplishment was a 'complete pastry cook.'" (The tradition of baking is especially rich in South Carolina, Georgia, and North Florida, in part because the availability of sugarcane, sorghum, citrus, and spices, but also because of a seemingly unlimited supply of enslaved Dominican workers who helped pastry and confection businesses thrive.)

And while the pain of enslavement reverberates for centuries, and through the centuries, too, black bakers have used their skills and savvy to create wealth, self-sufficiency, and generations of protégés to carry on their legacy and to build their own economic power.

Names and stories from history came alive for me as I researched further. Sally Seymour, "the founding matriarch of the greatest of South Carolina's African American dynasties," as Dr. Shields described her, was trained by one of Charleston's professional pastry chefs during the early 1790s. Once set free, she taught free and enslaved pastry cooks in the shop she established on Charleston's Tradd Street. Her network of business-savvy artisans and professionals went on to cultivate the next generation of apprentices, including her daughter Eliza Seymour Lee, Camila Johnson, Eliza Dwight, Martha Gilchrist, Hannah Hetty, Elizabeth Holton, Mary Holton, and Cato McCloud.

In the Colonial North, Jean Baptiste and Catherine Point DuSable of Santo Domingo, Hispaniola (today in the Dominican Republic), established a trading post at the mouth of the Chicago River on the site of modern-day Chicago, which included a bake-house along with a five-room house, horse mill, dairy, smokehouse, poultry house, workshop, stable, and barn. Samuel Fraunces, tavern owner and presidential chef and steward, created a wide variety of the highest quality desserts, such as cakes, tarts, jellies, syllabubs, blancmange, and sweetmeats at his New York establishment, the Queen's Head Tavern. Once-enslaved Phillis Wheatley, who became one of the most famous American poets of the late 1700s, was married to John Peters, who operated a bakery and a grocery in Boston. Tunis G. Campbell started a bakery in New York City after publishing *Hotel Keepers, Head Waiters, and Housekeepers' Guide* in 1848.

I asked myself: How could we not be inspired by Elizabeth Hewlett Marshall? She survived widowhood by working as a domestic, then opened a bakery in the basement of her home in what became New York's Central Park to support herself and her four children, her granddaughter Maritcha Lyons recalled in *We Are Your Sisters: Black Women in the Nineteenth Century*. Shouldn't we be proud of Harriett Owens Bynum, one of the important "race women" honored in *The Negro Trail Blazers of California*, a compilation of pioneering accomplishments? Bynum owned a bakeshop and a dairy in segregated Los Angeles, then became a realtor to ensure that the "poor class of colored laborers were given a square deal in the purchase of homes," she said with humility in 1915.

Activists Mary McLeod Bethune and Dr. Dorothy Height also boosted my baking enthusiasm. Bethune was an educator, human rights advocate, daughter of formerly enslaved parents, and founder of the National Council of Negro Women. Dr. Height, her protégé, became President and CEO of the NCNW. A woman of political influence, Bethune advised presidents and conferred a philosophical attitude of living to serve, which she said she left to "my people," and to those who shared her vision of world peace. In 1904, she founded the Daytona Educational and Industrial Training School, which is known today as Bethune-Cookman University, to cultivate the values of faith, courage, brotherhood, dignity, ambition, and responsibility as tools to enact equality.

Among other work and life lessons taught at the school, Bethune turned a spotlight on the connection between domestic science, baking, and self-reliance. Money earned by baking and selling sweet potato pies kept the school's doors open. Culinary students lived by her affirmation: "Cease to be a drudge, seek to be an artist."

Bethune's traditions flourished under Dr. Height's tireless leadership of the NCNW—a legacy of strong African American family values, cultural pride, and respect for diversity. Under her watch, the NCNW also published *The Black Family Reunion Cookbook*, a classic; in the introduction, Dr. Height spoke of the "power of breaking bread in the building of communities."

Dr. Height's and Bethune's hopeful aspirations encourage me. And I believe that remembering them can lead us to appreciate and embrace one another as extended family, celebrating what makes us unique and finding life-giving spirit in family traditions that create long-lasting memories. With their uplifting words and the ancestral wisdom of black pastry cooks, I can confidently spur my family's next generation to pick up some flour, sugar, chocolate, and a few eggs and bake a cake for Aunt M.

Classic Cakes

Cakes have been a big part of the Southern experience and African American cooks, who "learned the recipes from white homemakers using rudimental instructions, frequently excelled and became the baking experts," cookbook author and cooking teacher Nathalie Dupree asserted in the award-winning tome *Mastering the Art of Southern Cooking*. You wouldn't know it.

It took, for instance, the James Beard Awards, known as the Oscars for food folks, nearly thirty years to acknowledge that expertise. Finally, in 2018, the James Beard Foundation named an African American woman, Dolester Miles, Outstanding Pastry Chef. Dol, as she is affectionately called, is the powerhouse behind the coveted desserts featured in Frank Stitt's acclaimed cookbooks and restaurants in Birmingham, Alabama.

Dol, black cookbook authors, and other modern bakers call to mind a legacy of African American proficiency in baking that is much broader than even that defined by Arturo Schomburg. He presented a long list of puddings and pies to be included in the Negro cookbook he intended to publish during the 1930s but counted just a third as many cakes, cookies, and confections. This surprised me. African American cookbook authors at the time included familiar cakes with notable names in their collections—Lady Baltimore, Robert E. Lee, Scripture, No-name, and Election, plus other classics—some with African American heritage, such as George Washington Carver's Metropolitan Cake, and others, like Angel Food Cake, without it.

I believe the authors claimed ordinary recipes as their own because they knew in their souls what recipe copyright law contends: Change a recipe, and it becomes yours.

DEVIL'S FOOD CAKE

SERVES 10 TO 12

For generations, chocolate was a luxury food item that families stretched their budgets to afford, making its presence on our tables an expression of affluence. In flush times, bakers added extra chocolate to standard chocolate cake batter, which yields a deep, dark fudge cake known as devil's food cake. German chocolate cake, ennobled by a caramel, coconut, and pecan filling, was known as the "rich people's cake," Wilbert Jones explained in *Mama's Tea Cakes: 101 Delicious Soul Food Desserts.*

Chocolate-potato cake is an heirloom recipe, popular among early twentieth-century cooks from Kentucky to California, that might seem like a purely make-do improvisation for stretching valuable chocolate. But in fact, stirring mashed potatoes into the batter is a brilliant way to give the cake extra moistness. Fragrant with ground cinnamon, cloves, and nutmeg and studded with nuts, it may remind some of Texas sheet cake. I was not surprised to find that some cooks tossed raisins in the mix; African American families in California were active grape growers who marketed raisins for profit.

But back to the devil's food cake: This quick and easy recipe is a departure from standard mixtures that start by creaming together butter and sugar—what the old cooks meant when they said, "Bake a cake in the usual way." Coffee gives the batter a subtle richness. The cake is delicious topped with billows of fluffy white marshmallow frosting or a light buttercream or a chocolate cream cheese frosting. Baked in layers, it will make a lovely statement on your next special-occasion dessert table. A sheet cake is easier to serve and is de rigueur at the annual Martin family reunion.

Cooking spray (or shortening), for the pan

2 cups all-purpose flour, plus more for the pans

2 cups sugar

½ cup sifted unsweetened cocoa powder

1 teaspoon baking soda

¼ teaspoon salt

¼ cup vegetable oil

½ cup buttermilk

2 large eggs, beaten

2 teaspoons vanilla extract

1 cup boiling hot coffee

Chocolate Cream Cheese Frosting (recipe follows)

1 Preheat the oven to 350°F. Lightly coat two 9-inch round cake pans or a 13 × 9-inch pan with cooking spray or shortening. Cut parchment paper to fit the bottom of the pan(s). Coat again with cooking spray or shortening. Dust lightly with flour, then tap the edges of the pan to remove and discard excess flour.

2 In a large bowl, whisk together the flour, sugar, cocoa, baking soda, and salt. In a separate bowl, combine the oil, buttermilk, eggs, and vanilla. Using an electric mixer with the paddle attachment, beat the wet ingredients into the flour mixture on medium speed until the batter resembles hot chocolate, about 2 minutes. Stir in the boiling hot coffee and beat until well blended; the batter will be thin.

3 Pour the batter into the pans and bake until a wood pick inserted in the center comes out clean, 30 to 35 minutes. Cool the cake in the pans on wire racks for 10 minutes, then turn the cake out onto wire racks to cool completely.

4 When cool, frost with chocolate cream cheese frosting.

RECIPE CONTINUES

CHOCOLATE CREAM CHEESE FROSTING
MAKES ABOUT 3 CUPS

1 (8-ounce) package cream cheese, at room temperature
1 stick (4 ounces) butter, at room temperature
5 cups sifted powdered sugar
½ cup sifted unsweetened cocoa powder
2 teaspoons vanilla extract
1 to 2 tablespoons whole milk, as needed

In a stand mixer fitted with the paddle attachment, beat the cream cheese and butter until light and fluffy, about 3 minutes. Scrape down the sides of the bowl. Gradually beat in the powdered sugar and cocoa, blending in well between additions. Beat in the vanilla and enough milk to make a smooth frosting. Mix until light and fluffy, and it's ready to use.

POTATO CAKE

Kentucky Cook Book, Easy and Simple for Any Cook, by a Colored Woman [Mrs. W. T. Hayes], 1912

1 cup butter, 2 cups sugar, 2 cups flour, 1 cup hot mashed potatoes, 1 cup English walnuts, ½ cup milk, ½ cup melted chocolate, 2 teaspoons baking powder, 1 teaspoon cinnamon, 1 teaspoon ground cloves, 1 teaspoon vanilla, 4 eggs, yolks and white separated. Cream butter and sugar, add yolks, milk, chocolate, potatoes, spices, flour and a little salt and nuts. Bake in tins and ice with marshmallows.

POUND CAKE
SERVES 10

Some of the most decadent old-fashioned goodies I ever tasted—the kind of treats that are just too rich not to share—were baked by church ladies in East Cleveland. So, I once carefully bundled a tiny piece of pound cake left over from a bake sale and took it home to my pound cake-loving husband. He whooped and hollered like a spirit-filled preacher when he tasted the crumbs; if the fat-soaked napkin it was wrapped in had been edible, he might have eaten that, too.

He pleaded: "Find that woman and get her recipe!" I left her in peace and analyzed pound cake recipes instead.

Pound cake was a Martin family birthday tradition, adapted by my mother-in-law, Hazel, from a recipe in *The Original White House Cook Book*, by F. L. Gillette and Hugo Ziemann. Until the church ladies, I knew how to make it, but I had no desire to be the best pound cake baker ever!

The dense cake baked with a pound of every ingredient goes all the way back to 1796, when Amelia Simmons published *American Cookery*, a collection of English recipes adapted to native ingredients. Free woman of color Malinda Russell, who operated a pastry shop in Tennessee, also shared the recipe for pound cake in her cookbook from 1866. Over the years, bakers have de-standardized the pound cake formula using fewer farm-fresh ingredients and tweaking the original flavoring, experimenting with lemon-lime soda pop (as in 7-Up Cake), sour cream, buttermilk, brown sugar, flavored extracts, and chocolate. Some start the cake in a cold—not preheated—oven, as I do here.

Whichever version you like, the trick to perfect texture is a combination of butter and shortening, and a long, thorough beating to aerate the batter, making it light.

Softened butter or shortening for the pan

3 cups all-purpose flour, plus more for the pan

½ teaspoon baking powder

Pinch of salt

⅛ teaspoon ground mace

1 cup whole milk

1 teaspoon lemon extract

1 teaspoon vanilla extract

2 sticks (8 ounces) butter, at room temperature

½ cup shortening

3 cups sugar

5 large eggs

Fresh berries, for serving (optional)

Brandy Butter, for serving (optional; recipe follows)

1 Generously coat a 10-inch tube pan with butter or shortening. Dust lightly with flour, then tap the edges of the pan to remove and discard excess flour.

2 In a small bowl, whisk together the flour, baking powder, salt, and mace. In a liquid measuring cup, stir together the milk, lemon extract, and vanilla.

3 In a stand mixer fitted with the paddle attachment, cream the butter on medium speed until light, 2 to 3 minutes. Add the shortening to the bowl and beat for 2 more minutes. With the mixer on low speed, gradually beat in the sugar, 1 cup at a time. Increase the speed to medium and cream the butter and sugar together until light and fluffy, about 5 minutes. Scrape down the sides of the bowl. With the mixer still on medium speed, add the eggs one at a time, beating well after each addition, until they are incorporated well and the batter is light.

4 With the mixer on low speed, add the flour mixture in three additions, alternating with the milk mixture, and beginning and ending with the flour. Mix just until the batter is smooth. Pour the batter into the pan.

5 Place the pan on the middle rack in a cold oven. Set the oven to 325°F and bake until the top is golden and a wooden pick inserted into the center comes out clean, about 1 hour 15 minutes. Cool in the pan for 10 minutes, then invert onto a wire rack to cool completely.

6 Slice the pound cake and serve warm, garnished with fresh berries or brandy butter, if desired.

VARIATION

SIMPLE CHOCOLATE POUND CAKE
Omit the mace and lemon extract and sift ½ cup cocoa powder into the dry ingredients before proceeding with the creaming step.

BRANDY BUTTER
MAKES ABOUT 2 CUPS

1 cup unsalted butter, at room temperature
1 cup powdered sugar, sifted
¼ cup brandy

In the bowl of an electric mixer, beat the butter on medium speed until light and fluffy, 2 to 3 minutes. Gradually beat in the powdered sugar a tablespoon at a time, beating well after each addition, until the mixture is well blended. Beat in the brandy until the butter is light and fluffy. Refrigerate, covered, until firm.

LEMON TEA CAKE

SERVES 16 TO 20

Malinda Russell's classic lemon cake from her 1866 book, *A Domestic Cook Book*, reminds me of much more modern versions, which get extra moisture from a sweet lemon syrup. The sweet-tart lemon glaze on the cake in a cookbook published by the sorority sisters of Delta Sigma Theta is wickedly sweet, an update of the lightly browned butter glaze pioneers poured over classic pound or butter cakes. (The James Beard Award-winning pastry chef Dolester Miles's butter glaze is made tipsy with bourbon.) I mixed several techniques and loaded this cake with lemon zest and flavor to come up with a cake I bake at Christmastime in cast-iron kugelhopf or Bundt pans.

I have included lemon glaze here as the Barefoot Contessa, Ina Garten, and other contemporary chefs do; it is lovely as it drips along the peaks and valleys created by the decorative baking pan. You can also bake the cake in loaf pans and leave it unfrosted for easier handling.

Softened butter or shortening for the pan
3 cups all-purpose flour, plus more for the pan
½ teaspoon baking powder
½ teaspoon baking soda
1 teaspoon salt
¾ cup fresh lemon juice (from 5 to 6 lemons)
1 cup buttermilk
1 teaspoon vanilla extract
2 sticks (8 ounces) butter, at room temperature
2½ cups sugar
5 large eggs
¼ cup loosely packed grated lemon zest (from 4 to 5 lemons)
Lemon Glaze (optional; recipe follows)

1 Preheat the oven to 325°F. Generously coat a 10-inch tube or Bundt pan or two 8-inch loaf pans with butter or shortening. Dust lightly with flour, shaking to remove any excess.

2 In a small bowl, whisk together the flour, baking powder, baking soda, and salt. Set aside. In a liquid measuring cup, combine ¼ cup of the lemon juice, the buttermilk, and vanilla. Set aside.

3 In a stand mixer fitted with the paddle attachment, cream the butter on medium speed until light, about 2 minutes. With the mixer running, add 2 cups of the sugar, 1 cup at a time, while beating on medium speed until incorporated. Continue beating until light and fluffy, 3 to 5 minutes. Scrape down the sides of the bowl. With the mixer still on medium speed, add the eggs, one at a time, beating well after each addition until the eggs are completely incorporated. Beat in the lemon zest.

4 With the mixer on low, beat in the flour mixture in three additions, alternating with the lemon juice–buttermilk mixture, and beginning and ending with flour. Mix just until the batter is smooth.

5 Pour the batter into the pan and bake until a wooden pick inserted in the center comes out clean, 50 to 60 minutes.

6 Meanwhile, in a small saucepan, combine the remaining ½ cup sugar and ½ cup lemon juice. Bring to a boil, then reduce the heat and simmer 1 minute. Remove from the heat and stir the syrup for a few minutes to cool slightly.

RECIPE CONTINUES

7 With a wooden skewer, poke holes over the bottom of the cake. Gradually spoon the lemon syrup over the entire surface, allowing the cake to absorb the syrup between spoonfuls. Repeat until all the syrup is used. Let the cake cool in the pan 10 minutes, then turn out onto a wire rack set over a rimmed baking sheet (to catch any excess lemon glaze in the next step).

8 When the cake is completely cool, drizzle the glaze over the top of the cake, if using, allowing it to drip down the sides. Let it set before serving.

LEMON GLAZE

MAKES ENOUGH FOR 1 LARGE CAKE

3½ tablespoons fresh lemon juice
   (from 1 lemon)
2 cups sifted powdered sugar

In a small liquid measuring cup, combine the lemon juice and sugar and whisk until the glaze is smooth.

COCONUT-LEMON LAYER CAKE

SERVES 10 TO 12

Think about the modern-day cakewalk, and the image that comes to mind is of giddy children, prancing around in a circle to festive music, hoping fortune will smile on them and award them a cake when the music stops. But in the pre–Civil War South, the "cakewalk" was an exaggerated dance the enslaved performed near their cabins or in the woods to mock the ballroom pretension displayed by the plantation aristocracy. At the end of an evening of strutting, twirling canes, and tipping top hats, a prize was presented to the winning couple, "a towering, extra sweet coconut cake," Eliza Diggs Johnson, who was born on a Missouri plantation, recalled.

Although the dance was a parody of whites, it began crossing into popular culture in the 1870s through the minstrel stage, dance contests (such as the national "Cakewalk Jubilee" at New York's Madison Square Garden), musical plays, sheet music, and films; it entered American vocabulary through the expressions "takes the cake" and "that was a cakewalk." Charles Johnson, the "Cakewalk King," and his wife, Dora Dean, reclaimed the African American origins of the dance in an elegant performance on Broadway. Johnson's appreciation for the cakewalk sprang from the stories told by his mother, the aforementioned Eliza Diggs Johnson, according to an essay in *Africanisms in American Culture*.

Like so many things associated with plantation social life, coconut cake eventually became a centerpiece of African American special occasions, reserved for weddings, funerals, church suppers, and Christmastime.

For its base, cooks followed one of several butter cake formulas, each adapted well to all sorts of flavorings, toppings, and frostings, limited only by the baker's imagination. Some chose the simple 1-2-3-4 cake formula, which refers to the amounts of butter, sugar, flour, and eggs in the recipe; others preferred gold cake, in which the batter is enriched with egg yolks only; almond, coconut, or vanilla extract determined the cake's character; and the layers might be topped with a pineapple, lemon, or lime filling; but always, it was fresh coconut pressed into fluffy white mountain frosting that made the cake truly special.

The confectioners of old stirred the filling in a bain-marie, "a kettle set in a kettle of hot water," until it thickened. Next generations called that a double boiler. I updated the process by cooking the mixture in a saucepan. You will need to keep the heat low and your eyes on the pot to prevent the eggs from heating too quickly and curdling. Or, skip the fruit fillings. Spread the warm cake with your favorite jelly, or poke holes all over the cake and then brush the layers with fruit juice, as Dora Charles suggests in *A Real Southern Cook in Her Savannah Kitchen*, a book that sheds light on the complicated relationship between a black cook and her white employer and the recipes they develop together. Toasted coconut on the frosted cake makes a gorgeous garnish. I use less than suggested by bakers of previous generations, but let your taste buds decide how much coconut and whether you like toasted, untoasted (which is chewy and sweet), or a little of both. To surprise your family and friends with a bit of Creole lagniappe (which means "something extra"), stir some sweetened coconut into the filling.

Cooking spray or shortening, for the pan

2½ cups all-purpose flour, plus more for the pan

2 teaspoons baking powder

½ teaspoon salt

1 cup whole milk

1 teaspoon vanilla extract

2 sticks (8 ounces) butter, at room temperature

1¾ cups sugar

4 large eggs

Lemon Filling (recipe follows)

Buttercream Frosting (recipe follows)

1 cup sweetened shredded coconut, or more if desired

1 Preheat the oven to 350°F. Lightly coat two 9-inch cake pans with cooking spray or shortening. Cut rounds of parchment paper to line the bottoms of the pans. Coat again with spray or shortening. Dust lightly with flour, shaking out the excess.

2 In a medium bowl, whisk together the flour, baking powder, and salt. In a small bowl or measuring cup, combine the milk and vanilla.

3 In a stand mixer fitted with the paddle attachment, cream the butter on medium speed until light, 2 to 3 minutes. Gradually beat in the sugar until light and fluffy, about 3 minutes more. Scrape down the sides of the bowl. Add the eggs, one at a time, beating well after each addition until the eggs are completely incorporated. Beat in the flour mixture in three additions, alternating with the milk mixture, and beginning and ending with the flour. Beat just until the batter is smooth.

RECIPE CONTINUES

4 Pour the batter into the pans and bake until a wooden pick inserted in the center comes out clean, 30 to 35 minutes. Cool the cakes in the pans on a wire rack for 10 minutes, then turn out onto the wire rack to cool completely.

5 When the cakes are cool enough to handle, use a serrated knife to slice each layer horizontally in half to make 4 total layers. Place one layer, cut side down, on a serving plate. Spread with one-third of the lemon filling. Repeat with 2 more cake layers and filling. Top with the last cake layer. Refrigerate for 30 minutes to allow the cake to set.

6 Use a cake spreader or thin spatula to spread one-third of the buttercream frosting over the top and sides of the cake to coat the crumb. Spread the cake with the remaining frosting. Sprinkle the top and sides of the cake with the coconut, pressing gently. Refrigerate until ready to serve.

LEMON FILLING
MAKES 2 TO 2½ CUPS

3 large egg yolks, beaten
¾ cup sugar
2 tablespoons cornstarch
1 tablespoon grated lemon zest
½ cup fresh lemon juice (from 2 to 3 lemons)
6 tablespoons butter, at room temperature, cut into 4 pieces
½ cup sweetened shredded coconut (optional)

1 Place the egg yolks in a heatproof bowl.

2 In a medium saucepan, combine the sugar and cornstarch. Whisk in ½ cup water, the lemon zest, and lemon juice. Bring to a boil over medium heat, stirring constantly, then reduce the heat to low and cook until the mixture has thickened. Whisk one-third of the hot mixture into the egg yolks to temper them. Return the warmed egg yolk mixture to the pan. Cook and stir over medium heat until the mixture thickens and resembles pudding, about 10 minutes.

3 Remove the filling from the heat. Whisk in the butter, one piece at a time. Stir in the coconut, if desired. Place the filling in a small bowl. Cover with wax paper and chill until needed.

BUTTERCREAM FROSTING

MAKES ABOUT 4 CUPS

⅔ cup butter, at room temperature
5 cups powdered sugar
1 teaspoon vanilla extract
½ cup whole milk, as needed

In a stand mixer fitted with the paddle attachment, beat the butter at medium speed until light and fluffy, about 3 minutes. Scrape down the sides of the bowl. Gradually beat in the powdered sugar, beating until well blended. Beat in the vanilla and enough milk to make a smooth frosting. Beat until light and fluffy, about 2 minutes longer.

PINEAPPLE UPSIDE-DOWN CAKE

SERVES 8 TO 10

Skillet cakes go back to this country's Colonial times, when sponge cake and pancake batter were topped with apples, cooked apricots, prunes, or cherries and baked in a spider (a three-legged iron kettle) on top of an open flame, then inverted for serving. Annette Merson's 1987 *African Cookery: A Black Heritage* is a catalogue of recipes, tips for dinner parties, and decorating ideas from African nations. In it, Merson linked the upside-down cake to Liberia, where a crown of caramelized plantains or banana slices decorated gingerbread baked in a skillet.

Their contemporary descendant, pineapple upside-down cake, first appeared in 1926 when Dole held a pineapple recipe contest. The sticky-sweet treat increased in popularity, becoming a party favorite and a measure of a competent baker, during the 1940s and 50s. Improvisational soul cooks turned upside-down cake topsy-turvy, substituting canned sliced fresh peaches, pears, or fresh pineapple and rum for the classic topping of pineapple rings with a maraschino cherry center while retaining the original sponge cake base. Mine calls for crushed pineapple so that there is sweet fruit in every bite. And for a familiar taste of the South, try contemporary author and radio host Nicole Taylor's way: She taps into the funky boldness of chopped black walnuts instead of the pecans.

10 tablespoons (1¼ sticks) butter, at room temperature

½ cup packed dark brown sugar

1 (8-ounce) can crushed pineapple, drained, 3 to 4 tablespoons juice reserved

1 tablespoon dark rum (optional)

½ cup chopped toasted pecans

1 cup all-purpose flour

1 teaspoon baking powder

¼ teaspoon salt

¾ cup granulated sugar

1 large egg

⅓ cup whole milk

1 teaspoon vanilla extract

Sweetened whipped cream, for serving (optional)

1 Preheat the oven to 350°F.

2 In a 9-inch cast-iron skillet, heat 4 tablespoons of the butter over medium heat until melted. Stir in the brown sugar, 1 tablespoon of the pineapple juice, and the rum (or another tablespoon of pineapple juice if not using rum) and heat over medium heat until the sugar dissolves. Spoon the crushed pineapple on top of the butter-sugar mixture, and sprinkle with the pecans. Set aside.

3 In a small bowl, stir together the flour, baking powder, and salt. In a stand mixer fitted with the paddle attachment, cream together on medium speed the remaining 6 tablespoons butter and the granulated sugar until light and fluffy, about 3 minutes. Scrape down the sides of the bowl. Beat in the egg, milk, vanilla, and the remaining 2 tablespoons of the pineapple juice. With a wooden spoon, stir in the flour mixture until the batter is smooth.

4 Carefully pour the batter into the skillet, being careful not to disturb the pineapple topping. Bake until a wooden pick inserted in the center comes out clean, about 30 minutes. Let the cake cool in the pan for 10 minutes, then invert it onto a serving plate. Serve with sweetened whipped cream, if desired.

CARAMEL CAKE

SERVES 10 TO 12

For Jocelyn Delk Adams, the powerhouse behind the blog and book *Grandbaby Cakes*, making "real deal southern caramel cake" is a labor of love handed down through generations. She bakes her grandmother's rich yellow cake, accented with sour cream, in layers, and then tops it off with an old-fashioned icing cooked on top of the stove for 2 hours.

There is a shorter route to authenticity. You can frost this super-moist buttermilk cake with quick shortcut icings, such as Brown Sugar Buttercream Frosting or a hurry-up Caramel Icing.

Softened butter or shortening, for the pan

3 cups all-purpose flour, plus more for the pan

2 teaspoons baking powder

½ teaspoon baking soda

½ teaspoon salt

1 cup buttermilk

1 teaspoon vanilla extract

2 sticks (8 ounces) butter, at room temperature

2 cups sugar

4 large eggs

Caramel Icing or Brown Sugar Buttercream Frosting (recipes follow)

1 Preheat the oven to 350°F. Lightly coat two 9-inch cake pans with cooking spray or shortening. Dust lightly with flour, shaking out excess.

2 In a medium bowl, whisk together the flour, baking powder, baking soda, and salt. In a small bowl or liquid measuring cup, combine the buttermilk and vanilla.

3 In a stand mixer fitted with the paddle attachment, cream the butter at medium speed until light, about 3 minutes. Gradually beat in the sugar until light and fluffy, about 5 minutes. Scrape down the sides of the bowl. Add the eggs, one at a time, beating well after each addition until well incorporated. Add the flour mixture in three additions, alternating with the buttermilk mixture, beginning and ending with the flour. Beat for 1 minute more, until the batter is smooth.

4 Pour the batter into the pans and bake until a wooden pick inserted in the center comes out clean, 30 to 35 minutes. Cool the cakes in the pans on wire racks for 10 minutes, then turn them out onto wire racks to cool completely.

5 Wipe away any crumbs on the surface of the cakes. Place one cake on a serving plate. Spread the cake with half of the icing or frosting to coat, then place the second cake on top. Coat with the remaining icing or frosting.

CARAMEL ICING

MAKES ABOUT 2¹/₂ CUPS

1¼ cups heavy whipping cream
2½ cups packed brown sugar
5 tablespoons butter, at room temperature, cut into pieces
Pinch of salt
2½ teaspoons vanilla extract

1 In a small heavy saucepan, heat the cream over medium heat just until bubbles appear around the edges of the pan. Keep warm.

2 In a heavy-bottomed or cast-iron skillet, cook the brown sugar over medium heat until melted, 2 to 3 minutes. Keep cooking until it's turned a shade or two darker but not burnt, then gradually and carefully stir in the scalded cream with a wooden spoon. The mixture will bubble up. Cook and stir to a syrup or soft-ball stage on a candy thermometer, 234° to 240°F. Remove from heat and stir in the butter, salt, and vanilla. Beat with a wooden spoon until the icing is cool and has thickened to a spreadable consistency. Work quickly when spreading on the cake, as the icing sets up very fast.

BROWN SUGAR BUTTERCREAM FROSTING

MAKES ABOUT 2¹/₂ CUPS

12 tablespoons (1½ sticks) butter, at room temperature
1 cup packed light brown sugar
½ cup whole milk
3 cups sifted powdered sugar
½ teaspoon salt
2 teaspoons vanilla extract
¼ cup half-and-half, as needed

1 In a heavy-bottomed or cast-iron skillet, melt the butter over low heat. Stir in the brown sugar and milk. Bring to a boil over high heat and boil for 2 minutes.

2 Remove the pan from the heat and, with a wooden spoon, beat in the powdered sugar, salt, and vanilla. Beat until the frosting is cool and has thickened to spreading consistency. If the mixture becomes too thick, beat in the half-and-half 1 tablespoon at a time.

Spice Cakes

People of African descent have appreciated pungent seasonings going back to when the Ethiopian Queen of Sheba delivered gifts of abundant spices, gold, and precious stones to King Solomon. So I am not surprised that the nutmeg, cloves, and mace that brought riches to European merchants during the spice trade delivered prosperity to free and formerly enslaved pastry cooks, too.

Black cooks and spice cake go way back.

In the early nineteenth century, Mary Simpson heavily spiced cream cake batter, studded it with raisins and dried currants, and served "Washington Cake" in her basement pastry shop to a diverse crowd of New Yorkers to honor the birthday of the man she said was her former master, George Washington. Charity "Duchess" Quamino was known as Newport, Rhode Island's best pastry chef—especially praised for her frosted plum cakes, which she baked for events such as "Washington's Birthnight Ball." By 1922, this history was either unknown or ignored by mainstream cookbook authors, including the duo who published recipes on behalf of their "mammy," Caroline Pickett. The Washington Cake in *Aunt Caroline's Dixieland Recipes* is attributed to Martha Washington.

Although few explained its origins, black authors remembered spice cake in their cookbooks by many names. Molasses ('Lasses) cake is a plantation relic, mentioned often in the slave narratives; salt pork cake is sweetened with molasses and granulated sugar, spiced with cinnamon, nutmeg, cloves, and allspice, and studded with raisins. In hard times, spice cake was created from a few simple ingredients—flour, raisins, cinnamon, cloves, molasses or brown sugar, and water—a combination that evolved into a wartime recipe, known to several authors as "Milkless, Eggless, Butterless Cake."

Hardscrabble is just part of the spice cake legacy, though. When penny-pinching was no longer necessary, pastry cooks folded eggs, milk, and butter back into the batter. Eventually, dried fruit as the primary ingredient was mostly forgotten, replaced by the fresher tastes of homemade preserves, freshly grated apples, citrus, or chocolate. (Freda DeKnight even included a recipe for a spice cake moistened with tomato soup in her midcentury collection of middle-class recipes.)

Spice cake is still with us today, sometimes identified by the main ingredient; think carrot, applesauce, or winter squash cakes. Black cookbook authors also cling religiously to the recipe for Scripture Cake, a divine spice cake studded with figs and raisins. When I want to express reverence for these heritage recipes, I call them "soul cakes."

GINGERBREAD
WITH LEMON SAUCE
SERVES 12 TO 15

Booker T. Washington spent nine years of his life confined to a tobacco plantation in the Virginia piedmont, but he went on to become a noted author, orator, and founder of the Tuskegee Institute. In his autobiography, *Up From Slavery*, a vivid retelling of his upbringing in a cabin that doubled as the plantation kitchen house and the sweet potato bank, he described his passion for ginger cakes: "I saw my two young mistresses and some lady visitors eating ginger cakes . . . those cakes seemed to me to be absolutely the most tempting and desirable things that I had ever seen; and I then and there resolved that, if I ever got free, the height of my ambition would be . . . to eat ginger cakes in the way that I saw those young ladies doing."

African American cookbooks also carry on the ginger cake tradition—from the "old-time ginger cake" Abby Fisher baked in 1881 to author Vertamae Smart-Grosvenor's gingerbread in the 2001 cookbook *Vertamae Cooks in the Americas' Family Kitchen*. Verta dedicated the recipe to Booker T. Washington in a 2001 NPR interview to celebrate June 19, 1865. Juneteenth, as the day is known, is the day that the enslaved in Texas learned that the Emancipation Proclamation had set them free.

The essentials for gingerbread are usually the same: flour, butter, sugar, eggs, spices, and molasses baked until dark and lovely. You can experiment with sweeteners such as cane syrup, maple syrup, honey, and sorghum molasses, or try moistening the gingerbread batter with different liquids, such as coffee, milk, or buttermilk. Despite the name, gingerbread's mahogany crumb is light and cakelike, not at all dense like pumpkin, banana, or other quick breads.

This is my version of the recipe, developed with chef Joe Randall, which we published in *A Taste of Heritage: The New African-American Cuisine*. It is sweet and moist, fragrant with the scent of ginger and the distinctly bold flavor of molasses. Serve this gingerbread with a dollop of sweet Bourbon Chantilly Cream or a light garnish of warm Lemon Sauce.

Butter or shortening for the pan
2½ cups all-purpose flour, plus extra for the pan
2 teaspoons baking powder
1 teaspoon baking soda
½ teaspoon salt
2 teaspoons ground ginger
1 teaspoon ground cinnamon
½ teaspoon ground cloves
1 cup molasses
1 cup boiling-hot coffee
1 stick (4 ounces) butter, melted
½ cup packed dark brown sugar
2 large eggs, beaten
Lemon Sauce or Bourbon Chantilly Cream (recipes follow), for serving

1 Preheat the oven to 350°F. Lightly coat a 13 × 9-inch baking pan with butter or shortening. Dust with flour, tapping out the excess.

2 In a bowl, whisk together the flour, baking powder, baking soda, salt, ginger, cinnamon, and cloves. In a bowl or measuring cup, stir together the molasses and coffee.

3 In a stand mixer fitted with the paddle attachment, beat the melted butter, brown sugar, and eggs on medium speed until light. Beat in the flour mixture in three additions, alternating with the coffee-molasses mixture, beginning and ending with the flour mixture. Scrape down the sides of the bowl, then beat for 30 seconds longer.

4 Pour the batter into the pan. Bake until a wooden pick inserted in the center comes out clean, 30 to 45 minutes. Cool the gingerbread in the pan on a wire rack, then cut into squares and serve warm with lemon sauce or bourbon Chantilly cream.

LEMON SAUCE

MAKES ABOUT 1 CUP

½ cup sugar

1 tablespoon cornstarch

1 cup boiling water

2 to 3 tablespoons butter (to taste), cut into pieces, at room temperature

Grated zest and juice of 1 lemon

½ teaspoon vanilla extract

Pinch of salt

In a small saucepan, whisk together the sugar and cornstarch until well mixed. Gradually whisk in the boiling water. Bring to a boil over medium heat, then reduce the heat to medium-low and simmer until the sauce is thick and resembles syrup, about 5 minutes. Add the butter, lemon zest, lemon juice, vanilla, and salt, and stir until the butter has melted. Cool to room temperature to serve.

BOURBON CHANTILLY CREAM

MAKES ABOUT 2 CUPS

1 cup heavy whipping cream

2 teaspoons powdered sugar, sifted

2 teaspoons bourbon

In the chilled bowl of an electric mixer with chilled beaters, whip the cream to soft peaks. Sprinkle in the sugar and beat until blended, no more than 30 seconds. Add the bourbon, beating until stiff peaks form. Do not overbeat.

WASHINGTON CAKE

The Blue Grass Cook Book, Minnie C. Fox, 1904

1 pound of flour

1 pound of brown sugar

½ pound of butter

1 cup sweet milk

1 teaspoon soda, sifted with flour

1 pound raisins, stoned

½ pound of currants

½ pound of citron

1 cup of English walnuts, chopped fine

4 eggs, beaten together

1 teaspoon of cinnamon

1 teaspoon of cloves

½ glass of whisky

Bake in a 4-quart can, and in a slow oven.

SWEET POTATO–MANGO CAKE

SERVES 10

"Some of the very best dishes in the South were created by Blacks and this cake is a delicious example," Terry Thompson-Anderson wrote in 1988 in *A Taste of the South*. She praised an amazing, "well-loved cook" named Aunt Jessie, who started with a few lowly sweet potatoes and produced a marvelous nut-studded cake flavored with spices, orange—and a "healthy slug of whiskey."

This sweet potato cake, also known as yam cake, will remind you of the iced pumpkin bread that is so popular in coffee shops, served with the afternoon brew. The crumb is more airy than the pumpkin loaf, but it tastes just as sweet, thanks to studs of mango and the light orange-bourbon glaze that sinks into the cake's crust. The idea for including diced mango comes from chef Pierre Thiam's yam cake in *Senegal: Modern Senegalese Recipes from the Source to the Bowl*. The addition of orange flavor salutes Aunt Jessie.

Butter or shortening, for the pan
2¾ cups all-purpose flour, plus extra for the pan
2 teaspoons ground cinnamon
2 teaspoons ground ginger
1 teaspoon baking soda
1 teaspoon salt
1 cup vegetable oil
1 cup granulated sugar
1 cup packed dark brown sugar
1 cup mashed cooked sweet potatoes, at room temperature
1 cup finely diced mango
2 teaspoons grated orange zest
4 large eggs
1 teaspoon vanilla extract
¼ cup powdered sugar
1 tablespoon orange juice or whiskey, or half of each

1 Preheat the oven to 325°F. Generously coat a 10-inch tube pan with butter or shortening. Dust with flour, tapping out the excess.

2 In a bowl, whisk together the flour, cinnamon, ginger, baking soda, and salt.

3 In a separate large bowl, use a wooden spoon to beat together the oil, granulated sugar, and brown sugar until well mixed. Stir in the sweet potatoes, mango, and orange zest, stirring for 1 minute, until smooth. Whisk in the eggs, one at a time, beating well after each addition. Stir in the flour-spice mixture and the vanilla, mixing just until blended.

4 Pour the batter into the tube pan. Bake until a wooden pick inserted in the center comes out clean, about 1 hour. Let the cake cool in the pan on a wire rack for 10 minutes, then turn the cake out on the rack to cool completely.

5 In a small bowl, whisk together the powdered sugar and orange juice (or whiskey). Drizzle over the cooled cake.

JAM CAKE

SERVES 10 TO 12

As African Americans moved economically upward, recipes for this sweetly spiced cake started to feature store-bought strawberry, blackberry, or fig preserves as upper-class households abandoned scratch canning for less labor-intensive activities.

I reassembled this recipe with elements from across decades. This version has more sugar than wartime formulas, and butter replaces vegetable shortening—the "scientific discovery" of the early twentieth century. The cake retains its spice-forward flavor, moist texture, and hint of fruit sugar that comes from the jam in the batter. To turn a spotlight on the spice, double the amounts I give here; to accentuate the jam, here is a trick I learned from Patty Pinner's *Sweet Mornings: 125 Sweet and Savory Breakfast and Brunch Recipes:* Instead of beating the jam into the batter, pour the batter into the pan and pour the jam over the top. Use a wooden skewer or table knife to swirl the jam through the batter, then bake.

Softened butter or shortening for the pan

3 cups all-purpose flour, plus extra for the pan

1 teaspoon baking powder

½ teaspoon salt

1 teaspoon ground cinnamon

½ teaspoon ground cloves

¼ teaspoon ground allspice or nutmeg

2 sticks (8 ounces) butter, at room temperature

1¼ cups granulated sugar

4 large eggs

1 cup whole milk

1 teaspoon vanilla extract

1 cup blackberry or strawberry jam

Double batch Brown Sugar Buttercream Frosting (page 279)

1 Preheat the oven to 350°F. Lightly coat two 9-inch cake pans with butter or shortening. Dust with flour and shake out the excess.

2 In a medium bowl, whisk together the flour, baking powder, salt, cinnamon, cloves, and allspice.

3 In a stand mixer fitted with the paddle attachment, cream the butter on medium speed until light, about 3 minutes. Gradually beat in the sugar, ½ cup at a time, until light and fluffy, about 5 minutes. Add the eggs, one at a time, beating well after each addition until well incorporated. With the mixer on low speed, beat in the flour mixture in three additions, alternating with the milk, beginning and ending with the flour. Beat in the vanilla and jam until well blended and the batter is smooth.

4 Pour the batter into the pans and bake until a wooden pick inserted in the center comes out clean, about 30 minutes. Cool the cakes in the pans on wire racks for 10 minutes, then turn out onto wire racks to cool completely.

5 Wipe away any crumbs on the surface of the cakes. Place one of the cakes on a serving plate. Spread the cake with half of the frosting to coat, then place the second cake on top. Coat the top layer with the remaining frosting.

Cookies, as Small Cakes

The word cookie comes from the Dutch *koekje*, meaning "little cake." Until the mid-twentieth century, the small, flat, sweet cakes we know as cookies were called biscuits, small cakes, or wafers, one of the early American dishes caught in the blurry fusion of European recipes and native ingredients.

Beginning in 1866, when African Americans published cookbooks of their own without white authors "translating" for them, they included many recipes for small cakes, also known as cookies, which would appear on Arturo Schomburg's list of Negro recipes in the 1930s, such as Russian Rocks, Cream Cookies, and Walnut Wafers.

Bertha Turner portrayed small cakes both simple and elegant in her 1910 collection of recipes from the Negro women of California: The simple included sugar cookies, oatmeal cookies, ginger snaps, and a cookie laced with spice and raisins she called Old English Cookies; the elegant included "Mrs. Turner's Small Cakes," which involved a dough of butter, milk, egg whites, powdered sugar, and leavening and were flavored with lemon juice that was baked in sheets, cut in desired shapes, split, and filled with cream filling, then frosted with boiled icing *before* decorating.

Twenty years later, Dr. George Washington Carver offered recipes for peanut cookies in one of the bulletins he sent to Southern families to improve farming practices and improve nutrition, *How to Grow the Peanut, and 105 Ways of Preparing It for Human Consumption:* peanut cookies sweetened generously or lightly, and three types of peanut wafers, which were dropped or baked like bars, depending upon the amount of flour used.

Creative treats such as these, fun and dignified, counteract the recipes white authors disparagingly credited to their black cooks at the time. In 1922, for example, when Emma and William McKinney published recipes collected from their old mammy, Caroline Pickett, in *Aunt Caroline's Dixieland Recipes,* they gave her cookies names like Pickaninny Cookies, Plantation Cookies, Aunt Sug's Nut Cookies, and Mason and Dixon Cookies.

TEA CAKES

MAKES ABOUT 2 DOZEN TEA CAKES

There is a collectible cookie tin, festooned with gold script and a portrait of Mary McLeod Bethune, in the drawer below my oven. Back in 1996, "Mrs. Bethune's Tea Cakes" filled the box.

Developed as a fundraising joint venture between Etha Robinson and the National Council of Negro Women, Mrs. Bethune's Tea Cakes were a simple butter cookie—a tender cross between pound cake and shortbread, as Heidi Haughy Cusick described them in her 1995 cookbook, *Soul and Spice*. Tea cakes are not as sweet as sugar cookies and less fluffy than madeleines (the French tea cakes shaped like a scallop shell). They show up in black cookbooks—a lot.

A simple dessert, tea cakes played a key role in a proud tradition, Charlemae Rollins explained in *Christmas Gif': An Anthology of Christmas Poems, Songs, and Stories, Written by and About Negroes*. The game of "Christmas Gif" originated in the plantation kitchen. Rollins's grandmother was a bondswoman who described it this way: "Two people, meeting for the first time that day, would compete to be the first to call out 'Christmas Gif!', the loser happily paid a forfeit of a simple present—maybe a Christmas tea cake or a handful of nuts. There was more pleasure in being 'caught,' and having to give a present—the giving, though comically protested, was heartwarming to a people who had so little they could with dignity share with others."

Rollins's grandmother recalled that no long journey was ever made without taking along "a flour sack half-full of tea cakes."

Through the history of this recipe, I found the combination of butter, sugar, eggs, and flour usually flavored one of three ways. A hint of nutmeg seemed essential for some, while modern interpretations add a bit of citrus zest or extract. Cooks without access to spices baked plain dough, enriched with whole milk, evaporated milk, buttermilk, or sour cream.

With reverence for the old ways, and pulling from several recipes, here is my rendition of tea cakes, with baking powder added for a little extra lift. You can personalize them, too, substituting a pinch of cinnamon, allspice, or mace for the nutmeg or sour cream for the buttermilk.

3 cups all-purpose flour, plus more for the work surface

1 teaspoon baking powder

¼ teaspoon baking soda

½ teaspoon salt

¼ teaspoon ground or freshly grated nutmeg

1 stick (4 ounces) butter, at room temperature

1 cup sugar

2 large eggs

¼ cup buttermilk

1 teaspoon vanilla extract

Demerara sugar, for sprinkling

1 In a bowl, whisk together the flour, baking powder, baking soda, salt, and nutmeg.

2 In a stand mixer fitted with the paddle attachment, cream together the butter and sugar on medium speed until light and fluffy, 2 to 3 minutes. Scrape down the sides of the bowl. Add the eggs, one at a time, beating well after each addition. Scrape down the sides of the bowl again, then beat in the buttermilk and vanilla.

3 Gradually add the flour mixture, beating just until smooth and well blended. Divide the dough in half. Flatten each half into a disc. Wrap in plastic and refrigerate until chilled and slightly stiff, at least 1 hour, but overnight ideally.

4 Preheat the oven to 375°F. Line baking sheets with parchment paper.

5 On a lightly floured surface, working with one portion at a time, roll the dough to a ¼-inch thickness. Cut with a floured 1½-inch round biscuit cutter. Gather the scraps, reroll, and cut again. Sprinkle lightly with demerara sugar. Transfer the tea cakes to the baking sheets and space them about 1 inch apart.

6 Bake until the tea cakes are lightly browned, 8 to 10 minutes. Cool on the pan for 1 minute, then transfer to a wire rack to cool completely. The tea cakes will keep for about 2 weeks in an airtight container.

TEA CAKES

The Southern Cookbook: A Manual of Cooking and List of Menus, Including Recipes Used by Noted Colored Cooks and Prominent Caterers,
S. Thomas Bivins, 1912

Rub fine four ounces of butter into eight ounces of flour, mix eight ounces of currants and six of fine Lisbon sugar, two yolks and one white of an egg and a spoonful of brandy. Roll the paste the thickness of an Oliver biscuit, and cut with a wine glass. You may beat the other white and wash over them, and either dust sugar, or not, as you like.

EVERY-KIND-OF-COOKIE DOUGH

MAKES ABOUT 2 DOZEN COOKIES

As you can tell, I love to bake. So I was having an impossible time deciding which cookies to include and which to leave out of this book. My ancestors had no such problem. Their cookbooks feature dozens and dozens of irresistible sweet treats, some studded with nuts and fruit, the rest spiced, spiked, or iced, depending upon the whim of the cook. Thankfully, the Darden sisters came to my rescue.

Norma Jean and Carole Darden's family recipes and recollections have been published in multiple editions of *Spoonbread and Strawberry Wine* (1978), which includes a basic sugar cookie dough recipe from a close friend of their mother's. From Aunt Marjorie's cookie dough base, the Darden sisters made "at least nine varieties of crunchy cookies," all of them still popular today.

Building on that idea, here I offer a classic cookie dough base, with variations and some historical notes. The addition of shortening may seem old-fashioned, but it yields cookies that are light and maintain their shape.

2 cups all-purpose flour, plus more for the work surface

½ teaspoon baking soda

¼ teaspoon salt

6 tablespoons butter

6 tablespoons shortening

½ cup packed brown sugar

½ cup granulated sugar

1 large egg

1 teaspoon vanilla extract

1 In a bowl, whisk together the flour, baking soda, and salt.

2 In a stand mixer fitted with the paddle attachment, cream together the butter, shortening, brown sugar, and granulated sugar on medium speed until light and fluffy, about 3 minutes. Add the egg and vanilla and beat until well blended. Gradually add the flour mixture, beating just until smooth and well blended. Flavor the dough as desired (see Variations, opposite). Wrap the dough in plastic and flatten into a disc. Refrigerate the dough until chilled and slightly stiff, at least 1 hour.

3 Preheat the oven to 350°F. Line baking sheets with parchment paper.

4 For drop cookies: Use a ½-ounce cookie scoop or a tablespoon to drop dough onto the baking sheets. For cut-out cookies: On a floured surface, roll the dough out to a ¼-inch thickness. Cut into desired shapes. Use a spatula to transfer the cookies to ungreased baking sheets, spaced about 1 inch apart.

5 Bake until the cookies are lightly browned, 12 to 15 minutes. Cool on the pan for 1 minute, then transfer to wire racks to cool completely.

PEANUT BUTTER COOKIES

Travel with Bea Sandler, author of the 1970 *The African Cookbook*, to the marketplaces of Dakar with a simplified version of *cinq centimes* (five-cent cookies): Bake the sugar cookies as the recipe directs, then spread one side with peanut butter and sprinkle with coarsely chopped salted roasted peanuts.

CHOCOLATE CHIP COOKIES

When you want to splurge, as *The Soul of Southern Cooking* author Kathy Starr's family did when chocolate fit into the budget, add ½ cup semisweet or dark chocolate chips and ¼ cup chopped nuts to the dough just before finishing the mixing.

LEMON WAFER COOKIES

Indulge your whimsy as chef and TV personality Carla Hall suggests in *Carla's Comfort Foods*. Stir 3 to 4 teaspoons finely ground, high-quality loose-leaf herbal lemon tea or 2 tablespoons freshly grated lemon zest into the flour mixture, and substitute lemon extract for the vanilla.

MOLASSES-SPICE COOKIES

Bake cookies inspired by the "Creoles" in Mrs. T. P. (Sarah Helen) Mahammitt's *Recipes and Domestic Service: The Mahammitt School of Cookery* to remember the Creolized language, culture, and cuisine forged by enslaved Africans during the horrendous trade of molasses and rum for human beings. Add 1 teaspoon each of ground ginger, cloves, and cinnamon, and an additional 1½ teaspoons baking soda to the dry ingredients. Add 2 tablespoons molasses to the egg mixture. Bake as directed.

BENNE COOKIES

Use ¼ cup less flour in the dough, and blend in ¾ cup toasted benne or white sesame seeds just before the end of mixing. These will be more puffed-up than the thin, lacy benne wafers (page 25) and a departure from benne candy or benne crackers. (Enslaved Africans planted benne, a close relative of sesame, in gardens along the Southeastern coast, where the seeds are still believed to bring good luck.) This cookie was inspired by *Occasions to Savor: Our Meals, Menus, and Memories* by the Delta Sigma Theta Sorority.

HONEY COOKIES

The rich taste of honey was a common feature of many cooks' cookies; in the past, they would have harvested wild honey, but your local farmer's market may have local honey without the stings. Replace the granulated sugar in the dough with ½ cup honey, and add an additional ½ cup flour.

The Darden family enjoyed these variations to capture the tastes of the winter holidays:

Pumpkin Cookies: Add 1 *tablespoon pumpkin spice.*

Apple Cookies: Add 1 *tablespoon apple pie spice and* 1 *small apple, peeled, cored, and finely diced.*

Eggnog Cookies: Add 1 *tablespoon rum and* 1 *teaspoon ground or grated nutmeg.*

Fruitcake Cookies: Add 1 *tablespoon brandy and* 1/2 *cup chopped citron and nuts.*

Two Creole Favorites

Bread pudding and pralines, two beloved sweets associated with both the city Creoles of New Orleans and Cajuns in the country, vividly illustrate the way that black cooks transitioned unwanted leftovers into financial advantage.

Bread pudding is a frugal cook's way with stale French bread, which Creoles called "lost bread." It's one of the stunning desserts Crescent City cooks have produced for centuries, Nathaniel Burton explained in the collection of recipes and reminiscences he composed with Rudy Lombard, *Creole Feast: Fifteen Master Chefs of New Orleans Reveal Their Secrets*.

In personal profiles and recipes, the New Orleans culinary elite looked back through the years at their work in professional kitchens in Pullman train cars, merchant marine galleys, cooking schools, hotels, restaurants, and fine private homes. Their creative improvisation and style were perfected in "almost complete anonymity and frequently in a hostile environment," the authors wrote, but "they are proud heirs to the rich legacy of Creole cuisine they have inherited from Black professional cooks."

Bread pudding is one way Creole chefs showed off their creative whims, starting with regular stale bread, then stirring in favorite flavors to make it special—finely diced apples, fresh coconut, and drained crushed pineapple—and topping the dessert with whiskey, rum or hard sauce, fluffy meringue, or ice cream.

Pralines replay this improv story. Mirroring a treat once called "hard times candy" or "groundnut cakes," pralines originally were made with molasses (a by-product of sugar refining), then evolved to a boiled sugar syrup base when sugar was no longer a luxury. The process for making pralines was detailed this way in *Soul and Spice: African Cooking in the Americas*: "After the sugar syrup was heated until dark and caramelized, it was mixed with peanuts, pecans, benne (sesame) seeds, or sometimes cornflakes. A little butter might be added to make a creamy praline. The nutty confections were poured out onto corn husks to set up."

Women sold them from door to door in public areas of the city, throughout the African diaspora in the New World, Jessica B. Harris explained in *The Welcome Table: African-American Heritage Cooking*. "The legacy of the slave saleswomen still lives on in Brazil's *baianas de tabuleiro*, in the sweets-sellers of the Caribbean, and in the pralinieres of New Orleans."

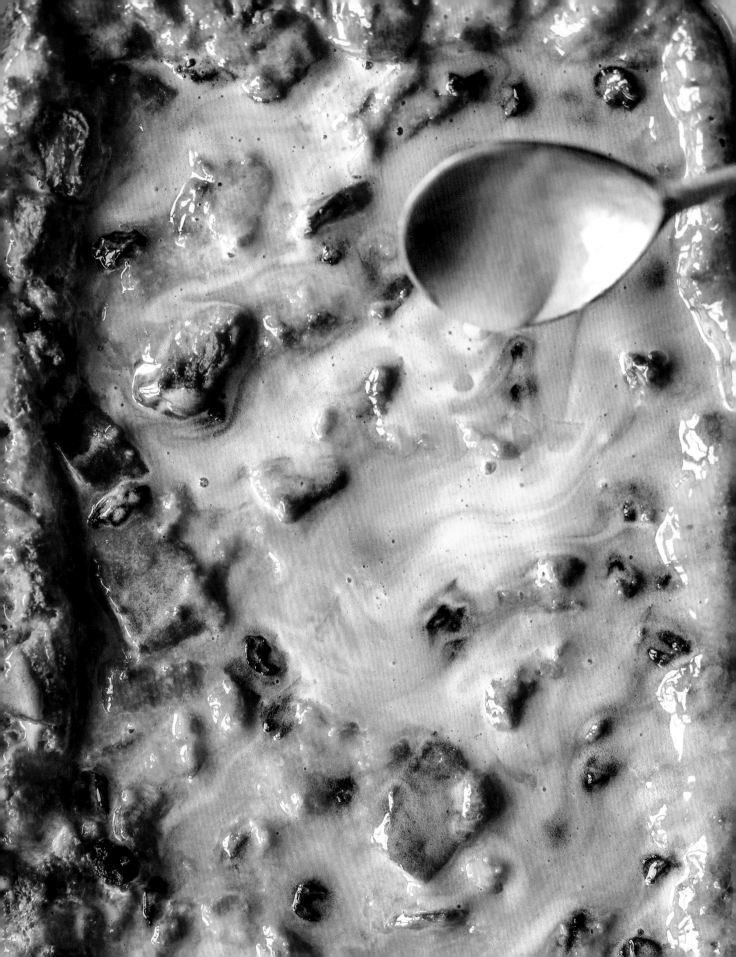

BREAD PUDDING
WITH WHISKEY SAUCE
SERVES 8

Annie Laura Squalls, the head baker at the Pontchartrain Hotel during the 1960s, was one of the accomplished cooks saluted in Burton and Lombard's *Creole Feast*. She shared her secret for making bread pudding, even if you don't have stale bread. "Put fresh bread in the oven, dry it out, then butter it like toast when you take it from the oven. Vanilla sauce goes nicely with it."

Chefs Leah Chase, Austin Leslie, and Louis Evans offered their own twists on "bread and butter" pudding in their cookbooks. Here are a few of them: Instead of soaking bread, toast dinner rolls or croissants and butter them generously before adding to the recipe. Try stirring in 1 cup peeled and grated fresh apple or diced pineapple. Swap in evaporated milk or light cream for the whole milk for a richer texture and flavor.

For a taste of Creole Los Angeles, I adapted my recipe from Homer's Great Whiskey Pudding from the restaurant Homer and Edy's Bistro. I have carefully protected the Creole recipes Edy Luke shared with me more than twenty years ago from the restaurant she and her husband owned and operated in West Los Angeles. The copy paper has yellowed, but the hand-written recipes are as dear as ever. In 2012, Edy honored her late husband's distinctive Creole style in an electronic cookbook, *Chef Homer's Taste of Old New Orleans*.

3 tablespoons butter, melted
1 pound sandwich or French bread, stale
4 cups whole milk
3 large eggs, beaten
2 cups sugar
½ teaspoon salt
1 teaspoon vanilla extract
1 cup raisins
Whiskey Sauce (recipe follows)

1 Preheat the oven to 350°F. Pour the butter into the bottom of a 13 × 9-inch baking pan.

2 Cut or tear the bread into 1-inch pieces. In a large bowl, soak the bread in the milk for 5 minutes. Crush with your hands to thoroughly mix. Stir in the eggs, sugar, salt, vanilla, and raisins and stir well. Pour the bread mixture into the buttered pan.

3 Bake until firm, about 45 minutes. Cool.

4 Heat under the broiler until lightly browned, or serve without browning, with the sauce on the side.

WHISKEY SAUCE
MAKES ABOUT 1½ CUPS

1 stick (4 ounces) butter
1 cup sugar
1 large egg, beaten
¼ cup whiskey, brandy, or rum to taste

In a heatproof bowl set over a pan of boiling water, stir together the butter and sugar until the sugar dissolves. Whisk in the egg. Cook, whisking constantly, until the sauce is thick and ribbony, about 5 minutes. Cool slightly, then stir in the liquor of your choice.

PRALINES

MAKES ABOUT 2 DOZEN PRALINES

These pralines are my adaptation of the Pecan Candy in *Cleora's Kitchens: The Memoir of a Cook & Eight Decades of Great American Food* by Cleora Butler. I traded molasses for her dark corn syrup and heavy cream for the milk, resulting in pralines that are thick and chewy. Decadent. For flat pralines, replace the cream with 1 cup milk.

1½ **cups packed brown sugar**
1½ **cups granulated sugar**
3 **tablespoons molasses or dark corn syrup**
1 **cup heavy whipping cream or whole milk**
4 **tablespoons butter**
2 **cups pecans, toasted and coarsely chopped**
Pinch of salt
1 **teaspoon vanilla extract**

1 Line a baking sheet with parchment or wax paper.

2 In a heavy-bottomed medium saucepan, stir together the brown sugar, granulated sugar, molasses, and cream over medium-high heat. Stir with a wooden spoon until the sugar dissolves.

3 Bring to a boil and continue to cook for about 5 minutes, until the mixture begins to thicken and forms a soft ball when a small amount is dropped from a spoon into a bowl of cold water, about 5 minutes. (Or use a candy thermometer; the temperature needs to reach 240°F.) Be very careful through this process, as the mixture is very hot and can burn severely.

4 Remove the pan from the heat and use a wooden spoon to stir in the butter, pecans, salt, and vanilla. Continue to stir vigorously until thick, 2 to 3 minutes. Working quickly, spoon heaping tablespoons of the mixture onto the lined baking sheet. Allow the pralines to cool completely. Store in an airtight container.

GROUNDNUT CAKES

Two Hundred Years of Charleston Cooking,
Blanche Rhett, Lettie Gay, and
Helen Woodward, 1930
[This recipe appears alongside a photograph of Maum Chloe, a groundnut cake vendor from James Island. The accompanying note explained that despite its name, "this makes a somewhat chewy candy similar to taffy."]

1 quart molasses
1 cup brown sugar
½ cup butter
4 cups peanuts, parched and shelled

Combine the first three ingredients and boil for half an hour over a slow fire. Then add the roasted and shelled peanuts and continue cooking for fifteen minutes. Pour into a lightly-greased shallow pan and allow to harden. Break into pieces.

Ice Cream

Augustus Jackson cooked in the Andrew Jackson White House before leaving to "stake his claim as an ice cream empire maker," Adrian Miller explained in *The President's Kitchen Cabinet: The Story of the African Americans Who Have Fed Our First Families, from the Washingtons to the Obamas.* Although historians used to say eggless ice cream was created by Dolly Madison, Miller notes that Augustus Jackson is increasingly credited with inventing it.

Later, Jackson ran a confectionery store in Philadelphia, where he sold ice cream in quart cans for $1 each, a truly luxurious, elite confection. His eggless style of ice cream became known as "Philadelphia-style," while early black cookbooks described egg custard-based versions of the frozen treat as "American-style."

Before there was ice cream as we know it, "snow cream represented all the joy of childhood," Freda DeKnight reminisced in 1948. She obtained a recipe from tenor Carl Jones, while he was on tour with the Delta Rhythm Boys. Dori Sanders, who remembered that her grandma "churned clabber-ready milk into buttermilk, using peach and strawberry jams to stretch her scant supply of sugar," also gave a vivid account of the thick and creamy snow cream in *Dori Sanders' Country Cooking: Recipes and Stories from the Family Farm Stand.* She made a boiled custard, set it in the refrigerator to chill, then stirred in chilled milk and a "big pail of clean, fresh-fallen snow."

PEACH-BUTTERMILK ICE CREAM

MAKES 1 QUART

Behind this recipe is a story the historian Marcie Cohen Ferris culled from the diaries of Freedom Riders imprisoned in Mississippi's dreaded Mississippi State Penitentiary, otherwise known as Parchman Farm.

When the college students plied a jailer with kindness and respect according to Dr. Martin Luther King Jr.'s philosophy of nonviolence for social change, the jailer was won over, to some degree—he arranged for them to be served ice cream every night. After the students were released, "they experienced the full hospitality of Mississippi's black community" at a dinner in their honor. Peach ice cream was served for dessert.

In memory of the peach ice cream featured in Minnie C. Fox's blissful 1904 collection of Kentucky recipes, *The Blue Grass Cook Book*, I made this frozen treat rich with cream, sugar, and fresh, sweet fruit and replaced the "morning's milk" she called for with the mild tang of buttermilk. Using a swirl of peach preserves that plays up the fruit flavor comes by way of a recipe by South Carolina peach farmer Dori Sanders.

1¼ pounds very ripe peaches, peeled and pitted (see Note)

2 tablespoons fresh lemon juice

½ cup peach preserves

2 cups heavy whipping cream

1 cup buttermilk

1½ cups sugar

2 large egg yolks, beaten

1 teaspoon vanilla extract

1 In a blender or food processor, puree the peaches and lemon juice. Measure out 1½ cups of the puree and transfer to a bowl (reserve any additional for another use). Stir the peach preserves into the puree. Set aside in the refrigerator.

2 Set up a large bowl of ice and water. In a medium saucepan, heat the cream and buttermilk over low heat until simmering, stirring occasionally. Add the sugar and stir to dissolve. Stir a small amount of the hot cream-sugar mixture into the beaten yolks to temper them, then stir the warmed yolks back into the pan while stirring. Return to a simmer, stirring constantly, and cook until the mixture coats the back of a spoon, 5 to 7 minutes. Do not boil. Remove from the heat and stir in the vanilla. Place a bowl into the bowl of ice water and pour the ice cream mixture into the empty bowl. Let stand in the ice bath until completely chilled, stirring occasionally, about 1 hour. (Alternatively, you can let the ice cream base chill in the refrigerator for a few hours or days before freezing in the ice cream maker.)

3 Stir in the chilled peach mixture and freeze in an ice cream maker according to the manufacturer's instructions. You may enjoy the ice cream right out of the maker for a soft-serve style, or pack it into containers and freeze for 8 hours or more for a scoopable consistency.

NOTE: To peel fresh peaches, bring a pot of water to a boil over high heat, and fill a large bowl with ice water. Blanch the peaches for about 10 seconds, until the skins loosen. Shock them in the ice water and slip the skins off. To pit them, simply split them in half and remove the pits.

SNOW CREAM

A Date with a Dish, Freda DeKnight, 1948

*Remove the top layer, and be sure the snow is clean.
Mix ½ cup sugar and 1 cup cream or milk with
1 tablespoon snow in a large bowl. Add snow gradually
until you get the consistency of ice cream. For variety
add: 1 cup crushed pineapple, mashed bananas, or
crushed sweetened apricots, peaches or strawberries.*

Pies

"There were groves of wild pecan trees down on the back acre on Grandaddy Bert Ferguson's farm in Charlotte, North Carolina," Sheila Ferguson recalled in *Soul Food: Classic Cuisine from the Deep South*. "Those tall sweeping old pecan trees were one beautiful sight and the fruits they bore were a real gift to us, as well as a test as to just how much nutcracking the human tooth could endure!" She then went on, of course, to talk about what might have been the destiny of those pecans: pie. "I'm told that Grandma Maggie would stack her pies up, one on top of the other, sometimes up to four or five of them, and when she sliced, she cut straight through the whole stack. The slices were narrower, of course, but the hunks were bigger and much more fun to eat."

What Ferguson didn't know was that this tradition of stack pies was common among old-school cooks. Charlemae Rollins shared the instructions for making them in her soul-era (1963) homage to black food folklore, *Christmas Gif': An Anthology of Christmas Poems, Songs, and Stories, Written by and About Negroes*: "Bake a sweet potato pie, a coconut pie, a custard pie, a mincemeat pie, and an apple pie. After removing from pie plate, stack each pie on top of each other. Press the stack gently, then cut into thin wedges so that everyone gets a taste of each pie."

Easier said than done, perhaps, but pie making has always been a hallmark of black baking. And single-serve pecan, buttermilk, and sweet potato pies kept the tradition of pie sharing alive in soul food restaurants, chicken shacks, and barbecue joints.

SOUTHERN PECAN PIE LACED WITH WHISKEY

SERVES 8

You can find standard pecan pie recipes on the label of the corn syrup bottle, but through the years I have encountered many inventive variations—whether predecessors or descendants. In slavery days, molasses pie, a cinnamon-spiced syrup-based pie without the nuts, was a Christmas treat. In later recipes, grated orange zest or coconut added an exotic perfume to the filling. Melted chocolate, chocolate chips, or cooked, mashed sweet potatoes spread on the crust gave tastebuds a surprise. And pie shells made from all sorts of baked goodies—from crushed ginger snap cookies and thin chocolate wafers, to graham crackers and zwieback toasts (old-time rusks)—have added variety.

But here is the time-honored version—sweet and gooey, packed with nuts—with one twist: The splash of whiskey or rum gives this spirited pie another layer of flavor and takes the pie's familiar syrupy sweetness down a notch.

1½ cups chopped toasted pecans, plus ½ cup pecan halves

2 tablespoons whiskey or rum

½ recipe Best-Ever Pie Crust (recipe follows), unbaked

6 tablespoons butter, at room temperature

1 cup packed dark brown sugar

¾ cup dark corn syrup

3 large eggs, beaten

¼ teaspoon salt

1 teaspoon vanilla extract

1 Place the chopped toasted pecans in a small bowl and toss with the whiskey until coated. Let stand 1 hour.

2 Preheat the oven to 350°F.

3 Roll the dough to fit a 9-inch pie plate, and tuck it in as the crust recipe directs.

4 In a stand mixer fitted with the paddle attachment, cream together the butter and brown sugar until light. Beat in the corn syrup, eggs, salt, and vanilla. Stir in the whiskey-soaked pecans. Pour into the pie shell, and arrange the pecan halves on top in an attractive pattern.

5 Bake until the filling is set but still has a slight jiggle in the middle, 55 to 60 minutes. (While baking, check to see that the edges of the crust aren't browning too quickly; cover them with foil if they are.) Cool the pie slightly, then serve warm or at room temperature.

BEST-EVER PIE CRUST

MAKES ENOUGH FOR TWO 9-INCH PIE CRUSTS

I use lard for my crusts because I love the rich flavor and short texture, but an all-butter dough results in an even flakier crust, should you choose to substitute more butter for the lard here. This recipe makes two crusts, for either two single-crust pies or one double-crust pie. Making the full amount is just as easy as making half of it, so if you only need one crust, freeze the other; that way there is always homemade dough on hand.

RECIPE CONTINUES

2 cups all-purpose flour, plus more for rolling

½ teaspoon salt

1 stick (4 ounces) butter, cut into ½-inch pieces and chilled

¼ cup lard or shortening, cut into ½-inch pieces and chilled

8 to 10 tablespoons ice-cold water

1 In a large bowl, whisk together the flour and salt. Sprinkle half of the butter and lard over the flour and use your fingertips, a pastry blender, or two knives to cut and mix until the mixture resembles large peas. Sprinkle in the remaining butter and lard and cut and mix to coarse crumbs. Sprinkle the dough with ice water, 1 tablespoon at a time, and use a fork to lightly mix until the dough just comes together and pulls away from the sides of the bowl. Gather the dough into a ball. Divide the ball in half. Press into two 1-inch-thick discs and wrap in plastic. Refrigerate for 30 minutes before rolling, or freeze for later use.

2 To blind-bake (prebake) the crust: Preheat the oven to 375°F.

3 Roll out the dough on a lightly floured surface to about 12 inches in diameter. Drape the dough over the rolling pin or fold it into quarters and transfer to a 9-inch pie plate. Press the pastry evenly into the pan, without stretching to fit. Trim the edges and crimp decoratively, as desired. Prick the crust all over with the tines of a fork. Cut parchment paper to fit the bottom and halfway up the sides of the pan. Line the pie shell with the paper. Pour in pie weights, uncooked rice, or dried beans to cover the bottom and sides of the crust. Bake for 12 minutes. Remove the paper and weights and bake the crust 5 minutes longer for a partially baked crust, or 10 minutes longer for a fully baked crust, until it looks dry and crisp.

SWEET POTATO PIE
WITH PRALINE TOPPING
SERVES 8

Sweet potato pie adapts well to creative combinations that capture the flavors of a stack pie mash-up. I've seen sweet potato custard mixed with pumpkin and coconut or made tipsy from praline liqueur, Frangelico, whiskey, or rum, but it is a cross between sweet potato pudding and a classic custard pie that we have here, with a caramelized pecan topping for good measure. You can make this pie without the topping, but why would you?

½ recipe Best-Ever Pie Crust (page 305), unbaked

1 pound sweet potatoes, unpeeled

½ cup packed light brown sugar

¼ cup granulated sugar

4 tablespoons (½ stick) butter, melted

2 large eggs, lightly beaten

½ cup evaporated milk or half-and-half

1 teaspoon vanilla extract

1 teaspoon grated orange zest

1 teaspoon ground cinnamon

½ teaspoon ground or freshly grated nutmeg

¼ teaspoon salt

Praline Topping (recipe follows)

1 Preheat the oven to 350°F.

2 Roll the dough to fit a 9-inch pie plate and tuck it into the plate as the crust recipe directs. Refrigerate until ready to use.

3 Place the sweet potatoes on a baking sheet and bake until fork-tender, about 1½ hours.

4 When the sweet potatoes are cool enough to handle, peel them and discard the skins. In a stand mixer fitted with the paddle attachment, beat together the warm sweet potatoes, brown sugar, granulated sugar, and melted butter on medium speed until smooth. With a wooden spoon, stir in the eggs, evaporated milk, vanilla, orange zest, cinnamon, nutmeg, and salt until mixed.

5 Pour the filling into the pie shell. Bake for 30 minutes. Remove the pie from the oven and carefully spoon the praline topping over the top. Bake until the topping is golden and the filling barely jiggles, 20 to 30 minutes more. Cool on a wire rack. Serve warm or chilled.

PRALINE TOPPING
MAKES ENOUGH FOR 1 PIE

Adding egg to praline topping is a modern twist. Unlike the crumbly topping that crowns Sweet Potato Casserole (page 197), this treatment creates a smooth layer that melts onto the custard.

3 tablespoons packed brown sugar
3 tablespoons granulated sugar
¼ cup all-purpose flour
1 egg
¼ teaspoon salt
3 tablespoons butter, melted
⅓ cup chopped pecans

In a medium bowl, combine the brown sugar, granulated sugar, flour, egg, and salt until well mixed. Stir in the melted butter and mix well. Stir in the pecans.

AUNT JEMIMA'S LEMON PIE

Aunt Caroline's Dixieland Recipes,
Emma and William McKinney, 1922
[Some cookbook authors relied upon the trademark image and name of Aunt Jemima to label African American cooks rather than to provide the name of a real person in their writings. This recipe may be an example of that kind of attribution.]

Six eggs,
One and one-half cups of sugar,
Two tablespoonsful of butter,
Three lemons,
Two tablespoonsful of flour,
One-half teaspoonful of baking powder,
One cup of milk.

To well beaten yolks add sugar, flour, milk, butter, baking powder, juice and grated rind of three lemons. Cook in double boiler until thick and then bake on a nice crust. After baking, make a meringue of the whites and bake a delicate brown.

LEMON MERINGUE PIE

SERVES 8

Lemon meringue pie is a nineteenth-century sweet made with a slightly tart lemon custard filling, sometimes called curd (an English type of preserves), and topped with billows of fluffy, sweetened egg whites. Its American roots trace to the old-time egg custard pies fashioned from eggs, butter, "something sweet"—molasses, sorghum syrup, or brown or white sugar—and a little flavoring, such as buttermilk, vinegar, vanilla extract, or lemon juice. That combination took the name "chess" pie, according to culinary legend, when an old cook who was asked to describe her intoxicating creation exclaimed, "It's 'jes pie."

With access to more lemons, plantation cooks worked more juice into the filling and thickened it with flour or cornstarch. The meringue put the egg whites to good use. It has been a staple on Southern and soul menus ever since. Adaptations abound.

Nancie McDermott, in her illuminating cookbook *Southern Pies,* saluted three African American cooks and chefs (all authors featured in *The Jemima Code*) and their lemon pies: Nathaniel Burton's New Orleans Lemon Pie, Leah Chase's Lemon Chess Pie, and Mrs. Natha Adkins Parker's Lemon Cloud Pie.

Here I present chef Joe Randall's Lemon Meringue Pie, adapted from the cookbook we published in 1998, *A Taste of Heritage: The New African-American Cuisine.* It is foolproof—none of that runny filling here; cooking the cornstarch an extra few minutes ensures that the filling sets up firm.

⅓ cup cornstarch

¼ teaspoon salt

3 large eggs, separated

1¾ cups sugar

2 tablespoons butter

1 tablespoon freshly grated lemon zest

½ cup fresh lemon juice

¼ teaspoon cream of tartar

½ recipe Best-Ever Pie Crust (page 305), blind-baked

1 In a heavy saucepan, bring 1½ cups water to a boil. In a small bowl or liquid measuring cup, dissolve the cornstarch and salt in ½ cup cold water. In a separate bowl, beat the egg yolks until thickened; set aside. Whisk the cornstarch mixture into the boiling water. The mixture will thicken considerably. Cook and stir over medium heat until it is almost translucent and resembles sour cream. Whisk in 1¼ cups of the sugar and bring back to a boil. Immediately remove from the heat. Beat 2 tablespoons of the hot mixture into the egg yolks, 1 tablespoon at a time, to temper them. Whisk the warmed yolks back into the hot mixture until combined. Whisk in the butter. Bring to a boil over low heat, stirring constantly, until the filling is thick, 1 to 2 minutes. Remove from the heat and stir in the lemon zest and lemon juice. Let cool for 30 minutes.

2 In the very-clean bowl of a stand mixer, beat the egg whites and cream of tartar until frothy, then beat on high speed until soft peaks form. Gradually beat in the remaining ½ cup sugar and continue to beat until stiff peaks form, about 2 minutes.

3 Pour the cooked filling into the prebaked pie crust. Spread the meringue over the filling, spreading to the edges of the crust to seal. Bake until the meringue is firm and golden, 6 to 8 minutes. Allow the pie to cool on a wire rack at room temperature, then refrigerate 3 to 4 hours before serving to help set the filling.

ACKNOWLEDGMENTS

NO STATEMENT OF THE EXCELLENCE OF THE COOKING OF AMERICAN HOMEMAKERS, WHO ARE REPRESENTATIVE OF EVERY RACE OF MANKIND, IS COMPLETE WITHOUT REFERENCE TO THE FINE COOKING OF THE NEGROES OF THE SOUTH, WHO ARE NATURAL GOURMETS. THEY SEEM TO HAVE INHERITED A SORT OF TRADITION OF GOOD COOKING, AND IT MAY BE THAT THIS WILL HAVE A LARGE PLACE IN THE FINAL DEVELOPMENT OF A REAL AMERICAN TYPE OF COOKERY.
—LOUIS P. DEGOUY, *THE GOLD COOK BOOK*, 1947

An adaptation of these words came to mind when I began thinking about how to express my appreciation for all of the blessings and grace extended to me by so many, in a space designed to recognize so few: No expression of appreciation for the assistance, support, and love that went into the making this book is complete without reference to the family members, lifelong and new friends, scholars, artists, and fans of *The Jemima Code*, who are representative of every race of mankind. They opened their hearts, shared family truths, and nudged this project along, and it may be that this will have a large place in the final appreciation of an expansive story of African American cookery.

To put it another way, it takes a village. And for me, a tribe of incredible women compose most of that village.

Before I get to them, let me say that this book would not have been possible without the pastors, spiritual leaders, and angels who provided me with guidance and comfort, and prayed with and for me through the dark times when insecurity and fear threatened to shut the whole thing down. Thank you for shining your light, Evan Black of Faith for Life Church in Austin; Philip and Sylvia Smith, Marcia and Trellis Stepter, and Denise Materre at Colorado Christian Fellowship; Jeanine Wade, Ana Dove Rodriguez, Jan Triplett, and the diverse women of Bible Study Fellowship, with whom I spent every Wednesday morning for seven years studying to understand my purpose.

I am indebted to everyone who has supported my efforts to reclaim my ancestors' reputations. That very long list includes those who bought *The Jemima Code* (you gave me the confidence and courage to tell my truth); the scholars whose research in Southern, women's, and African American studies schooled me; the chefs who dedicated their restaurants for book signings; the journalists who celebrated *The Code*'s debut with open minds; and so many friends who organized book parties, impromptu lunches, dinners, and happy hours that kept my fun-o-meter set on high, especially: the Hutt and Augustine Families (Heather, Ingrid, Jim, Annice, Hamilton, Harrison, Hugh), Nan Richie, Gina Harris, Joyce Turner, Sharon Gaston, Nikki Stinnette, Sedora Jefferson, Gale Ward, Todd and Joy Shorts, Monica McPherson, Adrienne Mayberry, and Michelle Ball; and I appreciate Wendolyn Washington of Jack and Jill of America; Roxann Chargois and Stacey Bell of the Town Lake Links; Carl Richie, Freddie Dixon, and the men of the Boule, who invited me into these circles of black excellence.

I am grateful for the tribe of women who became family along the way, helping me reconcile the European strands of my heritage: Karin Moss, Kelley Duvarney, Jackie Dielmann, Christy Ross, Luanne Stovall, June Jacobs, Nancie McDermott, Mary Margaret Pack, Lucey Bowen, Marla Camp, Virginia Willis, thank you for exchanging vulnerabilities that prove we are more alike than different. I have been blessed by the encouraging cards, emails, and texts that kept my gaze forward when industry barriers tried to block the way. Thank you, Nathalie Dupree, Ronni Lundy, Marcie Cohen Ferris,

Elizabeth Sims, Psyche Williams-Forson, Sandra Gutierrez, Charla Draper, Donna Pierce, Ellen Sweets, and Erika Webber.

Thank you one and all at my stellar literary agency, the Lisa Ekus Group: Lisa and Sally for surrounding me with warmth and love, respecting my vision, and helping me shape it into a proposal, and for your patience and guidance during stressful times; and for your assistance with promoting my work and arranging signings, Jaime Constantine and Sara Pokorny—you rock!

I owe so much to the team at Clarkson Potter for understanding my determination to present a larger vision of African American culinary history, and for going above and beyond to portray this story with such beauty and elegance. You went with the flow when I decided to share my platform as my ancestors had done, by uplifting the next generation of young black female food professionals. Thank you, Doris Cooper, for your expressions of confidence and support; Lydia O'Brien, for your administrative assistance; Stephanie Huntwork, for the genius that is evident in your designs; and Francis Lam, my incredible editor—you took a chance on an unconventional idea and then asked the just-right questions that kept me grounded and focused when I was tired and overwhelmed by the scope of this project. You are generous and compassionate. I have been comforted by your wisdom and care.

For the magnificent photographs in this book that made each dish spring from the page, I am eternally grateful to Jerrelle Guy and her partner, Eric Harrison. It took a year to find you, but the ancestors and I are blessed that we finally did. Your images, food styling, and prop choices went far beyond the average portrait to set a table that makes everyone feel welcome. You captured my respect and love for the ancestors and their long tables of hospitality. You are incredible. I also want to thank Pableaux Johnson, the talented and intuitive soul who took my amazing headshots. You sure know how to make a shy girl smile for the camera.

I wish to express my endless love for my family—a bunch of eager tasters who asked hard and sometimes annoying questions, forcing me to think through and to defend my opinions. Thank you, Bruce, for your love and encouragement and for never once asking me how much I spent collecting all of these cookbooks; Brandon, Jade, Christian, and Austin, for understanding the absence created between us when I answered the call to take up this work; Mom, for your organizational skills, helping me manage hundreds of notes and recipes and allowing me to make a mess testing recipes in your kitchen for nearly a year; and I am indebted to Derrick, my brother, LaTanya, my sister-in-law, and my niece, Aliya, for standing in the hard spaces for me when I was writing or on the road away from home. I also want to thank Margaret Bernstein for sparking three of the most important decisions of my life; without you I might still be writing about missing persons at a small weekly Los Angeles newspaper and I would never have met the love of my life.

Last, but certainly not least, I also must acknowledge and honor the ancestors whom I treasure for their wisdom, faith, and perseverance. When some people looked at you, they saw mere laborers and didn't even call you by your true names; I saw a glorious diaspora of bright stars using hospitality to express their hearts. You reminded me that I descend from a tradition of strong black women who observed beauty in the world around them and nurtured others no matter how limited or how few the resources and opportunities afforded to them. And through this you quieted my anxious spirit, gave me the courage to look back over my forty-year food industry career, and taught me to trust in my own culinary love language. Because of you, new vistas of self-awareness and self-confidence are mine. You have given life to the truism that you can't be what you can't see.

I proudly embrace your bandannas.

NAME INDEX

RECIPE INDEX